THE APOSTOLATE OF CHASTITY

THE APOSTOLATE OF CHASTITY

A Treatise for Religious Sisters

by

FERDINAND VALENTINE, O.P.

THE NEWMAN PRESS

WESTMINSTER · MARYLAND

IMPRIMI POTEST : FR. HILARIVS CARPENTER, O.P.
PRIOR PROVINCIALIS PROV. ANGLIAE
LONDINI : DIE V FEBRVARII MCMLIV

NIHIL OBSTAT : DANIEL DVIVESTEIJN, S.T.D.
CENSOR DEPVTATVS
IMPRIMATVR : E. MORROGH BERNARD
VICARIVS GENERALIS
WESTMONASTERII : DIE XXIX JANVARII MCMLIV

First published 1954
PRINTED IN GREAT BRITAIN

TO
MOTHER FOUNDRESS
AND
ALL SISTERS
F.M.D.M.

CONTENTS

FOREWORD

THE present volume is an attempt to set forth the vow and virtue of Chastity against the background of the religious life and the modern apostolate. Most of it will be intelligible, and I hope helpful, to all our sisters; but here and there, particularly in the chapter on 'The Chastity of Love', it will make more difficult reading. May I suggest, therefore, that those sisters who can gather the full content of meaning, especially from this chapter, should discuss it with others so that all may grasp the principles involved.

FERDINAND VALENTINE, O.P.

THE PROBLEM OF VOCATION

1

WHEN giving retreats to children the preacher is often conscious of a certain antipathy. This is particularly noticeable at our boarding schools. It is not due to a distaste for the retreat as such, but rather to a suspicion in the minds of the children that everyone is a little over-anxious to 'do them good' and that the motives are not always disinterested.

There may be nothing conscious about this attitude. It is usually an instinctive reaction against some kind of moral coercion. When the children are asked, for instance, whether they would like to be religious they often give the impression that this is a matter they would rather not discuss.

It is well to remember how easily one can seal up the heart of the modern adolescent. A chance remark to class-mates, such as: 'Sister has been asking me again whether I want to join the Order', and the mischief is done.

A similar attitude is noticeable amongst Catholic parents. How often, for instance, will they allow their daughter to enter religion 'when she is old enough to know her own mind', and yet raise no comparable objection to marriage. Such parents will sometimes go to extraordinary lengths to wear down the resistance of their child—by persuasion, threats, appeals to filial love and devotion and so on—till the whole family is living quite literally on the verge of hysteria. Why do sensible parents, and even good and fervent Catholic parents, sometimes behave in this way? Is it because they do not like parting with their child, or is the reason a little less obvious and due to ignorance or at least a complete misconception of the meaning of the religious novitiate?

Any adequate solution of this problem must deal with the primary cause and not with the excuses and specious arguments put forward when the whole affair gets beyond reasonable control. However reluctant we may be to face this issue, many parents are by no means convinced (could they put their motive into words) that their daughters are not being unduly influenced in view of their age and the serious nature of the step they contemplate. Parents know better than most of us how insecure any anchorage can be during adolescence. They can cope with a young girl's infatuation with a boy friend perhaps by drawing on their own experience. But what are they to do when their child becomes even more desperately infatuated with a religious sister or, in a sense, with Our Lord Himself? Such phases, we may be told, will pass; but on the other hand, are they not likely to endure at least as long as the school influences responsible for them? Parents have to be reassured not only by our arguments but by our conduct. They know quite well that their children would never be deliberately enticed into religion—such an idea is absurd. But in all fairness have they no grounds for uneasiness? Generally speaking, for instance, they do not appreciate that their daughters are not (or at least should not be) told to 'join' a religious order, but merely invited to 'try their vocation'. Parents must be made to understand that to enter a novitiate is merely to take the prudent step of sampling the religious life; and that there can be no question of keeping young aspirants if they are not suited, or if they, on their part, decide to leave. Most parents would be less reluctant to let their children go if they were confident that this acceptance of a call to religious life were every bit as free and personal as an acceptance or refusal of a proposal of marriage, and that precautions would be taken against any kind of self-deception.

But can they be sure when in fact entry into religion is given such an air of finality by priests and religious sisters; and the novitiate itself often considered more as an interlude for training than a time of decision? Can parents help wondering in such circumstances whether their children are not being swept into a difficult and even heroic way of life from purely human motives, as for instance to perpetuate their happy school relationship with an order or a group of sisters? Many vocations, we know, spring from inadequate human motives, but how can parents be reassured? Are we to blame them for wondering whether the risk is reasonable when the decision, and, as they think, the final decision, is about to be made before their children are sufficiently stable in character to judge for themselves?

The very delicate matter of inspiring vocations calls for the greatest discretion. It is not in essence a question of prompting our young girls with the desire of total dedication to Christ's service at the age, say, of seventeen or eighteen but of bringing them up to serve Him from their earliest years. By and large our methods of recruitment leave a good deal to be desired, and at times seem restrictive of human freedom. Moral coercion is not easy to diagnose, when it becomes, so to say, the very climate of one's life. A growing sense of insecurity overshadows the modern world, and this prevailing state of mind infects many of our religious communities. We worry, for instance, about the future of our house or order when its future or even its survival is one of the least important things to worry about. What matters, surely, is whether or not we live the life here and now we have professed to live and whether or not we do, here and now, what God wills us to do. We have to keep ourselves fit to be used as instruments of the Church. That is our primary duty. If God wishes to go on using us, all well and good; if not, then His will be done, as long as we die gloriously and die fighting. He may put us aside for something more appropriate to His work, or modify our life for the needs of our times. Whatever be His will, the one tragedy would be to fail Him through our own fault.

Religious orders, let us remember, derive their inspiration and their mission from the Church. They are her instruments; she brought them into being and they will pass when they have served their purpose. Could we look forward, say, two or three thousand years hence we should perhaps be surprised to learn how few of the orders as we now know them had survived. Rest assured the Church can raise up a greater than Benedict or Dominic or Francis or Ignatius amongst her religious founders and a greater too than Augustine or Aquinas among her doctors. We love to look back at the past glories of the Church and recall with a thrill of pride what she has already done, the development of her doctrine, the catalogue of her saints, the heroism of her martyrs; we rejoice in the art she has inspired. . . . But how short-sighted and unworthy it can be to recall merely the Ages of Faith that are gone and to forget the greater glories yet to come. Such thoughts help us to remember that it is to the Church that we, as religious, owe our first allegiance and not to our own particular order.

But alas, it is far too easy in these times to envisage our own order or congregation as an end in itself, thus accepting many situations as unavoidable which in fact do much to imperil the very fabric of religious institutions. Already we may have too much work to do, and it goes on increasing. We are asked to make new foundations to meet the growing demands of the modern apostolate; our members are scattered, overworked, and weary; and there is an increasing and imperative need for recruits. How are we to get them, and when we do is it easy to part with them should they decide to leave? We tend in such circumstances to make excuses, and almost in spite of ourselves to give candidates for profession the benefit of any doubt, creating by our thinking and behaviour a sense of emergency which makes some kind of moral coercion almost inevitable. 'God never so abandons His Church', writes St. Thomas, 'that suitable ministers are not to be found which are sufficient for the needs of the people; if those who are worthy are promoted and the unworthy set aside. And though it were impossible to find as many ministers as there are now, it were better to have few good ministers than many bad ones.'[1]

Nevertheless God does expect us to foster vocations to the religious life as such, and to inspire young people with the desire of following Christ in the way of the counsels. But how are we to do this? Wheat must be grown before it can be garnered, and these organic processes cannot be accelerated to suit our present need or convenience. However inadequate such an analogy, it is true to say that any attempt to isolate our need for recruits from the urgent need of relieving the general spiritual poverty of our time can be supreme folly. Vocations will not increase either in quality or quantity unless we strive to uplift the mass of our Catholic people, and particularly our children, to a greater realization of spiritual values, and recognize that this transfiguration must come mainly through the parochial life of the Church, supplemented by the generous co-operation of our Catholic teachers. There is no other way of safeguarding the integrity of the home or the dignity of parents.

But this does not mean that we should be content to let the flow of vocations subside, or forgo all legitimate means of inspiration. It is merely a question of priorities in working out a right and reasonable apostolic method. We shall replenish our religious houses here and now in proportion to our needs if we give priority to the spiritual advancement of all and particularly the Catholic home-makers of the future. The two vocations spring from the same roots. It is charity—the love of God—which brings forth the

[1] *S.T.*, Suppl., 36, 4, ad 1.

truly Christian family and every aspiration in young hearts to the positive and creative dedication of virginal chastity. In the words of Pope Pius XI, speaking more specifically of the priestly vocation:

> The first and most natural place where the flowers of the sanctuary should almost spontaneously grow and bloom remains always the truly and deeply Christian family. Most of the saintly bishops and priests whose 'praise the Church declares', owe the beginning of their vocation and their holiness to the example and teaching of a father strong in faith and manly virtues, of a pure and devoted mother, and of a family in which the love of God and our neighbour, joined with simplicity of life, has reigned supreme. To this ordinary rule of divine Providence, exceptions are rare and only serve to prove the rule.[1]

These things are mentioned here because it is often our undue anxiety to replenish our ranks by means of propaganda and other emergency methods of recruitment which tempts us to bring pressure to bear on aspirants. This tendency is inherent in a too naturalistic view of our needs which inevitably encourages wrong methods and a blind adherence to false principles. This state of mind grows upon us. Generally speaking, there is no question of a deliberate violation of justice.

II

The results of this tendency, however, are still to be seen in some of our novitiates. Thus novices in religion are sometimes given to understand that God will deny them the graces necessary for some other state of life should they return to the world, particularly if they are judged suitable for the order they have joined. They may not be told in so many words that they are imperilling their eternal salvation, but they are left in no doubt that they are taking a retrograde step or even a grave risk, and that they have only themselves to blame should anything untoward happen. Added to this, and as a salutary warning, instances are sometimes quoted of former novices who abandoned their vocation without just cause and what subsequently befell them.

Quite apart from the fact that the reasons for leaving a novitiate are often discovered only to the priest in the confessional

[1] *Ad Catholici Sacerdotii.*

there can be little doubt that religious sisters who constrain young souls in this way can do great harm. Indeed, isn't it possible that they may be responsible in large measure for the tragedies they deplore by allowing young people to leave the novitiate under a cloud, hopeless and despondent, and with a life-long sense of guilt? Whatever the motive for leaving, it is the fault of the authorities if those who have been into our novitiates do not take away with them an experience to be treasured rather than regretted in the memory of it. In the words of St. Thomas Aquinas:

> It is better to enter religion with the purpose of making a trial of the life than not to enter at all, because by so doing we are disposed to remain always. Nor is a person accounted to turn or to look back, save when he omits to do that which he has engaged to do. Otherwise anyone who did a good work for a time only would be unfit for the kingdom of God unless he did it always, which is obviously false.[1]

Let us repeat, for fear of any misunderstanding. It must not be supposed that these indiscretions are prevalent. But in this particular matter they may threaten any religious community to the serious hurt of souls if the wrong person is given charge of the novitiate. Traditional patterns of thought change very slowly.

A contributory cause of this situation should not be overlooked. Many young aspirants come to religion with the assurance that God has already given them a supernatural vocation. The danger of such an assurance is aggravated by the joy and thanksgiving of parents, relatives and friends and the general air of finality given to the leavetaking. Any confessor or director is of course quite justified in telling his penitent that she is offered a vocation, in the sense that all the faithful are given a general and external vocation to follow Christ in the practice of the evangelical counsels. It may also be true that the particular penitent shows every sign of having been given the grace of an internal, particular vocation which gives her the inclination and the firm resolve to enter the religious state. But what may not be true is the definite conclusion from observed states of soul, even those manifested in the priest-penitent relationship of the confessional, that a particular person has actually been given a supernatural vocation and is therefore a suitable candidate for religious life, to say nothing of her aptitude, physical, temperamental, mental and moral, for

---

[1] *S.T.*, 2–2, 189, 4 ad 1.

any particular order or congregation.[1] Nothing is easier than to induce impressionable young girls to think that all is settled even before they try. It is not the function of the confessor or director to assume the rôle of a novice-master or of novice-mistress. If he does so or at least does not make it quite clear that he cannot accept such a responsibility, what is to prevent young aspirants from seeing a diabolical temptation in every difficulty or natural incompatibility during the novitiate, or even, if they are stubborn and resolute souls, from carrying on grimly till their health breaks?

These girls, quite rightly, have the greatest confidence in the director who sent them. They will sometimes inform you that he is a very prayerful man of reputed holiness. This may be true, but in fact it only makes matters worse, because his decisions are supported by an unquestioned priestly integrity. But even if he were nearer to God than is generally supposed, he would still have no right to give the assurance we have mentioned, and if he did so he acted very imprudently. Generally speaking, the most such a priest can say on the evidence before him is that a particular soul has, as far as he can discover, no impediment which precludes her from the religious state; and that her constancy to prayer, and fidelity to her past resolutions, give every sign that God is calling her to religion. He may rightly conclude that there is every reason to suppose she should try her vocation, to make quite sure of God's will in this matter. But no priest or religious sister should ever presume to decide a religious vocation prematurely either by word, or, more especially, by adopting an attitude which takes it for granted.

Such decisions should be left to the novitiate. It is there that the aspirant on her part will have both time and opportunity to disentangle her motives. She may merely *wish* to become a religious, that is to say, have a preference for the end or purpose of religious life which is to love and serve God; or she may *will* to become a religious by also having the intention of adopting the means to this end or purpose, which are the counsels of perfection and a particular rule of religious life. But the only sure way of discovering this preference for the end as well as the means is by an actual experience of the life which provides the means, and not by any 'proving of the spirit' on the part of her spiritual counsellor or director before she enters.

[1] See Note 1, p. 215.

Similarly, in regard to the authorities to whom she has submitted herself. They and they alone, acting as they do in the name of the Church, can assess the fitness of a particular aspirant for their own way of life. Even so it is well to remember how carefully the whole question of vocation must be weighed in the balance under the guidance of the Church. If the authorities admit a novice to temporary vows, for example, the very temporary nature of these vows signifies in the eyes of the Church that her time of probation is not yet terminated, and that the conclusive signs of vocation cannot as yet be prudently determined. Conjecturally her vocation may be very probable. She may even have been given the grace of a supernatural vocation from early childhood; but the only sure and final decision on whether or not a vocation has been given is her admission by the Church to final vows. That is the outward sign of an inward grace conferred at profession or at some time previously.

We now begin to see, perhaps more clearly, the imprudence of any premature pronouncement on the question of vocation. In practice, a discreet reticence on the part of confessors and others gives a saving liberty of spirit to the well-disposed, who will usually have a specific vocation in mind; but they should always be encouraged to cleave to God's will whether this lead them into religion or not. It is this resolute intention to serve God as He shall see fit which solves many problems both for the aspirants themselves and for those directing them.

III

Many difficulties in contemporary religious life can be traced to fear; we cannot free the minds and hearts of young religious for a more positive approach to virginal chastity, unless we make every effort to exorcize their lives of this fear. The freedom characteristic of all true love should pervade every religious novitiate. One must expect there a prevailing normality and sanity—the whole life in which young people are encouraged to love and trust God in tranquillity and are not made too apprehensive by too strict a discipline nor dominated by a fear-love relationship towards the person in authority.

We shall have more to say about this later, but for the moment it should be recognized that the voice of God often goes unheard and unheeded in an atmosphere of disturbed and undisciplined emotions

—particularly a sentimentality which can be the individual's refuge from the demands of an ill-regulated régime. The sentimental aspirant loses touch with real objective values, becoming more than ever absorbed in subjective states of soul. She may even be carried through her period of probation on the crest of a phantasy-ideal too often confused with first fervour. This may be one reason why many such people declare themselves only after their first profession when they are brought grimly to earth by the demands of the modern apostolate.

Be this as it may, the main principle involved remains true and incontrovertible. The religious vocation is the offspring of charity, and charity, which is the love of God, cannot thrive in a heart victimized by its own emotions. To act from love is contrary to the very notion of servility whatever its exterior or interior cause, whether it be inordinate fear or respect, or an unreasonable admiration or affection for those in authority, or a certain subjectivism which is an affectation of love arising from a natural emotional tendency or disposition. The love of God, founded on divine Faith, demands an integral freedom of function, and through that freedom alone can a positive attitude to supernatural chastity flourish. That is why novitiate discipline must be ordered to a personal freedom in Christ through the loving worship of God, a positive unselfconscious approach which inspires young and ardent souls to carry out the divine will from a motive of love. For the rest they should be encouraged to leave themselves in God's hands that eventually they may be whatever He wills them to be, either great or small in His kingdom. Their prior vocation is to His will. 'Where the spirit of the Lord is there is liberty.'[1]

Loving worship alone can free the soul and found it in the basic virtue of true humility. Such humility cannot be cultivated by constantly dwelling on our evil tendencies or our past sins, or merely by submitting to humiliations, or by comparing ourselves with others more richly gifted. To be truly humble is not only to know our smallness or even to want to be small; it is to have the firm intention of being dependent on our heavenly Father, as the infant Christ was dependent, from a motive of loving trust, and as a means to this end to enthrone God in our lives by doing His will day by day, moment by moment. Humility is the child of worship and of love. Whatever be our place in the scheme of

[1] 2 Cor. 3. 17.

eternal Wisdom we should resolve to keep God where He has every right to be—at the very heart of things—and to rejoice in our privilege and power to reflect His gifts to His greater glory.[1]

This then should be the purpose of every religious novitiate if it is to avoid the difficulties we have discussed and to bring forth a truly Christian freedom of spirit. But in view of all we have said and insisted upon, it is a sad commentary on the lack of freedom amongst many of our novices when so often they go in mortal fear of failure. On their part they look upon the possibility of such failure as the threat of a dead-end frustration, the collapse of everything they have promised themselves, or else as a kind of deliberate apostasy. Their parents and friends expect them to get through; in the eyes of all concerned they have finally left home; to return is an open confession of failure, and a failure which is looked upon as a sort of family disgrace—a disloyalty inviting the divine displeasure. Sometimes, when they leave, such novices will refuse to face this public disapproval and take some job away from home. Added to this is the attitude of the sisters they leave behind who will sometimes look upon such a departure as a sign of their own unworthiness and undertake a community penance in reparation. The effect of all this upon the novice herself may well be imagined. If she goes through and is professed, the haunting experience of such anxieties is certain to constrict her heart. The novitiate gives tone to the subsequent life and apostolate of every religious; and what a joy it can be to look back and to know that her acceptance of Christ's love was a free and deliberate choice unblemished by anxiety or fear!

Fortunately most of our novitiates to-day are down-to-earth. But all with any knowledge of these matters will agree that the least enviable task of higher authority is to find the right person to supervise the early training of our sisters. Neither the good and fervent religious nor the experienced organizer, nor the disciplinarian—intrepid upholder of the letter of the law—is necessarily equal to this task; but rather the ordinary, intelligent woman who has given a mature heart and mind to Christ.

Religious chastity flourishes as a positive dedication in an environment of balanced tensions in which the free functioning of the person of the subject is encouraged. This calls above all else for prudent leadership. Many things can interfere with this

[1] Cf. *The Mother of the Saviour*, Lagrange; also *La Croix de Jésus*, p. 75.

normal development and restrict the freedom of function so essential to personal well-being. If this happens it is only to be expected that some of our sisters should be afflicted with a life-long negative bias in all that concerns religious chastity, and should habitually look upon it as a kind of necessary asceticism. With the best will in the world this frustrates the human spirit instead of liberating it.

Chapter 2

SOME PROBLEMS OF FITNESS

I

FORTUNATELY the prejudice is dying which suspects young girls of flocking to religion to nurse a broken heart—there are few Aïdas in the convents of the world. Modern society nevertheless brings forth a type of introspective adolescent who would appear to the inexperienced superior admirably suited to the religious life. Such people crave peace, solitude—remoteness from a rowdy and wicked world; they make few friends, feel drawn to prayer and have little desire to found a home of their own. When such aspirants enter as late vocations very little as a rule can be done for them, though obviously this does not apply to the late vocation as such.

These older women are often convinced that God is calling them and that at last they are free to occupy their predestined niche in the divine scheme of things; or else they look so forlorn and helpless, their worldly prospects overcast by the memory of past failures, that some motherly superior decides to give them a chance. At any rate many such unfortunate people sooner or later find their way to our convents and are not infrequently hailed as an answer to prayer.

But alas, the strains of the community *Te Deum* have barely died away before the dangers inherent in such a situation begin to reveal themselves. In these circumstances it is folly for superiors, whatever their need of subjects, to think that God, who can of the very stones raise up children to Abraham, will reward their patience and generosity.

The chief trouble is that these older people so easily settle down; they take their vocation for granted and are often with the greatest difficulty uprooted even after the briefest stay in religion. If those in charge hesitate they gradually begin to realize that such an uprooting will bring these novices almost to the brink of despair. But how are superiors to make any timely and confident judgement? They are not always women of great experience nor with

14

any extraordinary spiritual insight. Yet any delay will almost certainly do great harm. The longer these postulants stay the more grievous will be the wound when they are told to go.

Unfortunately the advice one can give superiors is not easily appreciated, especially if they persist in judging these cases by wrong standards. They will argue that these postulants have good health, are prayerful, obedient, intelligent. This may be true, but are they temperamentally suited for the religious life? It is not difficult to adjust oneself for a time to any environment, but to do so permanently is an entirely different matter. 'Then,' says the superior, 'let us wait and see.' But the difficulty is that in this particular instance one cannot afford to wait and see. The thing must be decided as speedily as possible. There is, however, one useful way of putting this temperamental fitness to the test. Some experienced superiors would say it was infallible, though others would prefer to say that at least it raises very serious doubts as to the temperamental fitness of these older women. The method is to decide whether or not they have a sense of humour. This may seem strangely incongruous until we remind ourselves what a sense of humour really is.

Now by humour is not meant a capacity for boisterousness, buffoonery or practical joking whereby we release surplus energy or, more usually perhaps in religious life, try to forget our morbid self-preoccupation; nor is it a natural joviality, which may spring too exclusively from a feeling of physical well-being; much less should humour be confused with wit which too often makes others look ridiculous and even contemptible. Humour is a far nobler thing. It is the feeling of surprise, the joyous shock of discovery in our appreciation of life's incongruities. To find these contrasts we must be self-detached, account ourselves of little importance, look outwards and not inwards, feel drawn to people and to things in thanksgiving, for humour is the reward of a will-to-community.

By this phrase 'will-to-community' is not to be understood a fixed determination to live with the community but rather the will to live in community as a grateful member of a crowd or group. Humour should be the natural endowment, more or less, of all those who seek to live in religion; and we see at once how it must flower under the impulse of the grace of vocation which unites us in our dedication, increasing our good neighbourliness in a community of interests and the common purpose of giving honour and glory to God.

'*Tu sei tanto grande ed io sono tanto piccolo*',[1] was the constant prayer of Gemma Galgani. Therein is the essential incongruity at the heart of things, that we are so small and yet can claim the interest and share the very life of the eternal King of Kings. We find ourselves and all else in the self-surrender of worship; the part is for the whole; the child for the family and the family through Christ our Lord is for God. Could anything be more sublime than the vocation of those who are uplifted into the life of God to be His children? Have we any right to share that life and love? Isn't it even absurd to suppose we have? More than that. Could anything be more incongruous than the contrast between what we are of ourselves and what we become by God's grace; the strange fact that He extends the romance of a divine and eternal love to you and me and the quite ordinary folk we see about us, the baker's boy, the sweep, the tramp, bearded and unkempt, taking his meal by the roadside? May we not say, then, that humour has its source in our Christian faith, in that man who walks the earth can still claim heaven as his birthright?

When we say, then, that the test of a true sense of humour is the capacity to laugh with others at one's self, this is hardly the whole truth. It is not merely to have the capacity for such laughter, but to discover a reason for it; not to resign one's self stoically to a fair give-and-take, but to discover in the laughter of others something very like a compliment. That is why true humour is akin to brotherly love and sympathy in a truly worshipful Christian and religious community. It binds us closer together and relaxes all undue tension.

But humour is not a transitory thing. We speak of a sense of humour which enables us to feel amused at many of the unexpected incongruities in life, a disposition or habit, a way of looking at life in a spirit of hopeful adventure; a Christian attitude of mind which looks for the *raison-d'être* of every created thing outside of ourself. Much of this spirit of hopeful adventure escapes us to-day. We tend more and more to plan our world and even our souls, seeking our *raison-d'être* within ourselves; and by trying in our pride to be 'as God' we lose all the fun of being a creature. It is the sure knowledge that God, *Rex tremendae majestatis*, is in our midst, all-wise, loving and powerful, that keeps us as Christians on the tiptoe of expectancy. Every day, every hour holds its divine secret, every fresh acquaintance is a surprise—a unique and

---

[1] 'Thou art so great, I am so tiny.'

unpredictable creation, every sunset is God's gift to crown the day.

And the unmistakable sign of this Christian attitude to life is laughter. When we can look outwards in our appreciation and love of things and people, we are at one with them and alive to life's incongruities, finding ourselves who dare call God a Father in the midst of so much that is odd. For to be odd in this sense is not to have everything out of place but only one—like the solemn novice who habitually twitches her nose, or the dignified novice who rolls as she walks, or the small novice with the voracious appetite, or the very large novice with the high-pitched voice, or the demure novice who is terrified of spiders, or a novice who speaks with a very precise and refined voice, or one who does not, and so on.

As can well be imagined, when such people live together in the close association of novitiate life anything might happen. But deliberately to forgather them in a free-for-all community recreation is indeed a courageous experiment and one which has a vital bearing on religious life. Few things escape the woman in the world; but nothing escapes the woman in religion. For this reason recreation can become for her either a means of self-isolation or of a bonding together in Christ, according to her attitude towards it. Only in the degree she approaches recreation prepared to think in collaboration with others and to be contradicted, to laugh with others at the risk of being laughed at, does this exercise become a self-revealing and purifying experience. It is meaningless when allowed to degenerate into a kind of masquerade in which our chief worry is the fear of discovery. But as a community exercise it can be the touchstone of religious life and especially of life in the novitiate, providing as it does, when reasonably conducted, one very important means of discovering whether the religious aspirant has the necessary will-to-community, and a general temperamental fitness for her vocation.

This statement is brief and perhaps inadequate, but it should be sufficiently clear to save the religious superior from a grave error of judgement. If the postulants we have referred to lack what is called community-spirit and have drifted towards religious life because they have found the society of others in the world irksome, how can they be expected to fit into religious life when a woman in religion is essentially a woman in community? The truth is that such postulants are, in the analogical sense, unchaste; their choice of the religious state is not, so to say, the choice between lovers, but merely between different ways of loving themselves. It matters little in one sense whether aspirants are sinners; but it is essential they should be companionable; and the one place in which this quality declares itself is not the chapel or the sanctum of the novice-mistress but the community-room at recreation. Novices who promise best, provided, of course, they are suitable in other ways, are those who manifest a sufficient sense of humour to mingle easily and joyfully with the rest.

But it does not at all follow that younger women, similar in character to these older postulants, cannot adapt themselves or be adapted to religious life. Because the novice-mistress has been warned against the impossible she must not hesitate to tackle what is merely difficult. Many young people come to religious life ill-suited to its demands, and the novitiate for all practical purposes is their final opportunity for any kind of re-education.

In the first place all those concerned in the training of these introspective girls must realize that severity, as, for example, the issuing of commands under obedience to mix with others or any drastic attempt to break through the shell of self-seclusion by ridicule, especially in the presence of others, will do far more harm than good. These young people are often the victims of joyless homes or the pampered offspring of indulgent parents. Whatever the cause and however grievously they may annoy others, their prime need is self-confidence. They must be inspired by every possible means to turn from their habitual indulgence in self-phantasy or day-dreams, in which many of them have sought an inner sanctuary since childhood, to the objective love and service of Christ in others. It is surprising how easily this can be done by the trustful and confident superior who appreciates the potential qualities of such souls.

But unfortunately religious of this type are often wrongly directed from the start, and can afterwards be readjusted only with the greatest difficulty, if at all. Their retiring disposition, their taste for a kind of spiritual literature which encourages their self-phantasy, their 'sense' or awareness of God's presence, their desire to be alone with God, the ease with which many of them turn to God in prayer—all these things, and a good deal more, may convince the novice-mistress that here at last is the finest material to work upon. But if she drives them still further into their self-isolation by giving them a target to aim at, or by encouraging them to become saints or model novices or even 'women of prayer'—or in any other way unduly stresses the subjective approach to religion—she will do irreparable harm. We shall deal with this more specifically later, but let us remark in passing that there is a whole world of difference between 'aiming high' in the spiritual life and 'loving much'. With beginners it is always difficult to discover where the main impulse towards perfection comes from—self or God. But the tendency to some sort of phantasy-ideal is such a danger in our own day that anything that might foster undue spiritual ambition must be avoided at all costs. It is much safer to say to these young aspirants, not 'Do you want to become a saint?' but rather, 'God is infinitely good and merciful, wouldn't you like to dedicate yourself without reserve to His service?' Both these invitations mean the same thing, but they are not always construed as meaning the same thing. We make progress in the spiritual life, not by multiplying our prayers or devotions or by giving satisfaction either to ourselves or others, but by trying to please God.

The love of friendship [St. Thomas tells us] seeks the friend's good; wherefore, when it is intense, it causes a man to be moved against everything that opposes the friend's good. In this respect a man is said to be zealous on behalf of his friend, when he makes a point of protecting his friend against whatever may be said or done against his good. In this way, too, a man is said to be zealous on God's behalf, when he strives, to the best of his ability, to prevent whatever may be contrary to the honour or will of God.[1]

St. Francis of Sales puts the same thoughts in other words:

I entreat you not to love anything too ardently, not even virtues, which are sometimes lost in an immoderate pursuit. . . . Let us be what we are, and strive to be that well, in order to do honour to Him who made us. Let us be whatever He wills, so long as we are wholly devoted to Him, but let us not be what we will, contrary to His intentions; for were we the most perfect denizens of heaven, of what use were it unless we be such according to God's will.[2]

II

The introspective tendency of many of our aspirants is often dominated by a morbid sex-consciousness. The modern world is

[1] *S.T.*, 1–2, 28, 4. [2] Letter of June 10th, 1605.

incapable of understanding the whole life crowned by divine love and ordered to a divine and supernatural purpose. To its narrowed vision the vow of chastity comes as a supreme challenge. It is indeed true to say that the pagan can no more understand the prerogatives and fruitfulness of a plighted troth to a divine lover than the brute animal can appreciate the delights of human friendship. That may seem grossly unfair; but if anything it is an understatement. The world's greatest mystery most significant of the divine power is not man the rational animal but man the son of God, partaker of the divine nature, who can love divinely.[1]

But this modern materialistic and anthropocentric way of life is a force to be reckoned with and it can have a very subtle and dangerous influence on the more intelligent aspirant. All her finest instincts rebel against any sort of unproductive womanhood unless she finds in religious chastity an integral though spiritual self-fulfilment. In other words, she has to be made to realize that the supreme dedication of her womanhood is at her disposal in the Christian apostolate in a loving collaboration with Christ who alone can fulfil and enrich her natural endowments. But if such religious do not appreciate the sublime nature of their vocation from their early novitiate days they tend to become too preoccupied with difficult natural readjustments and to overrate the seriousness of the problems confronting them. Chastity is a virtue which not only restrains our concupiscence but also purifies and releases our human love.

III

Another cause of morbid sex-consciousness is more widespread. The religious life calls for the normal woman, or at least one who can find her full maturity as a woman in religion. Lurking in the background of the minds of some aspirants is a strange and indefinable fear of sex, due partly to ignorance and partly to an anxiety-neurosis often passed on by parents. Few young people nowadays are completely ignorant in these matters; but it is a partial and inadequate instruction, sufficient to arouse curiosity, combined with the solemn warning that such curiosity is dangerous and may even lead to grave sin, which is so harmful.

It is not here a question of the validity of the vow of chastity but whether it can be wholly operative and fruitful if those who take it are to a large extent ignorant of its very nature. If the

[1] Cf. *S.T.*, 1–2, 113, 9.

young religious we have in mind are not prudently instructed on such matters in the novitiate, or, worse still, if those responsible see no need for such instruction, or, as sometimes happens, even confirm their charges in their ignorance by repressing their anxieties still further, who can tell what trouble the future holds? Such foolishness cripples the apostolate and degrades the most treasured and liberating influence of religious life into a nightmare. These young people must be made to realize that the gloomy hinterland of which they have been warned, far from being the abode of evil things, is the trysting place of the Angel of Annunciation. In other words, religious chastity is the deliberate setting aside of married friendship and human motherhood, things good and sacred in themselves, for a union which is more intimate and fruitful in the supernatural order.

Any other estimate of chastity is wrong, and may even be heretical. The Church could never be the guardian of chastity if she did not uphold the sanctity of marriage; the two in a sense are complementary. And she condemns any philosophy, any custom, which misprizes the dignity of marriage, whether this be defended by the advocates of civil marriage and divorce as in our own time, or by such groups as the Manichees and Eustathians in the early Church who taught that marriage was impure.

'If anyone preserves continence or virginity not because of the beauty and sanctity of this virtue', we read in Canon 9 of the Council of Gangra, 'but because he avoids marriage as something execrable, let him be anathema.'

Culpable ignorance of the nature and obligations of marriage predisposes some religious to a fear and even to a contempt of it. This may be implied rather than expressed, as, for example, when it is suggested that the God-fearing girl should pray for a vocation that she may find a safe refuge in religious chastity; the implication being more or less that marriage tends of its very nature to contaminate. Similarly, it may save much trouble and even embarrassment to lay down a hard and fast rule that 'the less young religious know about these things the better', but few half-truths have ever done more harm.

IV

A still more difficult problem arises from what appears to be a total ignorance in these matters. Apart from the vow's validity which is clearly the responsibility of those in charge, such young people run the grave risk of a life-long immaturity. At best they can offer Christ no more than the heart of a child. The 'little sister' aged thirty years or more, the Peter Pan of the community, is a very doubtful asset in the modern apostolate. Nothing could be more unwise than to put such religious in charge of adolescents, especially in our novitiates where their immaturity tends to perpetuate itself.

It would be a mistake to suppose, however, that our sisters are not alive to the urgency of this problem. The custom is growing of instructing all novices on the nature and obligations of the marriage state. All gloomy forebodings that this new departure was ill-advised have been confounded by the results. When such instructions are given with due discretion young religious have a better understanding and a more positive love of chastity, which in turn bears fruit in an increasing appreciation of the sanctity of marriage. It is those who have sought the higher creative union and the greater sacrifice of love who have the most perfect understanding of the true dignity of married life, and the inner secret of married happiness.

In spite of all we have said in this chapter, however, many of our sisters will still seek shelter behind the barricades of tradition. These difficulties, they will argue, are not new, and all in all religious in the past have not done too badly. Isn't it wiser, they will ask us, to leave all this unravelling to the Lord? Or again, if unsuitable candidates are actually received and become thorns in the flesh of the community, have they not a purifying influence and even an apostolic purpose? After all, God will take care of us if we try our best, and help us through our very mistakes.

But let us look at the other side of the picture. Advocates of *laissez-faire* in these matters should remember that God can indeed bring good out of evil, and in this case use our ignorance and incompetence for His divine purposes, but this does not exonerate us from all moral responsibility. Those with any experience of modern religious life know quite well there is a good deal wrong that could be remedied by an insistence on right method. Or, are we seriously to believe that such is the decay of religious life as a spiritual organism that it cannot determine for itself what is or what is not assimilable, and has not the vitality to dispose unsuitable material for such assimilation when this is prudent and necessary?

What, then, can be wrong? Two factors prevent religious from facing this problem courageously: first, the fears and anxieties about vocation already referred to, which shackle the innate common-sense of so many religious women; and, secondly, ignorance, or at least inadequate instruction on the means to be taken, consonant with our national character, towards spiritual perfection.

Our sisters will never cope with the present emergency unless they strive through conferences and discussions of the right kind to foster in their communities a reflective quality of mind through which new ideas, trends and even readaptations of rules and customs can be assimilated. They may complain, quite rightly, that these readjustments take time. But they should remember that this is not just another of the usual difficulties but a very unusual and critical emergency. Our sisters must awaken to realities. Something has to be done and done quickly. But it is of the utmost importance that these changes should come from inside and not from outside. Many young religious are leaving our novitiates before taking their vows, and even after final vows; and many who stay are restless and unstable. This is naturally causing grave concern and even a kind of panic in some quarters. It is even being suggested that a certificate of temperamental fitness, drawn up by some competent psychoanalyst, should be presented by every aspirant. This may surprise many sisters, but it goes to show the nature of the crisis when such a misguided and dangerous expedient is being seriously advocated.

To conclude. As we said at the beginning of this chapter, many introspective girls are to be found in our modern novitiates. We have tried to show that where this tendency is not too pronounced and the postulants are young enough to yield easily to the influence of a well-balanced novitiate environment they can be readjusted to the needs of religious life. We are perhaps a little too inclined to label these introspective girls as neurotics. The use of this term, especially in religion, can be misleading. In fact it may mean almost anything—a temporary bout of scruples, an undue sensitiveness, over-concern about one's health, moodiness and so on. There are few religious who have not a tendency to neurosis but they are far from being neurotics. All true neurosis is traceable to a grave conflict at the deeper levels of the human soul, and for Catholics and religious this is often related in some way to the confessional. Neurosis and sanctity are incompatible and mutually exclusive.[1] The obvious preventive and cure for such a tendency is to aspire to God and to regulate one's life by the directives of His love—a self-giving to others in sane living through worship.

One of the chief deterrents to this self-giving is fear in any form, particularly a servile fear of God and of God's representatives in religion; or fear of an ideal set forth in such extravagant terms that it either daunts the beginner or causes her to throw all discretion to the winds. The ideal of the true lover is to love more, not to love best. If this is insisted upon, the young aspirant will always realize her own true self in her loving service of Christ.

But any attempt to dominate young people and to refashion them to the mind, opinions and preferences of another is disastrous. We cannot forget all the experience that has gone to the making of us; we must be true to our past. This principle should be respected by those who have any influence on our spiritual life. All true spiritual change begins in the innermost recesses of the human person; it cannot be merely a superficial thing, something worn like a cloak. Any unnatural remoulding of the character begets an artificiality which rends the soul. The prudent novice-mistress builds upon foundations already laid. God's plan for each is unique and incommunicable.

We shall develop these thoughts in the following chapter.

---

1 See Note 2, p. 216.

Chapter 3

THE RELIGIOUS SISTER AND THE ADOLESCENT

I

WHAT matters most in the apostolate is a willingness to be used rather than an inner conviction that we have something to contribute.

This willingness to collaborate as an instrument towards God's eternal purpose must nevertheless spring, humanly speaking, from a natural disposition which helps to uplift the whole person of the religious in an ascension of mind and heart to God. True friendship is worthy of our human dignity even when our emotions are stirred; to plight one's troth to a human lover is a thing still more worthy; but to plight one's troth to Christ by an act of irrevocable and eternal dedication is the worthiest and noblest of all.

But this love at three levels should be within the capacity of all those who present themselves to our religious novitiates. That is the degree of normality demanded. This does not mean, of course, that they should have pledged themselves to any earthly lover, but that their capacity to love at the highest level should be the measure of their natural capacity to love at every other level, and, when they have taken the vow of chastity, a greater capacity to love humanly in the degree they love divinely.

This integral development of function presupposes a natural freedom of mind and heart, the tendency to look outwards, the disposition to pass one's self on, to make happiness in others rather than to seek it for oneself, to lose one's life to find it. If this movement outwards beyond the self is not characteristic of the later adolescent its later emergence is always a matter of some speculation.

It is not here a question of whether or not this natural disposition cannot be acquired gradually and laboriously under the influence of grace but of the need for establishing it as early as possible in the life of the child. This is a very difficult problem; but may we not suppose that the religious sister whose natural instincts are

25

freed, her heart expanded by her dedication to the loving service of Christ, will always be best suited for this task as the foster-mother of our children?

The difficulty is that although naturally speaking she may be fitted for it, her training in religion often impedes the growth and flowering of her natural gifts. She may be expert in the technique of education and yet fail because her deeper aspirations of mind and heart are not sufficiently in sympathy with her work. To train and educate the child and free its heart for Christ's service the woman must be drawn naturally as a woman to love the child. In marriage this attraction is chiefly exercised towards her own children, but in religion to her children in Christ, as the fruit of her virginity.

It is through the love of Christ, a willingness to surrender to His divine purpose, to work in double-harness with Him, that the natural womanly instincts of the religious grow large and generous enough for the difficult task before her. If this is true, it must be very evident that the compulsions which tend to creep into religious life not only keep us earth-bound by clipping the wings of the spirit, but also constrict our hearts. To love as Christ wills us to love, we must have complete freedom of function. Only on this condition can the vow of chastity release the human Heart of Christ upon the world, and the religious sister give her children the maternal love and care of Christ.

This is the first-fruits of chastity in the teaching apostolate. If the religious sister is to inspire an adult-mindedness, that is a natural will-to-community in her children, it is only reasonable to expect that her own training as a religious should have endowed her with this same quality. If many of our sisters in fact have not this influence on their children we must look for the cause in religious life and not in the schoolroom or in any neglect or ignorance of the pedagogic art. The reciprocal influence of the religious training of our sisters and the fitness for the religious life of our children, particularly adolescents, is therefore obvious.

But in practice the problem of a smooth transition towards a sense of adult responsibility is not easily solved for those who present themselves in our novitiates. The main difficulty would seem to be that for most aspirants the transitional period into adult life with its cognate physiological changes, spans their last years at school and their early years in religion. The task of the novitiate, generally speaking, is to steer them through the troubled waters of later adolescence; but school and novitiate should be linked by some kind of continuity, both of policy and of training, if this is to be effective.

How can this continuity be achieved? The answer, as we have suggested, should be sought neither in the novitiate nor school-room but in the factor common to both—the lives of the religious themselves, and particularly in their attitude towards religious authority. There can be little doubt that this problem of continuity insofar as it concerns religious should be seen against the background of the influence of modern life upon religious obedience. No religious teacher can exercise a right authority over the child if her attitude towards her own superiors is not predominantly supernatural. As her own authority *in loco parentis* is supernatural within the delegation sanctioned by parents, the command she exercises and even her technique as teacher take on the colour of her own obedience. Natural ends and motives, rewards, chastisement, personal influence—lawful inducements of every kind—cannot of course be excluded as legitimate means of inspiration in educating the child; but they should be used as means, that is, to encourage children to act with a due sense of responsibility from a right and supernatural motive.

This exercise of supernatural authority is therefore of primary importance. Immediate results may reward a too naturalistic approach to education, and it would seem that here we are at the root cause of at least some of our problems, as we shall see presently. But it is quite evident that those religious teachers whose submission to authority is vitiated by a predominance of natural motives, will induce similar motives in the obedience of those under their care. This must become the more harmful by reason of the immaturity and comparative helplessness of the child. Such an influence may get results, but all too rarely does it bring forth the woman from the child or inspire vocations.

The same truth may be seen perhaps more clearly from the opposite angle. Those religious teachers who submit joyfully and courageously to God's will as expressed through supernatural authority not only find personal security as women in religion but also grow in a sense of responsibility from a twofold aspect. First, by a healthy indifference to the person of authority in obeying the divine command as going forth from its human instrument primarily to please God and not to give satisfaction to the superior, nor through fear or any other human motive. Mixed motives are to be expected in some degree; but the submission of obedience, as such women see quite clearly, is meritorious and worthy of the dignity of a rational creature, only insofar as it is motivated by the love of God.

Secondly, this act of submission to the command of supernatural authority implies a responsibility towards the community with which the person commanded is identified. By her very status and profession the religious woman is a woman in community, participating in a common life, mentality and purpose which are informed and expressed through the directives and commands of legitimate authority. The act of religious obedience of its very nature binds all together and each and all to God. It is a surrender to God's will through the community inasmuch as it participates in a collective effort towards a common goal through a positive thinking-with authority to bring the community life and purpose to fruition.

It will be seen then that various inter-causal processes are operative in the apostolic purpose directing the act of supernatural obedience. There is a mutual causality between obedience and chastity. For chastity insofar as it is the release and diffusion of human love broadens our sympathy to embrace the community we serve and the faithful towards whom our common effort is directed. Again, this union of mind and heart in Christ through the operation of these vows and their corresponding virtues fosters of its very nature a psycho-physical maturity in the person of the religious. In other words, such a religious has a Christian and adult attitude of mind, the indispensable prerequisite in all those who have care of adolescents.

II

The same need for a personal maturity, and a positive will-to-community in our teaching sisters can be seen perhaps more clearly from yet another angle. It is man's duty to give God a rational service, to pass himself on and back to God his final Cause for His greater honour and glory. By this transference in a free surrender in Christ to God's creative plan, man is self-realized in all his dignity as God's son.

He is, then, as an individual primarily and finally responsible to God. But he finds his perfection and happiness in God through his relation to the plan and order of Divine Wisdom and not apart from it. Any approach to spiritual perfection therefore which encourages the phantasy that the spiritual life is merely an individual relationship, an enclosed garden, in which we find our perfection by loving God in isolation is both unnatural and unchristian. Our Lord could hardly have been more insistent on this. To love and serve Him we must love and serve Him in one another. If we do not love one another, that is to say, give our life in the loving service of others, our love of Him is void and sterile. Man by his God-given nature is a social being and in Christ by grace he gathers all things in his total self-surrender to God, as their unifying and rational principle.

Man, then, is one with all things inasmuch as he finds his meaning in relationship to the creation in which and for which he was made; he must live for the whole and not for himself in the surrender of self-interest when this contributes to the benefit of all. The primeval call to self-solicitude and self-sacrifice is the fundamental law of the universal conservation which extends to the Mystical Body whereby men are organically one in Christ. But it is not enough merely to know our oneness with Christ; we must go along together with Him. 'In Him we live and have our being.' The Christian life is a life in community whereby we love ourselves and our neighbour as ourselves, in that reciprocity of function essential to all organic life. The development of this sense of belonging to, being one with others in Christ—the sense of community founded on a healthy, natural social instinct—should be fostered and inspired during adolescence.

But it is no easy thing to bring forth this adult attitude of mind among adolescents who live in our modern society. It is only on *faith*—the sure knowledge that man is great enough to be God's son, and finds his greatness in his recognition of an utter dependence on God—that the Christian life can be built; it is only through *hope* that man can look forward to the complete self-fulfilment and the integral reconciliation of all life's aspirations in God; and as he needs power and confidence to step forward into a future known to God alone, it is only through *charity* that he can love God and all God's works, can be God's friend and son, and love all that God loves. For the Christian, God is enthroned, the first Cause of all things; whereas for the pagan, self is the centre of the cosmos whereto all else is a means to an end—self-exaltation. He puts his faith in a confident foresight; substitutes for hope his power to fulfil his own ambitions; and in the last analysis self-love for charity.

It is into this twilight of a Christian civilization that our children are born. They are called upon to grapple with the onrush of a pagan way of life in which selfishness and dissimulation are increasing, and men are concerned only with personal well-being and the transitory pleasures of this world. It calls for great courage to stand firm, undaunted and unscathed, in the midst of these tottering moral standards. And yet our children must be equal to this task or perish.

Thus the young religious sister soon begins to realize the part she must play in withstanding the forces of evil. She has not only to keep her own ideals unsullied but has also to prepare children for life, who are already crippled by its influence. She will soon discover, for instance, that she cannot remedy the mistakes of early home training, even in the lower forms and kindergarten of our schools. The Christian life is an integral organic thing; it must grow from birth and through the earliest years to a full maturity in which a personal responsibility to Christ and through Christ to society can be easily accepted. It is the privilege and prerogative of our Catholic parents to preside over and to foster this growth. Teachers and particularly teaching religious sisters are merely auxiliaries, but auxiliaries who in view of the waning influence of the home are assuming an ever-increasing significance.

In practice, however, this task of re-educating Catholic children can be heart-breaking. The religious sister knows quite well what she is called upon to do from the very nature of her vocation and yet at times she is the helpless victim of circumstance. To begin with, so many children pass through her hands, many of them non-Catholics, that any kind of personal influence would seem to be impossible. Further, she has to get results, to see that children work, for parents as well as the secular authority must be satisfied; and the first thing they ask for is a fitness for life, by which they usually mean the capacity to earn a livelihood. Added to this is the physical and mental strain of the sister's way of life. After a full day's work at school, she must fulfil her routine spiritual and community duties as a religious . . . Under such pressure it is not surprising that her novitiate ideals sometimes threaten to topple and that in her discouragement she decides almost as a counsel of despair to carry on, take things as they come, hoping in the end to save her immortal soul. Those who have had little experience of this harassing life with its dual obligations either side of the convent door can have little conception how easily it can get out of balance.

But the fact remains that the influence of our sisters is tremendous, in spite of these misgivings. This for two reasons: first, from their very status as religious women. It is no light experience nowadays for children, however numerous and whatever their religion, to come into contact with a truly Christian woman. If our sisters work together as a community, as a team, both inside and outside their convent, they create an atmosphere in any school, a temper of mind, a code of behaviour, which is the extension of their own life, a participation in the spirit of their order.

Secondly, the religious sister has a very real influence by reason of her vow of chastity. By this is meant that she has at her command, through her dedication, a wider and deeper devotedness which embraces the children under her care as her children in Christ; they can never be just her job. But this opportunity can never be appreciated unless virginal chastity becomes a dynamic drive in her apostolate. It is this infused virtue which brings forth in her heart the meekness, humility and patience required of her as teacher. We shall have more to say of this later; but for the moment, let us remember that chastity crowns and uplifts the natural endowments of the woman in a very special sense, widening her sympathies to embrace all those who in one way or another have been denied the influence of a good home; and that by the exercise of the virtue of magnanimity implicit in the grace of her vocation, there is no modern situation beyond her capacity.

Finally it must be emphasized once again that the secret of the religious sister's success and of her power to educate the child in the full sense of that word is to be found in her loving surrender to God's will. Fidelity to her supernatural dedication brings forth the woman, and the woman as apostle brings up the child, as one fit for life and particularly for life in religion.

III

Our argument, so far, can be briefly restated as follows:

First, if our children are to be inspired with the right supernatural intention to dedicate themselves to the loving service of Christ in religion, they must be guided from their earliest years to live for a supernatural purpose.

Secondly, this supernatural influence which is normally exercised by parents is devolving more and more on the teaching religious sister.

Thirdly, this fact demands a spiritual integrity on the part of our sisters. They can never inspire children to live for a supernatural purpose unless they themselves seek and lovingly embrace God's will as expressed through supernatural authority.

Fourthly, as the loving surrender to religious authority brings forth maturity of mind and the will-to-community, a similar surrender through the prudent exercise of supernatural authority by the teaching sister, must encourage a corresponding maturity in others, particularly in adolescents.

Fifthly, the growth of a sense of responsibility towards God and of the supernatural intention to serve Him, through such an influence, inclines adolescents freely to choose a total dedication to Christ in religion. This psycho-physical development towards adult-mindedness enables them to appreciate both the natural and supernatural significance of the vow and virtue of chastity.

Sixthly, it is the function of the novitiate to continue this influence begun in the school by bringing young aspirants under the rule of religious superiors who by a right exercise of their authority encourage a truly supernatural obedience. Only under such conditions can the freedom demanded by religious chastity and its future positive use be safeguarded.

One central truth emerges from the foregoing analysis, namely, that the training of our young aspirants depends, humanly speaking, on a right approach to the problem of adolescence, both before and during the novitiate years. A few further remarks may be helpful.

In the first place it would be a grave error to look upon the transitional period of adolescence as a crisis isolated from the child's life, that is from all that has already gone to the formation of its mind and character. For instance, those sisters in charge of older children, in their middle and later teens, often appear to bear the greatest responsibility. These children have to be prepared for an immediate future, and helped to decide upon a career. A sense of urgency often overshadows their training. But this should never obscure the fact that it is those sisters who are preparing the youngest children for a more remote future, and whose sacred duty it is to call forth a natural disposition which gathers the early impressions and experiences of early childhood around supernatural values, who have the greatest influence of all.

In the second place, as we said at the beginning of this chapter, the influence of religious must span the years of adolescence from the school to the novitiate. The crisis of adolescence strictly speaking is not due to the physiological emergence of sex but to the growing forth of the whole person towards life in community, a self-realization through our oneness with the common interests of our fellow creatures, of which sex is an integral part. No novitiate régime should retard this growth. Adolescence is a time of decision. It is not only a growing forth from the family circle into a larger world with its added responsibilities, but also presupposes a willingness to take this step and to assume these responsibilities. This decision can never be deferred without affecting the character and future of the child, either in the home, school or religious novitiate. But if the novitiate does not in fact help in this transformation, the fault does not lie with the novitiate as such, but with its mode and misuse.

But unfortunately it is often in the novitiate that this progress to maturity is halted. For instance, there is sometimes a tendency to extend a schoolroom discipline to young aspirants; or else the novitiate authorities tend to rely too blindly on traditional methods and lack sympathy for the best type of British girl who is often thought rebellious merely because she is uninhibited. Many young girls of this type brought up in our best schools are often clamped down on entering religion by an uncongenial foreign régime and mentality which destroys their freedom of function. However well-adapted these methods may be in other countries they do not help the British child, and if they are introduced during later adolescence can often be harmful.

Again, many novices enter religion straight from school; and in view of the inadequate training many of them have received, the first problem must always be that of self-adjustment to religious authority. It is the easiest thing in the world for those in charge of our novitiates to perpetuate a schoolgirl mentality which pays too obsequious an homage to natural incentives. To these young aspirants everything is new—rules, customs, habit—the whole environment. They have come to be good religious and to do so they must give satisfaction. If those in charge expect an immediate keeping of the rule, frown on the slightest misdemeanour, and look for an outward-inward development by cramping young souls into a sort of psychic straightjacket of rule and custom, then great harm will be done. It is not difficult to get immediate results in this way, when dealing with immature adolescents; and, humanly speaking, it may seem very satisfactory, for a woman loves things nice and tidy.

What these young people need most urgently, however, is not uniformity of behaviour, but a readjustment of mind in relation to religious authority. That is the one and only way to encourage freedom of function and a sense of adult responsibility. But often too much is expected of them and too quickly. If they are high-spirited girls, extraverted, with a saving sense of humour, their conduct is sometimes greeted with a good deal of eyebrow-raising and an occasional savage look or remark from one of the older sisters, 'Fancy a novice behaving like that'.

But why such surprise? Are we to expect young novices to be paragons of virtue or to parade the niceties of religious observance for the benefit of others? Surely it would be much more reasonable to exclaim, 'Fancy a silver jubilarian behaving like that'. Older sisters at least might be expected to have made good progress with advancing years.

Why is such exemplary conduct in fact invariably looked for in our novices? The answer is very revealing. To put it rather crudely, young people on entering religion are almost expected to be a little overawed by their new environment out of respect for the dignity of religious life or even as a kind of tribute to the rest of the community. 'Such conduct would never have been tolerated thirty years ago', some sister might remark. 'These young people seem to have so little respect for their elders!' But is it respect that is lacking? May it not be the expectation on the part of other sisters of a kind of deference which at least implies a predominance of natural motives? We are not defending rudeness or a want of respect due by the young to their elders, but rather commenting on a state of mind which can make excess of such respect an adequate motive for good conduct. When those about us are old or wise or learned there is every reason why we should pay special attention to what they say, and to the advice they give; but they have no authority over us just because they are old or wise or learned. Our conduct should be regulated by God's will, and He directs us through lawfully constituted supernatural authority. Our novitiates must indeed be governed by rules and customs consonant with their purpose as the proving ground of vocations. But how can young people be prepared for the modern apostolate if from the beginning they are not encouraged to stand on their own two feet, to live from a supernatural motive and to see Christ and not the headmistress in their superior. And how can their hearts be freed from fear and anxiety for a loving dedication to Christ when they feel as if they were being exhibited for inspection and approval—like gold-fish in a bowl?

A short time ago, a novice-mistress of great experience wrote as follows:

> . . . I cannot find out what they [the novices] are made of, if I correct them for the slightest transgression of the rule. My job is to teach them the rule, and especially why they should keep it, and to obey my commands in order to please God and not because I have my eye on them or to satisfy the Council. I instruct them as best I can. We have daily discussions on the spiritual life and on every aspect of the religious vocation. In addition to this I give them a loving care and I hope a fair example, but also a good deal of rope. I am not in the least distressed if the rule is rather untidy especially to start with. In my opinion it is better for young novices to grow into the rule and into a sense of the presence of God. Of course they must be corrected and at times severely; but they should be treated like young adult women and above all trusted. As my own dear novice-mistress used to say, 'A good mother mistress knows almost instinctively when to open both eyes or only one or neither; for a job done badly to please God is infinitely better than a job done well to please folk. . . .

That surely is wisdom. There is no other way of encouraging a salutary indifference towards the person of authority in our young aspirants so that their own personal responsibility to God may stand out as the primary duty of life.

It may here be objected that the above remarks may have held good for many novitiates at the turn of the century, but that they have little relevance in our own day. Much as one would like to believe this, it is unfortunately not true. The danger of natural motives and incentives in our religious life is perhaps more real to-day in the mid-twentieth century than ever before. Otherwise, why should the Church tighten up her legislation governing religious novitiates and extend the period of probation for those in vows? Surely because the supernatural intention of our modern aspirants needs to be more thoroughly investigated.

Again, the school for adolescents is undoubtedly the well-populated Catholic home. It is under the influence of this primary society that our children grow into a natural maturity. But can we say, generally speaking, that this is the function of our Catholic homes to-day?

Again, the influence of the Catholic school is ancillary to that of the home, but can our schools adequately counteract the disintegration of the home under modern conditions unless we insist more and more on supernatural values and encourage in our children that freedom of function which derives from their faith? This, we repeat, is the opportunity of our Catholic teachers, and particularly of our teaching religious sisters.

Is it not, therefore, reasonable to conclude with the above in mind that undue natural incentives and motives must be the plague of our novitiates? It should be obvious to any unbiased observer that a drastic readjustment of method is needed in many of our novitiates to remedy as far as possible the immaturity of young religious who are the offspring of an immature society. If our arguments still remain unconvincing, the observable facts of the situation are the final testimony.

In this context we would do well to ponder the advice of St. Frances de Chantal:[1]

Sister novice mistress, what would you have me say to your novices? I will tell them simply the thought that has come to me more than twenty times: This is, that I look at our daughters sometimes and I see, thank God, that they are walking aright; but it has come to my mind that they are walking a little too much through fear. I mean that it comes before my eyes that they are somewhat too much afraid of being seen by their Mistress and their sisters, and that they are too much afraid of transgressing, and that makes me think that they act rather through fear of being admonished than by the sole and single motive of pleasing God. Is not my thought true, dear daughters? If so you must rid yourselves for good and all of that defect, for, if you do your action for others, when you shall have your mistress no longer, you will become lax and will greatly try your superior. You ought to be much more careful to keep on your guard, not to transgress and to do well, when there is only God and you, than if you were in sight of all the world, of your superior, or of your mistress, and of all your sisters: for you ought to have such a respect for the eyes of God, that all care,

1 *Conferences*, p. 461.

all your study, all your attention should be not to displease Him and not to offend Him.

There is nothing more offensive to the eyes of God than to see a religious taking care not to fail or to commit acts of faithlessness in the sight of creatures, and thinking nothing of committing them before His divine eyes; as, on the other hand, there is nothing that pleases Him so much as to see a soul faithful whether in sight or out of sight of the eyes of her mistress, or for fear that her sisters will admonish her, and if she is not careful to keep this purity of heart, and to do everything to please God only, I tell and assure you that she will never be aught but a mere imitation of a religious. . . . I tell you again, my dear daughters, that if you do not as many good actions when no one but God sees you, if you are not as careful to keep yourselves modest and recollected when you are in your cells, and as much disposed to keep exact observance when you are alone, as when you are in the sight of your mistress, you will never be of any good in religion, neither for yourselves, nor for others, nor for the monastery. You will only be phantoms, masks and images in religion, who but occupy the cloisters and only serve there to give trouble and matter for mortification to the community.

IV

But with many immature minds to-day it is not the fear of failing to give satisfaction to others that provides the main drive but the fear of not giving satisfaction to themselves. This phantasy of perfection which is an extravagant spiritual ambition centring round an undue self-esteem, provides a norm of conduct not only in the presence of others but even in the presence of God.

Such self-phantasy can be encouraged by a too subjective approach to religious life. Exhortations to perfection may, for example, be so clothed in romantic, picturesque and pseudo-mystical phraseology that they feed the imagination of such young people, stimulate their day-dreams and even colour their own language when speaking to Our Lord in time of prayer. It is one thing to be simple, childlike and surrendered in prayer but quite another to be fantastical in the strict meaning of that word. At times the whole climate of a religious novitiate may give young aspirants the impression that they are expected to think and speak in this way, and to direct their behaviour and their work towards a phantasy relationship with Christ which excites emotional tensions of all kinds. To a certain type of modern adolescent this is deadly. The following quotation explains what we mean:

> One cannot be too careful to guard against inspiring adolescents with a stupidly sentimental piety towards the humanity of Christ [writes Jean Plaquevent]. The inevitably sexual colour of such feelings may permanently mislead the feminine soul, or by way of reaction, provoke in her an irrecoverable nausea on the subject of all devotion to Christ. The same danger is more rare, but should not be lost sight of, of possible perversions among adolescents, for at this critical age there is a margin of sexual indetermination. It is enough to say that, with regard to both sexes, religious teaching should be very carefully kept from too easy excitement of feeling. It is 'in spirit and in truth' that boys and girls both should be introduced to worship. The same prudence should be observed with regard to the Blessed Virgin.
>
> There are regrettable affective fixations towards their mother on the part of adolescents of both sexes which hinder interior freedom and the spiritual ripening of the individual. The transfer of filial devotion to the Blessed Virgin must not reinforce this fixation nor furnish a substitute for it, as so happens with misunderstood devotions which are vitiated at their affective base. They unman the male, and sentimentalize and weaken the maternal feelings of the female, whereas everything ought to rest on a solid and sure piety, rectified, purified and strengthened.[1]

If this is true, and such young religious are further encouraged in their phantasies by an extravagant presentation of the Christian ideal of perfection, who would care to be in the place of those responsible? The harm done to young souls in religion, particularly in contemplative orders, by the sudden and indiscreet projection of a highly mystical ideal against a background of emotional tensions is incalculable.

But even apart from this added complication one has to be careful not to excite any undue emotion in young souls. No one can polish floors with greater verve and enthusiasm than a young religious novice; she is working for Our Lord, and how she works! But no one is more likely to see herself reflected in the polished surface. Did Our Blessed Lady work in this way at Nazareth or was she

---

[1] *Lumen Vitae*, Vol. 5, 2–3. *Difference of Sex and Religious Instruction* by Jean Plaquevent, Director of the 'Institut Pédotechnique', Toulouse.

not rather content to do a normal day's work normally well to please God?

To seek perfection, to be in the way of perfection, to be perfect as our heavenly Father is perfect, to make progress in the spiritual life does not mean and cannot mean that we should be forever striving on tiptoe after an individual perfection by continually measuring ourselves against our own phantasy ideal. This kind of soul titivation in the mirror of introspection is corrosive.

To be in the way of perfection means one thing and only one thing, that we cease our strivings to get to our own self-appointed destination and rest content to go along in company with Christ, serving His convenience by going whither He shall choose in a moment-by-moment acceptance of His good-pleasure. The spiritual life is not getting somewhere but going with Someone, sanely and soberly as a Friend.[1]

To put this another way, less figuratively. Perfection is charity, and our progress in the spiritual life is measured by the degree of our charity. Charity means to love God—*velle bonum*—to will, do and be whatever is pleasing to God; to give ourselves and our service for His greater honour and glory according to His will. To examine our consciences therefore is not to look for stains on the soul, but for signs of His displeasure; or more colloquially, to sin is not to 'let ourselves down', but to betray a Friend. If we truly love God we do not give up our efforts because in our weakness we feel sorry for ourselves, but renew our efforts for His sake because we have offended Him. To grow in perfection is to become more and more Christ-centred, Christ-protective, and to stop trying to make a good job of ourselves.

We see then the need of protecting our young aspirants from the characteristic subjectivism of our time. This is much more dangerous for religious as it is so apt to manifest itself in many forms of self-seeking in the very name of Christ. One expects a good deal of enthusiasm, exuberance and imagination from normal young people; but these natural qualities must be used to lead them to an 'honest-to-goodness' collaboration with the divine will.

This demands great patience on the part of superiors. It is dangerous to drive souls faster than their grace. God's moments have to be awaited. As St. Teresa says, He does in one soul in a very short time what takes years of patient trial to bring forth in

[1] See Note 3, p. 217.

another. His movement is also imperceptible, at least in generous souls, so that they are scarcely aware of His gifts. It is therefore our duty to keep careful watch over young souls lest under the impulse of these graces they come to any harm. Every such grace is an added risk as the recipient is tempted to find in it a further motive for self-exaltation.[1]

This does not mean that we should be forever scrutinizing the motives and actions of others, but only that on realizing this danger we should act sensibly. It is only too easy to set young souls afire with enthusiasms and extravagant spiritual ambitions which obviously must thwart the divine supernatural activity. Of course nothing is good enough for God; but we have to be very careful to know the person to whom we offer such advice. So, too, we are called upon to do great things for Him in this Godless world; but the greatest thing we can do is to give Him a normal Christian service. The best mothers are not those who have set before themselves a high ideal of motherhood, but those who love their husbands and their children and forget themselves in the daily round.

If self-love is the principle on which we act [writes Father de Caussade], or if we do not rectify self-love as soon as we become aware of our preoccupation with it, we shall always be poor in the midst of abundance, at odds with God's order . . . I think that holiness corresponds to the love we have for the good-pleasure of God, and that the more His will and order are loved, no matter what they provide us with, the greater the sanctity. This is evident in the cases of Jesus, Mary and Joseph; for in their individual lives, there is more love than greatness and more form than matter, and we are not told that these holy persons sought the holiness of circumstances, but rather holiness in all their circumstances. We must, therefore, conclude that there is no special path which is the most perfect, but that, in general, the most perfect path lies in submission to the Order of God, in the accomplishment of our exterior duties as well as in our interior dispositions.[2]

---

1 'Oh, how blessed you are without knowing it. How beloved without understanding it. What great changes God effects in you, in a way that is the more assured the more secret and unknown to you it is. Our weakness it is, oh God, our wretched self-love, our pride, that brings it about that you are able to grant us graces only if you hide them from us, so that, in effect, we are unaware that they exist—this, lest we corrupt your gifts by appropriating them to ourselves by reason of our hidden, futile and imperceptible complacency. Here, dear Sister, you have the whole secret of the conduct of God.'—*Comfort in Ordeals*, J. P. Caussade, S. J., trans. Thorold, p. 100.

2 *Self-abandonment to Divine Providence*, Ch. 1, §8.

It is worthy of note that the one modern saint with a message for our time beyond all the rest is St. Thérèse. But her teaching of The Little Way has been frequently misunderstood. As a message to us it does not mean that we have neither the physical courage nor strength to do great things for God, when the faithful the world over are showing such heroism in the face of persecution. It means that the actual things we do matter little. We need not do great things to love God with all our hearts. It is the heroism of doing ordinary things with such love of God that we keep on doing them which pleases and glorifies Him. The merit of such actions is measured by their content of love and not by the magnitude or natural perfection of the deed. There is a great difference between doing a thing more perfectly for the love of God and doing a thing with a more perfect love of God.

v

A similar problem deriving from self-phantasy appears in our novitiates under another form. Many young people to-day are better educated than the youth of thirty or forty years ago. They show talent and promise. It might be supposed that the novitiates to which they go, belonging to the active apostolate and particularly to the teaching orders and congregations, are better equipped to foster maturity of mind and heart by reason of their intellectual background.

Furthermore, these young people have come from a world in which woman is emancipated. They want to give their services to Christ, sometimes admitting quite frankly that they have much to contribute and have chosen one particular order among many as the best vehicle of their talent. They are often full of new and startling ideas. They have heard, so they tell us, the creaking machinery of old antiquated apostolic methods. How, they will ask, can a Victorian superior cope with the young people of this new age? Why will they not open their convent doors to the saving tide of the Elizabethan renaissance, and send young sisters to learn their crafts at appropriate centres, and above all release the flair and talent of modern young religious who know what the world needs, from the petty and cramping restrictions of a too shortsighted exercise of religious authority?

Unfortunately it is precisely these young sisters 'with ideas' who seem to suffer from the most mysterious psychogenic disorders of one kind or another under the strain of the modern apostolate or who leave religion before taking their final vows and, alas, even afterwards. The truth is that this kind of phantasy-apostolate is dangerous and mischievous because it is rooted in a wrong system of values which sooner or later must bring it into conflict with the redemptive method of Christ. It racks the minds and hearts of its advocates because it is inherently self-contradictory.

But what can be the solution of this problem? Must the work of Christ suffer from the ambitions of young extremists on the one hand or be paralysed by the obstinacy of traditionalists and die-hards on the other? Let us make one or two suggestions.

First: In her need for vocations the modern superior sometimes forgets that young aspirants should enter religion to receive and not to give. Their one desire should be to put themselves at God's service. Once we allow aspirants to enter, so to say, on their own terms, as, for example, with the firm conviction they have a message of saving missionary importance to the older generation, the burden of responsibility rests on those who receive them. We are well aware that some modern writers ask for a new sympathy towards these talented young people. The religious superior should, of course, use the material at her disposal to the best advantage; it is her duty in conscience to do so. But on the other hand any tendency either explicit or implicit to receive such candidates on condition they will be allowed to trade their talents as they shall think fit, is subversive of the right order of things. They enter religious life as suppliants. The fruits of their apostolate will depend not so much on their talents as on the mercy of God through a participation in the divine oblation of Christ; and this offering may well include the sacrifice, as the order shall decide, even of their own natural gifts. Unless they see this quite clearly they should never be admitted.

But the argument may still be pressed. Such a policy, we may be told, will estrange many suitable candidates from religious life. Not all these young people leave; some make very good religious. In our present need of vocations, therefore, why should we not take the risk and even in a sense readjust our traditional attitude to accommodate the requirements both of the modern intellectual and of those who tell us that their happiness and well-being depends upon the free expression of their natural potentialities? 'After all,' these young people will argue, 'why should I squander my gifts, my previous training and my acquired proficiency through a refusal to insist they shall be used profitably in God's service? That is why I have come to this particular order which is dedicated to such services as I can render.'

But the point is this: although it is almost certain that the order will use these gifts in the apostolate, it cannot guarantee to do so. From the point of view of the religious authority such previous training may satisfy one kind of fitness test, whereas the insistence on a kind of contractual arrangement that it will actually be used shows a complete lack of moral fitness insofar as it disregards the Church's apostolic method. This does not mean, as we have said, that the views, methods and talents of such aspirants may not be appropriate to the apostolate. But however true this may be it should never obscure the fact that God saves the world on His own terms and not on ours. He regardeth the humility of His hand-maiden and not her talents. If, therefore, superiors receive those with the necessary qualifications for their order—say a university degree, or previous training for school or hospital—and forget the one thing that matters, or too easily give such aspirants the benefit of the doubt when presented for profession, they will bring grievous hurt to souls and the apostolate of their order. This is a matter of principle. What proportion of these young people actually stay is irrelevant. When a young person requests admittance to an order or congregation she is asked: *Quid quaeris?* What seekest thou? and she answers, *Misericordiam Dei et vestram*—God's mercy and yours.

Secondly, we should never assume that the more intellectual girls who enter religion are necessarily the more mature. Imma-turity is not incompatible with high intellectual ability and accom-plishment. Indeed far from it. One of the greatest needs in the apostolate is the *woman*. It matters little comparatively speaking whether she be learned or even efficient; but she must be a woman, as mature, unpretentious, work-a-day, self-forgetful as the mother of many children, if she is to be worthy of the privilege of caring for souls in Christ's name.

Still, however true this may be it does not answer the question we asked ourselves, namely, How are we to reconcile the modern, intellectual and emancipated girl to a largely reactionary religious authority? We had rather hoped the answer would be self-evident in view of all we have said. Perhaps, however, it would be better to add a final word.

The answer is simply this; such a reconciliation depends in large measure on the conversion of religious authority. All superiors must realize that religious life, particularly that of religious women, is in a state of acute emergency. This is the view of the Holy Father himself, as we shall see later. If superiors refuse to read the signs of the times then nothing can help them. Religious institutions must have the vitality to readapt themselves from within or perish. That is the choice of every organism when confronted with a new environment and the religious life is no exception. The test of this immanent vitality is whether or not any order or religious institution has a true conception of supernatural obedience and whether or not it intends to make such obedience practicable through the right exercise of true supernatural authority. That is the core of the whole problem. It is not a question of allowing religious sisters to do as they think fit but of making it possible for them to do as they are told from a right supernatural motive. No act is more purifying than that of religious obedience; but no act should be more responsible and free, because of its nature it is ordered to the loving service of Christ, to whom alone the religious made herself personally responsible at her profession. More difficulties than one cares to enumerate can be traced to a wrong conception of obedience from our novitiates onwards. It matters little whether things get done, but what matters profoundly is that they should be done with a sense of supernatural responsibility. There can be no freedom of function or power of readaptation in any religious order where this is not recognized. The penalty of servility in any form must be immaturity, mental stagnation and dwindling vocations.

It follows that we must not only approve the modern young woman's struggle for self-realization, but show her and the world that this can be achieved in and through the religious life. There is no question here of compromise but merely of giving the religious woman freedom to live a whole life. Of course it is quite wrong to let these young people crash through the barriers of legitimate authority under the impression they can remould the apostolate of our sisters; but this very difficulty surely should convince us of the need for some kind of readaptation. Must it be said that what secular education can do to give the woman a sense of adequacy in our times cannot be done even better inside our religious institutions? Or must it be admitted once and for all that we are so lacking in self-criticism that we refuse to see the error of our ways?

Chapter 4

THE RELIGIOUS SISTER AND THE
MODERN WORLD

WE are sometimes told that religious sisters cannot address themselves to the needs of our times unless they have had experience as adult members of society before entering religion. This would appear to give the late vocation a definite advantage.

Is this true? It does not seem to be so. Apart from other difficulties, such people, generally speaking, lose the overall viewpoint and lack the natural adaptability of those who reach maturity in religion.

However, in the opinion of many, both Catholics and others, the comparatively sheltered life of the religious sister produces a type of woman completely out of touch with the contemporary world. For example, it has sometimes been said by reputable Catholics and even by notable ecclesiastics, that schools run by our sisters are satisfactory for girls up to the age of thirteen or fourteen but that adolescents can best be prepared for modern life in secular schools under secular teachers. This judgement has often held true in the past and may even have a limited application in our own day; but this disability is not inherent in the religious life as such.

Granted an integral freedom of function it can be said without any qualification that the religious woman is not only equal to any task set before her in schools, hospitals and institutions of every kind but that no one is more competent to fulfil it.

Why must we necessarily have had experience of the world to help those who live in it? When this subject is debated in some quarters one would almost think that the apostle could only help the sinner by sharing in his sin. The apostle need not have been a thief to help the thief. Indeed he can help the sinner far more by showing forth the opposite virtue to his vice in being Christ-like. Our Lord's method was to take over the burden of sin for love of the sinner; and following His example the apostle needs compassion rather than 'experience' in the restricted meaning of that word. And it is the virtue of supernatural chastity which opens his heart to such compassion.

Again, what do we mean by experience? Usually we mean an experimental knowledge of an environment and of those who come under its influence, the nature of their reactions, their difficulties, advantages and so on. But is environment the simple thing we generally make out? We speak of the rural environment, the urban environment, the religious environment and so on, as though these simple phrases exhausted the infinite content of that expressive and meaningful word. Every environment has of course its physical features—the hills, the plains, the sea, climate, architecture as well as the cruder furniture of the modern town. But it has also many intangibles which enshrine a common historical experience of a people or locality, and which together with the physical features we have mentioned go to the formation of a common mentality; for instance, language, customs, art, literature, folklore and religion. The only way of sharing in the mental background of a people, therefore, is to be native to that people. It is from such a participation in a common mentality that sympathy and patriotism are derived. Such too is the argument for a native clergy and native religious apostles.

Our answer then to the question, Can a religious sister minister to the needs of the modern world from which she herself is comparatively isolated? must be in the affirmative, provided she is native to that world and is a mature woman, and above all compassionate, that is to say, one who can identify herself with the people by sharing as far as possible in their present experience.

Now compassion implies two things: love and knowledge. A love of the sufferer and a knowledge of the evil threatening him. The question at issue then is this: Can a religious sister engaged in the active apostolate appreciate the dangers threatening those under her care? The answer, as we shall find, is most definitely—yes. Even contemplative nuns are sufficiently in touch with the plight of the modern world to spur them on in their apostolate of reparation. But clearly the active sister needs a wider knowledge because her work brings her more closely into contact with souls. How is she to acquire this knowledge in view of the restricted nature of her life? We suggest in two ways; first, directly, in pursuance of her normal apostolic duties, though this contact is strictly limited by the Church. Secondly, indirectly, as a member of a community.

Every community is an apostolic unit, at least in theory. But it should also become so in practice, through the participation of each religious in a common experience and effort. Every sister as a community woman should be interested in the community activities as a whole. With this in view every superior should strive to keep her sisters united at all costs. It is not merely a question of sisters helping one another in a spirit of fraternal charity. In some religious houses, for instance, the sisters and even the superiors will roll up their sleeves to lend a helping hand in the kitchen or laundry. This is not what we mean. We are rather concerned with the sisters helping one another to think and so creating a common mind. This is a different matter and its demands can be very exacting. But once the superior is convinced that her community must think-together if it is to function smoothly and creatively as a single apostolic entity she can do much to inspire the right situations. At recreation, for instance, or by presiding over discussions in which a free exchange of views is encouraged, or by her own individual efforts in gathering the interest of each member of the community, whatever her work, into the common apostolate.

On the other hand a situation in which the round of duties of one set of sisters is completely out of touch with that of others, or in which a few sisters know all about the community and its work and the rest nothing, is humanly speaking intolerable, and from an apostolic point of view completely sterile. In no community should sisters be expected to mind their own business in these matters when all communicable information about their religious family *is* their business whether they be house-sisters or officials. It is sometimes explained that such a situation has its practical advantages where women are concerned or that as all the sisters are working for the same Lord and towards a common purpose these things should not matter. Sisters must do as they are told and rest content with such information as the superior deems fit to impart. This is not the general attitude of religious authority but it is frequent enough to cause considerable alarm.

The cold fact remains however that the human mind is God-made and must function as God intended. The competent military leader not only tells his men what to do, their local objective; he goes round and explains why they are going to do it, and how it fits in with the general plan of attack, and how much depends on their co-operation. In this way the ordinary soldier is not just a tactical unit acting blindly, but shares in the general strategy. In army phraseology he has been 'put into the picture' as far as security allows.[1] In this way the common soldier is given confidence both in his commander and in himself. One of the chief factors in the morale of any army is the general feeling that all ranks are being trusted, and treated like intelligent human beings.

Similarly with our sisters. Every member of a community must be incorporated in the general strategic plan of the apostolate if she is to have a contented mind. Religious sisters are not saints, and it encourages dangerous phantasies to pretend they are by making them grind away at some particular job day after day, just because they have been told to do it. The job may be necessary, but, humanly speaking, it is often in itself unrewarding unless it can be given a meaning. What an inspiration it can be for such sisters 'to be put into the picture' of the general apostolate of the community, and to realize how their work fits into the world picture of the Church's apostolate! But the trouble is that too many superiors expect the spirit of faith and of prayer to make up for this default on their part in purely human inspiration. The outcome must necessarily be a kind of survival of the fittest, spiritually speaking. Those who have a great love of God can find a certain peace even in such mental segregation; but others, being spiritual pedestrians like most of us, are mentally frustrated; they grow disgruntled and even bitter, without quite knowing why.

In these circumstances it is not difficult for those in authority to put the onus on others and even in a certain sense on the Lord, when in fact they themselves are failing as a means of inspiring a common mind and a real community of interests. Some may object that a religious should do as she is told for the love of God. That is perfectly true; and we defend to the utmost of our power every implication of supernatural obedience. But this in turn presupposes that the superior acts from a similar motive. If she does not, then, naturally speaking, she may create unbearable tensions for which she is responsible. The superior must be obeyed implicitly in utter surrender of mind and heart, but this does not give her the right to command imprudently. She may even commit a grave sin in commanding when it would be an equally grave sin for the subject to disobey.[2]

---

[1] See Note 4, p. 218.

[2] Absolutely speaking no one commits sin in exercising a right. But sin may be committed in the manner of exercising that right. E.g., it is conceivable that a religious superior may assign a sister to a foreign mission where in the prudent opinion of the doctors her health will be endangered. The superior could insist on the

A right-functioning obedience can only be safeguarded as far as lies within the superior's power by a right-functioning authority. For this reason prudence obliges her to govern her community, not in spite of, but through the common mind. She can never, supernaturally or even naturally speaking, get more out of her community than she finds there. Her functions are restricted by the material at her command. How then is she to discover and actualize the potentialities of her community, mental and spiritual, unless she reduces as far as possible all internal tensions in the creation of a common mind, through the expression of which she can prudently direct all and each towards a common purpose? From the superior's point of view it is her duty to guide and direct this creative stream into the right channels; from the subject's point of view the superior's command must be obeyed simply because it is commanded. If we want to use an instrument to the best advantage we must know how it functions and what are its limitations. In this sense the superior has more to gain by inspiring a free-functioning common mind than anybody else.

On the other hand we have sometimes heard superiors object that discussion, however discreetly conducted, or any means of giving religious sisters freedom to voice their opinions, will introduce so much criticism, uncharitableness and insubordination into any community of women that the superior's life would be unbearable. This we firmly refuse to believe. But, in any case, we are here chiefly concerned, not with means, but with a definite and urgent need. Our sisters are so skilled in the pedagogic art that they themselves, surely, can be safely given charge of the means, once they see the urgency of the need. And with regard to the above objection, are our sisters so lacking in the spirit of supernatural obedience that the personal influence of the superior is a *sine qua non* of peace and decorous behaviour? Isn't it the experience of every religious, man or woman, that it is precisely those who refuse to think-with the community who tend to become singular and even to give themselves a nuisance value?

Let us remember, too, that if young women are being given a free-functioning mind in contemporary society, the reaction to any kind of mental frustration is going to be a still graver problem in the future. The task of uniting every member of our religious

subject going to this mission and the subject would be under a grave obligation to go. But the motive of the superior could be personal dislike, jealousy, or even revenge or hatred, etc., and she may commit a sin and even a grave sin in commanding her to go.

communities in a common mind must therefore be undertaken promptly and firmly; and on two levels: supernaturally in being 'one mind and heart in the Lord', and naturally by observing the natural laws of human association. It is difficult to see how any religious authority can ignore the latter with a clear conscience.

Apart from such arguments, however, the fact remains that many superiors in this country and abroad are putting these principles into practice and with conspicuous success, even contemplative communities and notably the Mother-house of Carmel at Avila. Amongst active orders particularly, group-discussions are being encouraged, addresses given by competent sisters on matters concerning their common apostolate, always followed by questions and a free exchange of opinion. Even lecturers from outside are invited to address the sisters, at the discretion of the superior, on child-welfare, for instance, or nursing technique, care of the old and infirm, pronouncements by the Holy Father, the foreign missions and so on. Addresses, too, by priests on the spiritual and religious life, all followed by discussion.[1]

There are of course many difficulties. But what matters most is the formation of a reflective mind in our sisters from their earliest years in religion. This may or may not endure; but if the sisters themselves are alive to their best interests as apostles, and superiors devise every possible means of inspiration, for example, through discussions at retreats and at the weekly conferences over which the priest presides, attendance at lectures, group-meetings with sisters from other orders doing similar work and so on, then success is assured. But the urgency of this need for readaptation should be brought home to all.

With this in mind it should be remembered that whenever in the past any aspersions were cast on the competence of our sisters as apostles this has seldom been for their lack of worldly wisdom. Rather it was an indictment on their lack of adaptability to the needs of the time. The complaint was, quite frankly, that our sisters were shackled mentally by reason of their very vocation as religious. We have tried to show that whenever this was true it could never be attributed to the influence of the religious life as such but rather to its mode or even to its decay.

Finally, a word on the sister's indirect experience through her contact with souls. The religious sister may not live in the world but if she is a normal uninhibited woman, native to her aposto-

[1] Cf. Appendix 2, 'Discussions in the Novitiate', p. 203.

late and large-minded through the influence of her community life, she can judge causes from effects and through her intuitive gifts arrive at a very balanced judgement of the dangers of modern life.

Even so our sisters can never be expected to be ultra-modern in any sense. This is a great safeguard in dealing with souls. The gibe—'old-fashioned'—may be acceptable when applied to method but it can be very misleading when applied to culture. It is one thing, for example, to speak of certain modes of religious dress or habit as old-fashioned, or even methods of running schools and orphanages; but it is quite another to speak of the basic Christian culture of our people as old-fashioned. The trouble is, so often, that new methods may be very appropriate as methods to the needs of our time, but unfortunately they are not infrequently advocated in the name of a supposedly new culture which may even dismiss the Ten Commandments as an outmoded code of moral behaviour. Religious sisters do not, of course, think in this confused way; but there can be little doubt that the advocates of the new naturalism tend to do so. Those religious apostles who are thought to be conservative, or old-fashioned, may in fact be more faithful than any of us to the Christian principles underlying the culture around them. This is only mentioned here because true sympathy, humanly speaking, wells up spontaneously and un-reflectively from the depths of the human soul. Our religious sisters have more in common with the people of our time than mere superficial differences brought about by the ever-changing face of the modern world will warrant. It is a remarkable fact, for instance, that many parents to-day realize this, and will send their children for preference to a convent school to make contact with what is old and stable in modern life, and to prevent them from being contaminated by the false values around them.

The nature of woman is eternal, and however it may be modified superficially and accidentally it must always remain unalterably the same. Moreover, it can never be questioned that the noblest and most sublime expression of this eternal idea is to be found in the person of Our Blessed Lady; and that the state of life most closely associated with this ideal of perfect womanhood is that of virginal chastity professed by our sisters. In the degree they are faithful to their state will they be the highest expression of Christian womanhood.

What the world needs and indeed what it expects from our

sisters is not primarily a sympathy with such modifications of woman's functions as may please contemporary thinkers, or fall in with the schemes of those who replan our social life; but a restatement in the living example of the nature of woman. If the modern woman is in revolt against her environment, then every effort must be made to help her to secure a characteristic function in modern society which harmonizes most closely with her deepest desires as woman. We may sigh for the time, long-since past, before the onrush of the industrial revolution when the woman had an honoured position in the home worthy of her dignity, and was expert in many domestic crafts. But those days are gone, never to return.

In the struggle for new Christian forms, however, a dual process is at work, the one which drives our spiritual roots still deeper and by which we cling ever more tenaciously to what is true, timeless and unalterable in the midst of a swiftly changing society; the other which seeks a mode of life within that society consonant with the deepest aspirations of the Christian soul. Both these processes are necessary; but which of them should be given priority in our thinking and effort? In other words, applied to the matter under discussion, is the Christian woman more likely to accommodate herself to the needs of the new society by an increasingly aggressive insistence on woman's rights or rather by a deepening realization through a life of prayer and self-dedication to God's will of her essential dignity as woman as expressed in the archetype of Mary? There can be little doubt where the emphasis should fall. This surely gives an added significance to the vocation of our sisters.

Again, by reason of her vow of chastity, the heart of the religious sister is ennobled by a truly Christian sympathy which gives her a helpful indirect experience of the difficulties and frailties around her. Her compassion and humility enable her to listen and to learn. It is not the duty of the apostle to shape souls to his own image, but to remove as far as possible every obstacle to an integral freedom of function that they may receive the image of God through the operation of grace. This is notably true of children. We are tempted to make them grow up instead of letting them grow up; and to stamp them with our own individuality. In our aloofness we measure their ignorance against our knowledge, their immaturity against our adult-mindedness, and too often strive to control their behaviour to suit our personal preferences and even idiosyncrasies. This is the way of pride and not of humility and love, and it should teach us at least one important lesson, that the real obstacle to a true Christian sympathy in dealing with souls, especially children, is our own sin and not our lack of experience, or our comparative isolation from the world as religious.

The above brief observations should help us to decide whether or not the religious life as such brings forth women who are immature or who lack initiative and a sense of personal responsibility. If this ever seems to be true and to be justified by facts it should make us more than ever resolved as religious to keep our novitiate methods of training under constant supervision; and above all to teach our younger sisters to appreciate the maturing influence of true supernatural obedience both through adequate instructions and conferences, and the right exercise of supernatural authority.

How woefully mistaken are those who imagine that religious life as such tends to encourage servility, indecision and a total disregard for human values; or those who think that wherever a true sympathy and mature broadmindedness are to be found within their ranks this must be attributed to a rare courage which dares to find a personal independence in the face of the restrictions of higher religious authority. It cannot be repeated too often that it is not supernatural obedience but its disregard, a too naturalistic conception of obedience, which is responsible for the negative qualities characteristic of some religious women. The obvious remedy is to supernaturalize both our life and our work, and not to clamour for readjustments in our relationship with authority in the name of a modern subjectivism with its senseless insistence on the need for self-expression, and on the sacrosanct nature of personal talent. The woman, Christ's woman, is infinitely more fruitful in the apostolate than the woman of exceptional ability who has little appreciation of supernatural values. The more naturally gifted we are, the more we tend to blaze our trail to God's kingdom and to get lost in the short-cut. The guiding voice of the spirit can easily be drowned in the hubbub of modern techniques and the competitive scramble for results and prestige.

These things are more than local or domestic issues; they have a tremendous significance in our time when homes are disintegrating and the influence of parents correspondingly weakened.

Our children are largely at the mercy of a pagan society, over-whelmed in many instances by a sense of frustration and inade-quacy, with its attendant anxiety, introspection and rebellion. This is the new generation which our sisters are called upon to prepare both for life and for life in religion. How can they be equal to this supremely difficult task unless they themselves are willing instruments in the hands of Christ? Above all let us recognize the importance of the transitional years of adolescence both in our schools and novitiates. This will mean in some cases a radical change of method, if a healthy progress to adult-mindedness begun in the school is to be continued in religion. But perhaps what is needed at the moment more urgently than anything else is courageous thinking, however tenaciously we may cling to tradi-tional methods and customs.

'We have a very special reason in speaking to you,' said Pope Pius XII, addressing the heads of religious orders and congrega-tions of women gathered in Rome.[1]

> You know that orders of religious women are going through a serious crisis; we refer to the decrease in the number of voca-tions; though this crisis has not yet overtaken every country. And even where it is most serious its intensity is not everywhere the same. But already it is alarming in a number of European countries. In one district where vocations for religious orders of women were flourishing twenty years ago, they have dropped by half. Nevertheless, whereas formerly serious difficulties stood in the way of the vocation of young women, to-day exterior conditions of life seem to be attracting them to it, so that it would appear we must be on our guard against false and imaginary vocations.
>
> We do not wish to discuss this crisis in detail, though it gives us grave concern. . . . To-day we want only to address our-selves to those, whether they be priests, laymen, preachers, orators or writers, who have no word of approval or praise for a virginity which is vowed to Christ; and who for years, despite the warning of the Church, have, contrary to Her mind, preferred on principle marriage to virginity, and who go so far as to say that marriage alone is the one means of safe-guarding the development and perfecting of human personality. Those who speak and write like this should consider their responsibility before God and the Church; and they must be accounted amongst the principal offenders of whom we can

[1] On 15 Sept., 1952. Cf. *A.A.S.*, 1952, XIX, p. 823.

only speak with sadness; particularly when in the Christian world and indeed everywhere else appeals are becoming more insistent to-day than ever before for the help of our Catholic sisters, which time and again have to be regretfully declined. Indeed, our sisters have even found it necessary to close down hospitals and educational centres of all kinds from lack of vocations.

Let us then on Our part advise you as follows:

Take care in this crisis that your customs, and the life or ascetic practices of your religious families do not become a barrier and a stumbling block. We refer to certain customs which if they formerly had a meaning in another cultural context have no such meaning to-day and which would hinder a truly good and courageous girl in her vocation. . . . Let us return for a moment to the question of clothing. The religious habit should always express your consecration to Christ; that is what all expect and desire. For the rest let the habit be suitable and satisfy the requirements of hygiene. We were pleased to see during the course of the year how one or another of the Congregations had achieved practical results in this respect. To sum up: in those things which are not essential adapt yourselves reasonably and with a discreet charity.

Having said this we now give you, dear daughters, two urgent words of advice:

(i) In regard to your maternal affection in ruling your sisters:

There can be little doubt, as psychology claims, that the woman in authority does not succeed as easily as the man in striking the right and exact balance between severity and kindness. This gives yet another reason for cultivating your motherly gifts. Never forget that the vows demand a great sacrifice on the part of your sisters as well as yourselves. They have renounced their families, the happiness of marriage and the intimacy of home life. This is a high and rewarding sacrifice of decisive importance in the Church's apostolate, but it is sacrifice none the less. And it is those of your sisters with the noblest and most sensitive hearts who feel this detachment the most keenly. It is here that the words of Our Lord can be applied wholly and unreservedly in our own day: 'He who having put his hand to the plough and looks back is not worthy of the kingdom of God.' But the order should replace the family as far as it can, and you, superiors-general, must be the first to instil the warmth of family affection into the common life of the sisters.

In addition you yourselves ought to be motherly in your

outward bearing and in your words, both spoken or written,
even if at times you have to hold yourselves in; but let this restraint above all be exercised over your innermost thoughts
and judgements, and as far as possible over your feelings. Every
day ask Mary, the Mother of Jesus and our Mother, to
teach you to be motherly.

　　(ii) In respect of the training of sisters for the work incum-
bent on them by their vocation.

Do not be mean or niggardly, but broadminded in this
matter. Whether it is a question of education, teaching, the
care of the sick, artistic or other work, the sister should be able
to say to herself: 'The superior has provided me with a training
which puts me on an equal footing with my colleagues in the
world.' Give them also the opportunity and means of keeping
abreast of the latest thought and developments in their profession.

Chapter 5

THE RELIGIOUS SISTER IN TRANSITION

I

IT is said that when the late Father Bertrand Wilberforce divested himself of his habit at the end of the day he would leave it in the middle of the floor. He argued that this saved him the trouble of looking for it the following morning. But as everything else seemed to find its way there sooner or later his argument lost much of its validity. In the words of an old religious sister when she heard this story, 'Wasn't that just like a man?' But on the other hand how many priests have remarked in making their perilous way over the highly polished floors of our convents: 'And isn't this just like a woman?'

So much in lighter vein. But there are more serious differences in the mode of religious life of men and women and we would like to examine these a little more carefully.

First, in their approach to work. It is sometimes said rather vaguely that our sisters, generally speaking, do more work than their brothers in religion. As far as one can tell, this is hardly fair on the men. But they certainly do work very differently. One always feels, for instance, that religious sisters would get through more work if they had more leisure. However debatable this might be, many of them would certainly be happier if they had more time to do as they pleased.[1] It is no answer to reply that women are never happier than when 'doing something'. There is a certain element of truth in this, but the question is whether it would help them if they were given more opportunity to do as they pleased, and, if they pleased, to do nothing. A full day's horary, one job succeeding another with split-second regularity, may seem very admirable. It is undoubtedly true that in many of our convents an unpunctual chaplain can throw the whole daily routine out of gear. But without defending even the occasional unpunctuality of chaplains, may not such a nicely scheduled existence cause a good deal of mischief in the lives of the religious themselves?

[1] See Note 5, p. 219.

Many superiors will argue that a full and crowded day improves the community silence, prevents gossip and so on. If this is not an instance of the remedy being worse than the disease, it is surely the wrong prescription.

Again, we may be told that sisters must work in this way as there is so much to do. If this is true then there are two obvious remedies: either more sisters or less work. One can imagine an experienced Reverend Mother throwing up her arms in horrified exasperation at such a suggestion:

'More sisters, Father. But where from, pray?'

'Well, dear Mother, if you cannot get more sisters perhaps you could streamline your work?'

'Streamline, indeed! When we already polish the floors from the mains.'

And she has the last word.

But two things must be said. Isn't it possible that the complaint, 'we have too much to do', is evidence not so much of overwork in foot-pound output of energy, but of a wrong attitude towards work, which can make people less efficient because they expect to feel tired? The cause of this wrong attitude may be an absence of right motive for working.

But let us suppose that our sisters do work from the highest motive. Can there be any doubt that the breathless existence many of them lead does more harm than anything else to their spiritual lives? Somehow or another they have got into the way of working hurriedly, their minds one move ahead of their hands, distracted by the urgent need to get on to the next job. This emotional ferment is both unnatural and unchristian. Such religious live in a state of continual tension which ends by robbing them of all functional co-ordination. They begin to make mistakes, to be unpunctual, forget obediences, break things, pray with endless distractions. And, what is worse, their emotional state drives them to work still harder in an effort to escape from themselves.

There is only one way of gearing down such a restless existence that is at all practicable, and that is by the right use of leisure, if we may repeat a word which is anathema to our sisters. And by leisure is not meant the usual respite we call recreation, but time off to gather up the loose ends of the day, and do as they please within the scope of rule and custom. The distinction between working quickly and working hurriedly is clear enough; but the one sure way of increasing our capacity to work both well

and quickly and to avoid undue haste is to be given time of our
own. In the words of Père Lacordaire, 'it is a prudent man who
understands the reasons for taking his ease and how to take it.'[1]

We are far from pretending that this problem is easily solved
when a radical solution may depend on our willingness to remove
more fundamental causes. Higher authority can spend many a
weary hour balancing the personnel of this house and that to
enable each to work as a team; and how often she has to admit
defeat! But she knows in her heart of hearts that the real trouble
has been caused by others in her position who have taken on more
work, founded more houses than she had sisters to staff, hoping for
an increasing flow of vocations which never materialized. An old
and experienced bishop once said in our hearing, 'the first consideration of any superior in making a new foundation should be
the souls of her own sisters.'

Nothing increases the religious sister's sense of inadequacy
and causes more discouragement than to be perpetually faced
with the demands of a life which are beyond her normal capacity.
This spectre of overwork has a disastrous effect on the spiritual
lives of whole communities; and it is not surprising that St.
Francis of Sales should tell us that next to sin this is the greatest
curse in religious life.

Further. One of the chief needs in the modern apostolate is a
free functioning mind. Our work must not be of such a nature, or
carried out in such a way, that it prevents us from co-ordinating
the contents of our minds through the frustration of all subconscious mental activity. Automatic and repetitive work, and
normal day by day routine duties can assist such an activity
provided leisure is used creatively. But on the other hand, when
our work is not only unceasing but begets a mental restlessness and
an anxious preoccupation with the urgent need to get things done,
we live at such a self-conscious and superficial level that all mental
co-ordination and integration is impossible. Such a way of life
brings the mind of many a religious sister in conflict with its own
demands. The mind craves unity and order, and if this is withheld,
it becomes the prey of every kind of extravagant and dangerous
fancy.

Secondly—and this leads us to the main argument of the present
chapter—the natural dispositions of men and women in religion
would seem to differ widely. This may be due principally to a

[1] See Note 6, p. 220.

difference of sex. It is sometimes said, for instance, that, generally speaking, women are more excitable and emotional than men, less self-reliant and more introspective. The emotional level of the average religious woman is certainly greater than that of the religious man. But it would be unreasonable to conclude that this is necessarily harmful. On the contrary, it might be compatible with high virtue. The woman, from her point of view, might just as reasonably protest against the staid, phlegmatic, unfeeling and heartless religion of men. It would almost seem, therefore, that this problem is insoluble, at least as far as the judgement of one or other of the sexes is concerned.[1]

Yet is this quite true? It is difficult for any man taking his own reactions as the norm, as he usually does, to judge what degree of emotion is connatural to the woman. Absolutely speaking, the problem is still more perplexing because we do not know how far the character of the modern woman, to say nothing of the man, is reactive to environment. Nevertheless it does seem possible to discover from its causes whether the relative emotionalism of woman is excessive, particularly the emotions of fear, timidity and discouragement which, as we have seen, play havoc with the spiritual life of the religious sister. These emotions at any rate seem to be reactive to the modern society in which woman finds herself, through a prevailing sense of inadequacy and insecurity; and they may be increased immeasurably through faulty training in the home, and school, and particularly in the religious novitiate.

The acceptance of the inferior status of the woman in modern society must therefore be taken into serious consideration in deciding the method of training and the nature of the apostolate of religious sisters.

It is clear to the most casual observer that woman to-day is largely out of context in modern society. This state of affairs has been accelerated by the impact of the machine and the physical sciences which has swept away the old order of things and created an industrialized and mechanized society which in turn has made necessary highly centralized economic and political systems. A closed domestic, local or national economy is no longer possible. The people in one country depend for their daily bread upon those of another, supply and demand fluctuating under the influence of imponderables such as international relations and the internal

[1] See Note 7, p. 221.

stresses of nations. The result has been to create populations which are increasingly nomadic, insecure, and dependent upon the state. The home as we knew it is disintegrating.

But the tragedy has been that these things have come upon us so swiftly and violently. Woman, in particular, has had little opportunity of rehabilitating herself to the changing conditions of domestic and social life and is reacting against her lot with all the violence of frustration, in her anxious search for a domestic and social meaning. She has to fight against the deeply rooted prejudice that all her gifts are domestic in character, as though her inevitable lot were to become man's auxiliary and dependent, to be used as he thought fit, on the assumption that superfluous women are a social problem rather than a social asset.

Unfortunately, through her temporary displacement, woman finds herself more than ever in direct competition with man in the social struggle for recognition. She is claiming not only equality of status but also in a sense similarity of function. As a result her qualities of mind and heart are being relentlessly compared with those of man, now a rival more than a co-partner, and she is generally being proclaimed his inferior before her natural gifts have even been tested. In the general view she is timid by nature, over-anxious, unreasonable in argument, narrow-minded, lacking concentration and persevering effort, incapable of speculative enquiry, ruled by her heart and her intuitions rather than her head, and so forth.

There is obviously a substratum of truth in this assessment; but how much? On the other hand how far are these qualities merely reactive? Unfortunately, woman's inferiority is so taken for granted that subconsciously she herself has come to accept it. From her earliest years she is greeted affectionately and even proudly as one to be loved for her feminine charm and good looks; one to be protected, but over whose education parents need not worry unduly. Any attempt to think or act otherwise is viewed with patient tolerance especially by fond parents who see their daughter as a potential wife and mother, forgetting that she may be a wife without a home and perhaps without a family, and may even not get married at all.

Can we wonder then that in her present search for rehabilitation woman should be irritated and in her instinctive reaction to this sense of inferiority should overcompensate and lose all sense of direction? But it may well be that the passing of the home as we knew it will bring forth even greater things from the dead ashes of failure, frustration and despair in the restatement of womanhood and of its significance both in domestic and social life.

This is woman's moment in history. Man has held the field for so long in all social and intellectual life, and has had so many opportunities of acquiring confidence in his own abilities that the present comparative achievements, both social and intellectual, of men and women can hardly be taken as evidence of their comparative capacity. For this reason, whilst admitting that woman's qualities are ordered to her function as wife and mother, this does not mean that she is inferior to man in her other gifts or that she has no social purpose as woman. If she herself takes this for granted by lowering her self-esteem through her willingness to be humoured and used for man's purposes she does a great disservice not only to herself but to mankind. Her principal struggle is against herself and her first emancipation must be the victory over her own fears. The condition of such a victory, and in a sense the very victory itself, will be found in her ability to restore social chastity amongst us by her example and moral influence as woman. But this must come about through a positive appreciation of this virtue and not merely through the knowledge that social lust is her enslavement.

We begin to see then that woman is not man's rival but his co-partner in domestic and social life. 'In the day that God created man,' we read in the book of Genesis (5. 2–3), 'He made him to the likeness of God. He created them male and female; and blessed them; and He called their name Adam, in the day when they were created.'[1]

These words surely mean that there is an organic oneness, spiritual and psychological, in the relationship between the sexes, and that each discovers and realizes itself precisely in its relationship to the other. For just as in marriage the man and woman are one 'in the flesh', so in the male and female relationships of human life in society man and woman must be interdependent 'in one mind', and indeed interdependent at every level of life, even, as we shall see later, in the Christian economy of Redemption.

What matters most then in our human life is not the equality or precedence of the sexes in relation to one another, but their right functioning in relationship to one another; not pride of place but happiness. We are not happy when functioning *first*, but when functioning *right* according to our God-given nature. This right

1 See Note 8, p. 222.

functioning can be brought about only in the union of the sexes, by first restoring this creative union in the primary society of the home that through its influence men and women may be inspired to work together in a creative mental and moral union for the good of society. As the true functioning of the former calls for a union and oneness in Christ, so too does the latter.

II

Let us now review the whole question we have been discussing from the opposite angle—that of Christian marriage—that we may see more clearly how it affects the apostolate of our sisters.

Pope Pius XI writes in the Encylical Letter, *Casti Connubii*:

False teachers who try to dim the lustre of conjugal faith and purity do not scruple to do away with the honourable and trusting obedience which the woman owes to the man. Many of them even go further and assert that such a subjection of one party to the other is unworthy of human dignity, that the rights of husband and wife are equal; wherefore, they boldly proclaim, the emancipation of women has been or ought to be effected. This emancipation in their ideas must be threefold, in the ruling of the domestic society, in the administration of family affairs and in the rearing of children. It must be social, economic, physiological—physiological, that is to say, the woman is to be freed at her own good pleasure from the burdensome duties properly belonging to a wife as companion and mother (We have already said that this is not an emancipation but a crime); social, inasmuch as the wife being freed from the cares of children and family, should, to the neglect of these, be able to follow her own bent and devote herself to business and even public affairs; finally, economic, whereby the woman even without the knowledge and against the wish of her husband may be at liberty to conduct and administer her own affairs, giving her attention chiefly to these rather than to children, husband and family.

This, however, is not the true emancipation of woman, nor that rational and exalted liberty which belongs to the noble office of a Christian woman and wife; it is rather the debasing of the womanly character and the dignity of motherhood, and indeed of the whole family, as a result of which the husband suffers the loss of his wife, the children of their mother, and the home and the whole family of an ever watchful guardian. More than this, this false liberty and unnatural equality with the husband is to the detriment of the woman herself, for if the woman descends from her truly regal throne to which she has been raised within the walls of the home by means of the Gospel, she will soon be reduced to the old state of slavery (if not in appearance, certainly in reality) and become as amongst the pagans the mere instrument of man.

This equality of rights which is so much exaggerated and distorted, must indeed be recognized in those rights which belong to the dignity of the human soul, and which are proper to the marriage contract and inseparably bound up with wedlock. In such things undoubtedly both parties enjoy the same rights and are bound by the same obligations; in other things there must be a certain inequality and due accommodation, which is demanded by the good of the family, and the right ordering and unity and stability of home life.

As every society however small must have its head, the husband is the natural head of the home; but he is not empowered to do as he thinks fit, but what is right and within the appointed sphere of his authority. Obedience is due to him in domestic matters, in which he is head of the house; in the choice of a place of residence, for example, or the management of the family income, the discipline of the children; but he has no rights over his wife's personal affairs, over her conscience, or politics, or property, or what she reads, or how she dresses, or how she spends her leisure-time. Further he has no power to command if he is unreasonable and he has no claim to obedience should he order something sinful or foolish.

The relationship between man and wife thus crudely stated would be almost meaningless to those who are happily married. Imagine, for instance, a non-Catholic reading through the rules and constitutions of a religious order. He might study them word by word and yet never understand them if he were ignorant of the spirit which brings them to life. So too with the mutual obligations of man and wife. These can have little meaning unless we remember that married partners are bonded in Christ.

It follows, therefore, that in the degree that marriage is deprived of this supernatural life in Christ it must tend to degenerate into a mere convention held together by human respect or by fear, or at least by some other inadequate human motive. In such circumstances it is hardly surprising that the husband should become the usurper of power as though authority were vested in him as man and not as husband. This is obviously much more likely to happen in Catholic marriages in which the outward forms are more rigidly held together by a common Faith.

The truly Christian marriage is a fusion of two human lives, in the sense that it is a union of minds informed by a common belief, and a contractual union of wills which directs two lives towards a common, accepted purpose and experience. The Christian family is therefore a supernatural organism in which the free-functioning of the husband as head is dependent upon the contrasting and complementary free-functioning of the woman as wife and mother. It is this reciprocity of function of two people united in love and loyalty to Christ which brings freedom, happiness and contentment into the Christian home.

Children brought up under the aegis of such a home acquire an unbounded love and respect for their parents. But what is more important still, the dignity and freedom of the woman as woman is revealed in the living example of a truly Christian mother; and the girls acquire a self-respect and self-confidence in their destiny as women. On the other hand, when girls find their own mother unhappy and self-piteous, complaining continually of her lot as wife and mother, it is only to be expected that they will envisage their own future with foreboding and anxiety, convinced either that marriage is a pitfall to be avoided at all costs, or at least a state of life to be divested of as many irksome duties as possible.

Is this picture exaggerated? In one sense it may be. Apart from the fact that even Catholic families tacitly accept the social inferiority of the woman, we cannot say that such families are either very good or very bad. In a large number of Catholic homes conditions are far from satisfactory, and, what is more to the point, it is from such homes that the majority of our aspirants to religion are recruited. The good Catholic family is the best training ground for the religious life, but we have to face the fact that if we insist on an ideal home background we are likely to get very few vocations indeed. This partly explains why so many young people entering religion suffer from the disabilities we have mentioned.

Without attempting to trace all the causes of these things, there are several observable facts which sometimes alarm those in charge of our novitiates. For example, the children of the non-Catholic home are often better prepared for life and, should they be given the faith, better suited for life in religion than the children of many Catholic homes, particularly those nominally Catholic or in which the parents are failing in their responsibilities. When the Catholic marriage ceases to function aright the children often suffer from a more grievous sense of inferiority, with its attendant emotional disorders, than the children of non-Catholic and even non-believing families around them. This is chiefly due to the domestic tensions created by the inner conflict of a fixed and unalterable mode of life that has lost its Christian meaning.

Again, many of the characterological disorders noticeable in aspirants of good Catholic stock can be traced to ignorance. In districts and countries traditionally Catholic the need for a thorough and well-balanced Catholic education seems less urgent. But it is a tragic mistake to infer that because such people are practising Catholics they do not need instruction in the life of the spirit, or because their marriages are crowned with the nuptial Mass and blessed with children that Catholic women and mothers do not need a thorough instruction in Christian mothercraft. This becomes all the more imperative when we remember that in all probability the children of these families will spend their lives in a totally different and even pagan environment. Let us insist, not only does a faith rooted in the culture of a country demand a more thorough religious education to prevent mental stagnation, but the very nomadic nature of modern life which uproots individuals and even whole families, transporting them to alien lands, makes such education more and more urgent and even a matter of conscience for those responsible.

There is hardly any need to pursue this investigation. But even the brief remarks we have ventured to make lead us to the inescapable conclusion that many characterological disorders manifested in religious life and which have been examined in the preceding pages of this book are due to ill-regulated Catholic marriages. This points to a long-term policy if we are to inspire young people with a love and preference for the religious state, and to ensure a temperamental fitness. Our policy should be vocations *through* marriage and never, even implicitly, vocation *instead* of marriage, which may suggest that the religious vocation is in some way an escape from the hazards of married life.

The radical cure for all our difficulties is to be found in a religious education which deepens the life of the spirit, and destroys the illusion that a traditional and pietistic Catholicism will safeguard our children from the many pitfalls of the modern world. Everything which tends to debase the supernatural purpose of the Christian marriage must be opposed, particularly the mixed marriage and the tendency of the modern girl to rush into marriage through ignorance of the dignity of married life and the real nature of married love. Many of our girls refuse to see the risks of choosing an unsuitable partner through a deep sense of fear and anxiety. If, for instance, we take the two words—bachelor and spinster—and listen to their overtones we see at once that the former is a freely chosen way of life whilst the latter implies a kind of stigma. The spinster is one who has been rejected. Many young girls feel the disgrace of this more than we realize, and through their lack of confidence overcompensate and take unnecessary risks.

What then is the alternative? The religious vocation? Emphatically—No. We should never encourage our girls to think in this way, but try to free their minds, make them confident and purposeful by pointing out courageously that many vocations are open to them as Catholic women in society. If this is emphasized in all our teaching, it will restore that much needed self-respect and sense of power in our girls which will prevent many an indiscreet and precipitate marriage. And especially will it encourage them to seek the highest vocation of all in religion.

Our sisters must at all costs grasp this truth. They will be rewarded most generously with vocations if they will give priority in their thinking and in all their apostolic activities to the restoration of self-confidence in our Catholic girls, and try by every available means to dispel that sense of inadequacy which enslaves the women of our time.

We see then the urgent need for a whole life of normally balanced tensions in our convents, if sisters are to be worthy of this apostolate. They themselves are the children of the modern world and are equally infected with the prevailing lack of confidence and its attendant emotional instability. Their first victory must be won in their own hearts.

But this is not quite as simple as it might seem. The sense of inadequacy amongst religious women tends to make them timorous and self-distrustful on the one hand, and on the other this very disability works towards an undue self-assertiveness by way of compensation. This inner instinctive drive becomes a source of great danger when we consider the relationship between subject and superior, and the dread results of lack of confidence or its opposite in either one or the other. Our religious sisters must not only understand the principles governing supernatural obedience and the right exercise of supernatural authority; they must have the courage to put these principles into practice. Unless they do so, even naturally speaking, their apostolate will be crippled. Nothing so warps the character of the woman as any tendency or pretence to serve Christ from natural motives, particularly fear in its many manifestations. The obedient religious is one who does as she is told fearlessly and lovingly to please God and never merely to give satisfaction to others, even the superior. Her complete supernatural surrender is the royal road to freedom of spirit, to that self-confidence and sense of personal responsibility to God and God alone, which must radiate from her life and activity as Christ's apostle.

When we ponder the influence of our sisters in their active apostolate we can see how much depends on this victory over themselves as women. If they succeed they will bring forth in our Catholic girls that confidence in their capacity as women and a will-to-community which are so needed to-day. But let us repeat, this can only be achieved by mature and responsible women in whom the supernatural infused virtue of obedience is operative and whose hearts are freed and ennobled by virginal chastity.

III

The full stature of the woman has still to be manifested in the life of society. This fact must be seen as a challenge to our sisters; they must be given every opportunity to realize their full potentialities in every branch of science, literature, art and general culture connatural to the life and mind of the woman.

To some this statement may seem unreasonable. They will tell us that the range of the woman's apostolate as a religious should be restricted to or at least directly related to such duties as a woman normally fulfils in the home. But are these the inviolable limits of the apostolate of our sisters, or commensurate with their natural endowments? We are not here voicing the need of higher education as such but merely expressing the hope that all the potentialities connatural to the woman will one day be released into the Christian apostolate by our sisters; and that this will not only be found compatible with the supernatural purpose of their vocation but will, under obedience, have that purpose as its inspiration.

A new development of this kind can never spring from the ambitions of the religious subject however talented; it must come from a definite policy on the part of those in authority who believe that women in religion have qualities of mind and heart which have yet to be fully and courageously explored in the service of Christ. This is precisely the present trend both in Europe and America where a beginning has been made in spite of reactionary elements. It is only fair to point out that wherever this disapproval is to be found, whether among the sisters themselves or others, it is mainly due to the acceptance of the intellectual inferiority of the woman or to the suspicion more generally felt that she can scarcely be trusted in her quest for truth. The woman's place is in the home; but 'the fact is', writes Pope Pius XII,

> that woman is kept away from the home not only by her de-
> clared emancipation, but often also by vital necessity by the
> need to earn her daily bread. It is therefore useless to preach her
> return to the home as long as conditions continue which in many
> cases force her to remain absent from it. And here is the first
> aspect of the mission in social and political life which presents
> itself. . . . A wide field is opened to woman's activity, an
> activity primarily intellectual or primarily practical, according
> to the capabilities and qualities of each individual.[1]

Similar extensions in the apostolate of our sisters may be expected principally amongst those devoted to the education of
Catholic youth. Many of us in spite of our protestations to the
contrary may still look upon these changes with a certain repug-
nance. But surely if our sisters are not worthy of our encourage-
ment in their desire to give a corrective feminine emphasis in the
practical application of truth to human affairs, then there is
something radically wrong with their religious life. Are we to
suppose that women are less proof against the dangers of the intellectual and scientific life than men? If we persist in thinking they
are, and by undermining their confidence cause them to over-
reach themselves, it is not a pleasant thought that we may soon
be blaming them once again for mistakes and excesses which we
ourselves have done a great deal to encourage.

Let us repeat our conviction once again: woman has still to
manifest her full potentialities to the world. And as the Christian
woman is the highest ideal of womanhood, we must expect such a
manifestation to come mainly through our religious sisters. If
woman is more true to her God-given nature through her love of

[1] *Questa grande vostra adunata.*

Christ, she is never more so than when her heart is dedicated exclusively to the loving service of Christ. Our sisters can never show forth these qualities to the world unless they are more widely accepted in every branch of modern culture in keeping with their religious state, and take every opportunity as apostles and teachers to draw forth the natural talent of those under their care, by founding colleges and universities for women and by participating insofar as their rules permit in every branch of cultural and scientific life. We can only repeat that if the lives of such religious women are relentlessly directed to a supernatural purpose, particularly in respect to supernatural authority, all our fears are groundless. If we still persist in voicing them we are giving yet another instance of our determination to perpetuate woman's subservience and inferiority.

Our sisters must break down this prejudice in the name of Christian womanhood both by their work and their example, and restore the dignity of woman in the home and in society; not in a spirit of revolt inspired by self-love but through a love of truth and their own characteristic interpretation as women of basic human values. When the Christian woman is functioning according to her nature she is functioning freely and is thereby self-fulfilled in her surrender to the love and will of Christ. That is her *Magnificat*, whether she is serving Christ in society or in the home or in religion. If this revolution of love is not inaugurated by our sisters who are dedicated to Christ through a life of virginal chastity, where else can we expect it to begin; or by what other means can the Christian woman regain her freedom?

One final thought. We are often inclined to think that the biological changes of adolescence are its essential characteristic whereas this crisis is in reality an integral reorientation of the human person towards social life and responsibility conditioned by such biological change. Similarly it is an error to suppose that the purely biological differentiation of the sexes is the one essential factor in the husband-wife relationship of marriage, whereas the formal cause of this relationship is to be found in the contractual union of two *persons* of different sex; and though its primary purpose is to beget children it has a secondary purpose in promoting a community of mind and of life; and this may become the one and only purpose through a free and mutual agreement to practise perpetual continence from some worthy motive. Such a union is a true marriage, as in the case of Our Lady and St. Joseph,

and it bears abundant fruit insofar as it is the unselfish and intimate union of mind and life for a social and spiritual purpose.

So, too, the less intimate man-woman relationship in society is
a complementary relationship of persons of different sex which
brings forth a community of life and of mind in the interests of
society, through a mutual influence and collaboration conditioned
by difference of sex. But we must bear in mind that the right
functioning of this association can be promoted and safeguarded
only by the practice of chastity, the moral integrity of the sexes.
Any violation of this fundamental condition of a creative social
collaboration promotes from the very nature of things an anti-
social disunion and independence which brings about an unequal
struggle for sex supremacy. Outside the creative act of marriage
this surrender of woman is, of its very nature, an enslavement
which sacrifices her dignity and destroys her influence. Above all
the social violation of chastity brings in its train a licence which
degrades the national mind and character by introducing a
selfish and individual purpose into a social collaboration ordered
to the interests and perfection of the race. In the face, therefore,
of modern thought, practice and propaganda we should recognize
and acclaim the virtue of chastity as the bulwark of a creative
and progressive society, at every level of social life.

We must conclude then that whilst marriage is the association
of the sexes *par excellence* which brings about by one identical
organic act the union and perpetuation of the race, it would be
an error to suppose that this creative function covers the total
significance and use of sex association, either in the home or in
society.

As children of God [writes Pope Pius XII], man and woman
have a dignity in which they are absolutely equal; and they are
equal, too, in regard to the supreme end of human life, which
is everlasting union with God in the happiness of Heaven.
To have vindicated and proclaimed this truth, and to have
delivered woman from a slavery as degrading as it was contrary
to nature, is one of the imperishable glories of the Church. But
man and woman cannot maintain or perfect this equal dignity
of theirs unless they respect and make use of the distinctive
qualities which nature has bestowed on each sex; physical and
spiritual qualities which are indestructible, and so co-ordinated
that their mutual relation cannot be upset without nature itself
intervening to re-establish it. These peculiar characteristics
which distinguish the sexes are so obvious to everybody that

nothing short of wilful blindness, or a doctrinaire attitude as disastrous as it is utopian, can ignore or fail to see their importance in the structure of society.

Indeed, this co-ordination of the sexes through the characteristics peculiar to each is such as to extend its influence to every single manifestation of the social life of man.[1]

We must say then that whilst woman's place is in the home, it is not exclusively in the home; she cannot forgo her duty to society in the broader and secondary issues of sex association. Even as a married woman she will have opportunities of fulfilling this duty after her family has grown up and her primary obligations satisfied. Or again as an unmarried woman she may forgo marriage altogether to fulfil these social duties, embracing a profession or devoting herself to some other form of social service; or she may enter religion to devote herself to the higher spiritual well-being of society, preferring the way of perpetual chastity not only to safeguard her integrity as woman but also as a means to union with Christ, that in, with and through Him her influence may embrace the world to the full extent of her being as woman and spouse.

But the key to this vocation of woman whether in the home, the world or in religion is chastity. It must be abundantly clear that the religious sister promotes the well-being and salvation of her sex not only by her example but by the promulgation of the creative power of chastity through every possible avenue of her apostolate.

Every woman without exception is under an obligation—a strict obligation of conscience, mind you!—not to remain aloof; every woman must go into action, each in her own way, and join in stemming the tides which threaten to engulf the home, in fighting the doctrines which undermine its foundations, in preparing, organizing, and completing its restoration.

This is one motive calling the Catholic woman to enter on the new path now opening to her activity. But there is another: her dignity as woman. It is for her to work with man for the welfare of the *civitas* in which she enjoys a dignity equal with his, and here each sex has its part to play according to its nature, its distinctive qualities, its physical, intellectual, and moral capabilities. Both sexes have the right and the duty to work together for the good of society, for the good of the nation. But

[1] *Questa grande vostra adunata.*

it is clear that while man is by temperament more suited to deal with external affairs and public business, generally speaking, the woman has a deeper insight for understanding the delicate problems of domestic and family life, and a surer touch in solving them—which, of course, is not to deny that some women can show great ability in every sphere of public life.

It is not so much that each sex is called to a different task; the difference is rather in their manner of judging and arriving at concrete and practical applications. Take the case of civil rights for example; at the present time they are equal for both sexes. But just think how much more intelligently and effectively these rights will be used if men and women pool their resources in using them. The sensibility and delicacy which are characteristic of the woman may perhaps bias her judgement in the direction of her impressions, and so tend to the prejudice of wide and clear vision, cool decision or far-sighted prudence; but on the other hand they are most valuable aids in discerning the needs, aspirations, and dangers proper to the sphere of domestic life, public assistance and religion.[1]

Questa grande vostra adunata.

Part Two

DEDICATION

Chapter 1

INITIAL PROBLEMS

THE Christian attitude towards virginal chastity bewilders the modern world. Apart from the usual dissentient voices, many sincere and religious folk are convinced that perpetual chastity and particularly any kind of general invitation to follow this counsel is unreasonable and even unnatural.

It is sometimes asked, for instance, why the Church should accept without question the natural law of self-preservation and yet provide so many exceptions to that of race-preservation, especially when that law has been unequivocally reaffirmed by the divine command—'Increase and multiply and fill the earth.'[1]

Although one has little hope of convincing those who ask this and similar questions it is helpful now and again to examine the natural foundations of our vow. To begin with, there is an obvious difference between the two obligations mentioned. The former is laid upon the individual, the latter on the race. The ultimate good of the rational species does not depend merely on its numerical increase by carnal generation but also on the willingness of the individual acting in the name of the race to use his sexual life reasonably for the well-being of society. In this matter all restraint and even complete and perpetual renunciation is praiseworthy if it is directed towards the common good.

But even if marriage is an obligation laid upon the race and not on the individual, the argument continues, virginal chastity is in fact impossible for all. St. Paul says, for instance, 'But everyone hath his proper gift from God: one after this manner, and another after that. But I say to the unmarried and to the widows: It is good for them if they so continue, even as I. But if they do not contain themselves let them marry. For it is better to marry than to be burnt.'[2] Is it not imprudent, therefore, to advocate virginal chastity for all when many people lack the necessary disposition?

But St. Paul is not speaking of the disposition but rather of the

---

[1] *Genesis* 1. 28.   [2] 1 Cor. 7. 7–9.

will-to-chastity. This argument can be disturbing only insofar as the two are confused. A religious under the stress of grave temptation, for example, might conceivably be tempted to regret her vow, and permit some form of the above argument to weaken her resistance. She may argue that the burden she has taken upon herself is intolerable. And if so, how can she be held responsible for the 'way she is made'? But may not this apparent impossibility be due not so much to an unsuitable disposition or to any physical cause but to a gradual undermining of the will-to-purity through neglect of prayer and the encroachment of a deep-seated self-love? It is not sufficient to love chastity in the sense of wanting to be chaste, she must will to be chaste, by taking the means provided by her vocation to build up a chaste mind. If she refuses she can hardly pretend that God has not given her the right disposition when the formation of such a disposition is within her own power.

A further argument comes from the opposite extreme. If all the people choose the state of virginal chastity what is to become of the world? This question may be answered by asking another. In the words of St. Jerome, is it very likely that virginal chastity will ever become popular enough to endanger the future of the race? And even if it did, may we not argue with St. Augustine that as the world will come to an end when the number of the elect is completed, is it not conceivable that God will bring this about by the universal practice of virginal chastity? Such a view is neither contrary to Faith nor the natural law, however incompatible it may seem with the predictions of Our Lord.

Again, the modern pagan will argue that whether it is contrary to the natural law or not, there can be no doubt that any such rigorous restraint of the sex impulse inflicts an irreparable hurt on all those who practise it. As man and woman are mutually complementary it is unreasonable to urge them to forgo a natural completeness to which each is entitled. And not only unreasonable but harmful, bringing in its train many grievous psycho-organic disorders. To be happy we must function according to our nature.

To many people this argument seems unanswerable. Even religious will sometimes refuse to face it squarely because they fear no answer can ever satisfy them. Such people should realize that by deliberately closing their minds to all rational investigation they must gradually begin to accept chastity as a discipline and remain forever ignorant of its power as a positive function in the apostolate. It would be an extraordinary thing indeed if we religious were condemned to an unnatural existence and to become the oddest of all God's creatures through our efforts to be Christ-like.

To solve this problem let us make two points as briefly as possible. In the first place we know, as Catholics, that our Divine Lord brings us a total and threefold reconciliation—to God, to one another and to ourselves. Any degree of frustration at any level of the human soul is incompatible with the theocentric life begotten in us through the redeeming grace of Christ. It is painful to have a limb further dislocated before it can be reset; and so in the Christian life our personal readjustments to God's will are often painful and difficult. But one result of this asceticism is the harmonious and integral functioning of our human nature even in this life.

Our Lord has told us explicitly that after death there will be no marriage or giving in marriage. In other words, in heaven the sexual function will be eternally quiescent as the merest symbol of the higher rapture of the Divine embrace. In that God-man relationship each glorified soul will find an integral personal happiness. We must therefore say, either that man here below is divinely organized as a person to this eternal life which is the very purpose of his creation, or he is not. If he is, then it is only to be expected that as grace is an actual participation here and now in the eternal life and love of God, he who is vowed to virginal chastity will find personal harmony in the degree of his love of God as expressed in his unconditional surrender to the will of the divine Lover. On the other hand any serious disorganization of his person of whatever kind, or any abnormal failure in those human qualities which make him acceptable in a normally constituted Christian society, must be attributed to his refusal to pass himself on in love, worship and self-forgetfulness, and to see in his vow a further means of a more perfect union with the divine will.

This argument must have a considerable force, even for the pagan. The sex-function of its very nature is an act of the race, because its primary purpose is the continuation and preservation of the race. The promulgation of any system of thought or behaviour therefore which tries to resolve these problems in terms of personal well-being may in the actual circumstances of our fallen nature be a crime against the race and create frustrations at a deeper level of the human soul. If the main problem of our times is to find sufficient reason for the unselfish service of others, the perversion of the sex-instinct and function which is the symbol and the highest natural expression of such a service must bring grievous hurt both to the human race and to the minds and lives of the individuals concerned.

Further, for the modern pagan, the solution of the problem of chastity may be found in the correlation of sex and the well-being of society. If society realizes collectively the perfections of our human nature more than is possible in a single individual, it may be considered in the human order of things to have the greater claim on man's allegiance, sometimes transcending personal interests, particularly in that act whose primary purpose is social. If this is granted, there is no reason to suppose that individuals may not have the duty of living chastely and even of living in perpetual chastity for the good of society.

Man is by nature a social animal and the sex-function is primarily directed of its very nature to the good of the race; it is therefore inconceivable that chastity, either married or virginal, should bring serious hurt to the psycho-organic life of the individual. But on the other hand if this social responsibility is flouted and the well-being of the individual made the norm of the right exercise of the sex-function, such is the innate tendency of man as we know him towards every form of self-seeking that all social relationships will be profoundly disturbed. Once this twist has been given and we are all expected by prevailing opinion to look inwardly to our self-interest as the norm of our social conduct, then any solution of this problem is impossible. The sluice-gates having been opened, how can we prevent the flood of selfish thinking which distorts truth to the grave detriment of society? It is seldom those most conversant with informed scientific opinion who are most intimately in touch with the ordinary folk, but writers and professional men who adopt the scientific jargon of to-day to support outmoded and discredited theories. Under the influence of this pseudo-scientific bombardment people become too conscious of the workings of their body and mind, and the easy prey of functional disorders of every kind, mesmerized by their anxious preoccupation with personal well-being.

Treating of this matter Father Henry Davis, S.J., writes:

It was held for a long time that continence was impossible for the married and for celibates. Doctors lent their authority without much scruple to the widespread conviction that absolute chastity was dangerous to young men; at the present time there has been a change of opinion in this respect, and it is admitted, not only by medical opinion but by the majority of the enlightened public, that continence has no dangers provided that it is the physical outcome of a moral attitude. The so-called sexual necessity of young people is often produced artificially through the nervous system under constant stimulation of an erotic nature. Under these stimuli there is increased desire; on the other hand, desire diminishes, and continence therefore becomes easier, if occasions of this sort and their recall by the mind are sedulously avoided. It is, in fact, chastity of the mind which makes possible and renders easier physical chastity while immoral thoughts or intentions make it difficult or unbearable.

To confuse continence and chastity is an error. One who is chaste can be continent without much effort and without disorder; one who is not chaste can be continent only with great difficulty, and if he achieves it, it is often at the expense of his physical and mental health. It is not chastity which is anomalous, it is continence plus impurity; that is the real danger, and it is there that we must seek for the causes of nervous disorders which have been wrongly ascribed to continence as such.[1]

And finally let us ponder the wisdom of Jean Guitton:

If sensual desire were not intensified by the excitements of imagery and the artificial idea of its exigencies, it would be very much more easily moderated. In rude ages the cult of the Virgin has recalled this possibility. As Auguste Comte perceived, the idea of the Virgin did much to make virginity possible; to give it the characteristic, which it has always had in the Catholic West, of appearing easy. It is a reproach to the Reformation, according to Harnack and Foerster, that it had the effect of compromising this achievement. By obliging priests and religious to marry, not so much out of respect for marriage itself as to make a ritual protest against clerical celibacy, the Reformation lessened that human liberty which it was its professed object to exalt. The absence of the cloister and the obligation of marriage suggested that continence was both impossible and inhuman. In a world where marriage is conceived as the only normal state, the imagination, so powerful in this sphere, makes virginity unrealizable, or at any rate gives it a certain air of impertinence.[2]

[1] *Moral and Pastoral Theology*, Vol. II, p. 175. In the last paragraph Father Davis quotes Doctor Pasteau's *Étude Médicale sur la Chastité chez l'Homme.*
[2] *The Blessed Virgin*, pp. 164-5.

Chapter 2

THE VOW AND VIRTUE OF CHASTITY

LET us now consider the nature of religious chastity and the relationship between the vow and the virtue. This can perhaps best be done in the form of questions and answers, even though, for the sake of clarity, some repetition and overlapping will be necessary. The questions will be as follows:

(i) What is meant by the vow of chastity? (ii) Is chastity a virtue? (iii) Is chastity a moral virtue? (iv) Is chastity an acquired moral virtue? (v) Is chastity a supernatural infused moral virtue? As this last question is by far the most important, we shall deal with it at length, and then conclude the chapter with one or two practical applications.

I

What is the vow of chastity? Clearly the virtue of chastity is not confined to the religious state. Married partners have to practise it by exercising a reasonable marital restraint; and indeed this mutual co-operation is a source of great strength in facing the many problems of family life. But even the vow of chastity is not proper to religious; it is taken by the clergy of the Western Church and at times by layfolk.

By definition the vow of chastity is a promise, freely and deliberately made to God, to abstain absolutely from all voluntary sexual pleasure, and all interior and exterior acts conducive thereto. It will be seen, therefore, that as long as this vow is valid we do not afterwards sin against the vow by observing it from any motive whatsoever. For example, the overriding motive for keeping the vow in some emergency may be self-respect or shame. We may even commit some other sin in preserving our integrity, but we do not break our vow.

The vow of chastity is co-extensive with the virtue. It is therefore a violation of the vow of chastity to trifle with phantasms, which we know from experience will excite sexual emotions and desires, even though these are not consummated by any exterior sensuous act.

Why then, we may ask, is the vow necessary and even more pleasing to God if the virtue of virginal chastity may be exercised without taking the vow? Would it not be more meritorious to practise this virtue under the free impulse of love than under a kind of compulsion? No, and the reason is this: it is more meritorious to perform a good action under vow because the vow is an act of the virtue of religion, the noblest of moral virtues, by which men give due worship and reverence to God as the Creator and supreme Ruler. To observe one's vow of chastity, therefore, is an act of the infused moral virtue of religion which is more meritorious in itself than an act of the infused moral virtue of chastity. It is clear, then, that he who loves God finds an additional perfection in formally consecrating his human desires and emotions to God's service. St. Thomas writes:

It is better and more meritorious to do one and the same deed with a vow than without it, and this for three reasons:

In the first place because to make a vow is an act of religion which is the chief of the moral virtues; and as the more excellent the virtue the better and more meritorious the deed, so the act of an inferior virtue is the better and the more meritorious for being commanded by a superior virtue, whose act it becomes through being commanded by it, just as the act of faith or hope is better when commanded by charity. Hence the works of the other moral virtues . . . are better and more meritorious when they are performed in fulfilment of a vow, since in this way they belong to the divine worship and are like sacrifices made to God. That is why St. Augustine says: that not even virginity is honourable as such, but only when it is consecrated to God and cherished by godly continence.[1]

Secondly, (it is better and more meritorious to do one and the same deed under a vow) because he who vows to do something and does it subjects himself to God more than he who merely does it, for he subjects himself not only in regard to the act, but also in regard to the power to perform the act, because in future he cannot do something else. Even so, as St. Anselm remarks, 'he who gives the tree with its fruit gives more than he who gives the fruit only'. That is why we thank even those who promise to make us a present (for he who promises us something already gives it to us in so far as he binds himself to give it, just as a thing is said to be made when its cause is made, because the effect is contained virtually in its cause). That is

---

[1] *De Virg.*, VIII.

why we thank those who offer to make us a present as well as those who actually make us a present.

Thirdly, (it is better and more meritorious to do one and the same deed under a vow) because a vow gives us firmness and inflexibility in willing to do what is good and this belongs to the perfection of virtue, just as obstinacy of mind aggravates our sin, and is called a sin against the Holy Ghost.

Then St. Thomas quotes St. Paul: 'Each of you should carry out the purpose he has formed in his heart, not with any painful effort; it is the cheerful giver God loves'[1] and asks in view of the fact that some fulfil their vow sorrowfully under the constraint of its very obligation, whether it would not be better to act without taking a vow? And he answers:

The necessity of compulsion, in so far as it is opposed to the will, brings sorrow; but the necessity from a vow in so far as it strengthens the will, does not bring sorrow but joy. That is why St. Augustine wrote to Armentarius and Paulina: 'Repent not thy vow, thou shouldst rather rejoice that thou canst no longer do what thou mightest lawfully have done to thy detriment'. But [continues St. Thomas] granted that the will to fulfil the vow still persists, even should the very deed, considered in itself, become joyless and grudging it would still be more meritorious than it would have been without the vow as the fulfilment of the vow is an act of religion which is a greater virtue . . .[2]

It is clear therefore that in vowing ourselves to virginal chastity we intend, amongst other things, to take the prudent precaution of safeguarding the deeper and more noble aspirations of our hearts against any vacillation or weakness in times of temptation.

The vow of chastity binds us under grave sin. If we transgress we offend first against the virtue of religion, secondly against the virtue of chastity; and in some cases, by the exterior violation of chastity, we commit a sin of scandal, which has a special gravity by reason of our vocation as apostles. It may be a sin of active scandal and offend against charity if it occasions the sin of another by word or deed which is or appears to be evil to the person scandalized. We say 'appears to be' because our own conscience can never decide the moral rectitude of another. Such scandal may be a mortal sin if we know that the person scandalized is thereby put into the serious occasion of mortal sin. If the other's

[1] 2 Cor. 9 7 (Knox).   [2] S.T. 2–2, 88, 6; and ad 2.

sin is not only foreseen but intended, that sin also is committed by the one who gives scandal.

But scandal caused to others by a good action on account of their evil dispositions is called 'pharisaical'. The peculiar incidence of scandal in the life of religious apostles is due to our profession as the upholders of right and Christian conduct. We are trusted, respected, and what we do and cause others to do can be a sort of guarantee that it is both right in itself and for them, instituting perhaps some subtle deviation from their habitual behaviour which may lead even to moral disaster.

II

Is chastity a virtue? Yes, chastity is a virtue or good habit. A habit in this sense is a permanent quality in a faculty of our soul, acquired through repeated acts, and disposing us to exercise that faculty readily, easily and with pleasure.[1] Once acquired, a habit is with difficulty lost. A virtue is a good habit that is a lasting quality in a faculty of the soul acquired by repeated acts which disposes it to good rather than to evil. Chastity therefore is a good habit acquired by chaste living whereby we restrain concupiscence, that is to say, voluntary pleasure arising from the sexual appetite, or the interior or exterior acts conducive to such pleasure, following the dictates of reason. The pleasure attaching to the sexual appetite is God-given and cannot therefore be sinful in itself; but the desire of it and the surrender to it may be sinful if the sexual appetite is not directed to the purpose God intended.

A certain confusion has arisen in the use of words to connote chastity as, for instance, purity, and even virginity. It might be helpful to define these terms, at least as they are used in this book.

Purity. The confusion is here especially noticeable. Sometimes this term is made synonymous with chastity or again with decency (*pudicitia*); or again it is used to include chastity and decency, which is the meaning we shall give it here.

Decency. As chastity is a virtue which moderates according to right reason all venereal pleasure but chiefly that of the principal or consummated act, so decency is a virtue which moderates to the rule of reason venereal pleasure chiefly in its secondary or non-consummated external acts, for example, looks, conversations,

[1] See Note 9, p. 224.

touches, embraces, kisses, which are however related to the principal act because they are of their nature enticements to it or its preliminary expression or at least its external sign and accompaniment. These secondary external acts therefore may be sinful because they are of their very nature ordained to the primary act.

For this reason undue and inordinate expressions of affection are accompanied by a sense of shame sometimes called a sense of modesty, which helps us to safeguard the virtue of chastity. To lose this sense of shame through indiscreet and senseless behaviour is to tear down the natural defences of chastity, and to leave the soul open to more grievous temptations.

Virginity. 'To keep free from the experience of venereal pleasure', says St. Thomas, 'has an excellence worthy of greater praise than merely avoiding inordinate venereal pleasure; wherefore virginity is a special virtue which is related to chastity as magnificence is to liberality.'[1]

Virginity is therefore the highest form of chastity. It is twofold; first, *physical virginity* which belongs to the virtue of virginity only insofar as it is the physical sign or indication of the virtue; but it does not belong to the virtue essentially since virtue is in the soul and not in the body. Hence it is possible to be a virgin in body without having the virtue of virginity as, for example, an unbaptized baby. On the other hand there are many virgin martyrs in heaven crowned with the aureole of virginity with all its heavenly rewards and privileges who on earth lost their physical virginity as the result of an outward violation to which they gave no inner consent.

Secondly, *moral virginity*. Virginity as a virtue is perfect chastity, that is, the firm intention of abstaining always from venereal pleasures. The virtue of virginity not only excludes the external act or sexual function but also all deliberately entertained desire for such intercourse. This is what is usually meant when the word 'virginity' is used. To put it more simply—to be a virgin means never to have consented to consummated venereal pleasure in thought or deed. To lose one's virginity means deliberately to give way to such a desire with or without the consummated act. If this unlawful loss of virginity is brought about through desire only and not followed by the full experience of venereal pleasure, then virginity can probably be restored by repentance. But as the

[1] *S.T.*, 2–2, 152, 3.

essence of virginity is the perpetual abstinence from all such venereal pleasure, it is obvious that one single act fully consented to
and experienced can bring about the loss of this virtue. Not even
God can make an actual breach of this virtue non-actual. But
although in such a case the virtue of virginity would be irre-
coverable this does not apply to chastity, which is always recover-
able; and indeed heroic chastity is quite compatible with the loss
of virginity as in the case of St. Mary Magdalene and St.
Augustine.

When the term virginal chastity is used in spiritual books it
must be taken as synonymous with perpetual chastity unless
otherwise stated, that is, the firm intention of abstaining from all
venereal pleasure in the future. Nor must it be considered that
the loss of virginity as such introduces any impediment into the
Christian apostolate. It is indeed possible that the virtue of infused
chastity may be more intense in one who is not a virgin than in
another who is.

III

Is chastity a moral virtue? Yes, chastity is a moral virtue. Moral
virtue perfects our natural tendencies by bringing them under the
sway of right reason. A moral virtue then is a habit perfecting
man's will and lower appetites to dispose him to act in accordance
with the dictates of reason; first in his relationship to God and
his neighbour as, for example, in the moral virtue of justice;
secondly, in relationship to himself as in the moral virtues of
fortitude and temperance. Fortitude is the moral virtue which
disposes man to face those evils which he most dreads and to
resist the inclinations of mere recklessness. It involves the control,
not the absence, of fear. Temperance, on the other hand, is the
moral virtue which inclines a man to control his natural appetite
for sensual pleasure.

The moral virtues like the faculties of the soul which they perfect
are very numerous; but all of them can be reduced to the four
cardinal virtues of Prudence, Justice, Fortitude and Temperance.
Of these, the one which concerns us here is temperance, of which
chastity is a subsidiary. Temperance as above defined is a moral
virtue which enables man to control his natural sense-pleasure.
This sense-pleasure is twofold—first, the pleasure attaching to
self-preservation in the use and enjoyment of food and drink,

which is moderated within the proper limits of propriety by the subsidiary virtue of abstinence; and secondly, sexual pleasure attaching to the preservation of the human species, which is moderated to the requirements of reason by the moral virtue of chastity. The purpose of chastity is therefore the control of venereal pleasure.

IV

Is chastity an acquired moral virtue? Yes, chastity is an acquired moral virtue. This question has more than an academic importance. As we have already seen, if virtue is a good habit it can obviously be acquired by doing and continuing to do what is right and reasonable, so that even a pagan can acquire the natural virtue of chastity with or without supernatural help.[1] But the motive inspiring such virtue in his case would remain natural, for instance, self-esteem, or to free the mind for the service of truth. Such acts having a natural purpose or motive can never be supernaturally meritorious.

V

Is chastity a supernatural infused moral virtue? Yes. An infused moral virtue may be defined as a perfection of our natural faculties which does not depend upon repeated acts as in the case of acquired moral virtues, but is immediately implanted by God as a principle of supernatural activity in the soul, enabling it to perform meritorious acts. Clearly every effect must be proportionate to its cause. For example, an animal acts instinctively; it cannot act rationally. Man, on the other hand, being a rational creature can perform rational acts; but these acts are natural. If he is to perform supernatural acts, these obviously must proceed from a supernatural principle of life within him, which is called grace.

Through the merits of our Redeemer, man once again participates in the supernatural and divine life of God. At Baptism this supernatural elevation of grace is infused into the essence of his soul, and with it are also infused the three theological virtues of Faith, Hope and Charity, which have God Himself as their immediate object, and the gifts of the Holy Spirit; and together with these the infused moral virtues of Prudence, Justice, Fortitude

1 See Note 10, p. 225.

and Temperance, which are concerned with the means to be employed in attaining union with God our last end. The object of these infused moral virtues therefore is not God Himself, but the regulation of our life according to His will from the supernatural motive of love.

Chapter 3

THE CHASTITY OF LOVE

LET us now reconsider more carefully and formally the questions we asked ourselves in the foregoing pages, more especially the difference between the acquired and the infused virtues.

First, we return to the notion of the acquired virtues. The human, rational soul is a substance, and as such is not immediately operative, but needs faculties through which it may act. There are as many faculties of the soul as there are operations of the soul specifically different. These faculties are very numerous and fall into various groupings. There are the *cognitive faculties*; first the intellect, which is the faculty of thought, including attention, abstraction, judgement, reflection, self-consciousness; and then sensitive cognition, including the external senses and the imagination. Then there are the *appetitive faculties*; first the will (the intellectual appetite), which directs itself to whatever is good as set before it by the mind; and the sensitive appetite which is inclined to whatever is good as apprehended by the senses, and in which the passions reside.

A passion then, psychologically speaking, is the intense inclination of the sensitive appetite, accompanied by organic modifications. It is synonymous with what is now commonly called emotion. A passion of its nature is involuntary though the will can influence it indirectly. These passions are either concupiscible or irascible insofar as the sensitive good presented to them is easy or difficult of attainment. The passions in the concupiscible part of the sensitive appetite are love, hatred, desire, aversion, joy, sadness; and in the irascible part, hope, despair, courage, fear, anger . . .

All the faculties are interrelated and co-ordinated under the simple directive impulse of the rational soul. Two things here must be borne in mind:

First; as a soul unregenerated by grace is a natural principle of life and activity, the faculties through which it acts are also natural and can be ordered only to a natural end or purpose. The mind, for instance, cannot apprehend divine truth, nor can the will love other than humanly.

Secondly; the operations of the soul are often involuntary, as, for example, in autonomic glandular functions and reflex activities of all kinds; but most of those which affect human behaviour, as in the case of the passions, are at least indirectly under the control of the will. In other words, the soul through the will exercises choice in accepting or rejecting whatever good is apprehended by it.

Those faculties then which are under the direct or indirect control of the will can acquire habits through the repetition of acts to which its consent is given. The free will is therefore the efficient cause of these habits, good or bad. But if virtues are good habits, it is important to remember that in a sense not all 'good' habits are virtues. We may use the word 'good' either in the absolute sense to signify moral perfections, as when we speak of a 'good' man, or in the relative sense to signify a perfection in some physical or human function or faculty, as when we speak of a 'good' violinist or 'a good memory'. A good habit, therefore, may mean two things: good in the relative sense that this particular habit modifies and even perfects a particular faculty of the soul; or good in the absolute sense that the motive or purpose of the will causing the habit is good because it helps to make him who wills a *good man*. When we say virtue is a good habit we mean good absolutely speaking—a morally good habit.

An example will make this clear: An expert burglar may be habitually abstemious because abstemiousness sharpens his wits and so helps him to take other people's property. He may undoubtedly have the habit of abstemiousness through a life-long discretion in this matter but he would not have the virtue of abstemiousness. But if this habit is not good, morally speaking, because his motive is bad, neither is it bad, morally speaking, insofar as it is a habit. It is even relatively good, psychologically speaking, because through it a particular faculty of the soul is functioning aright. It is important to be quite clear about this distinction between the psychological aspect or perfection of virtue and the virtuousness of virtue.

If the human will then is the efficient cause of acquired moral habits, good or bad, what is the function of the will when the soul is elevated into the divine life by sanctifying grace? The ultimate purpose of such a soul is not the perfection and co-ordination of its faculties towards the good natural life, but a supernatural and divine union with God here and now which will bring it to its ultimate goal in the Beatific Vision. If therefore a soul is possessed of supernatural life and destined to live for this supernatural purpose, it must possess supernatural faculties to achieve that end, for natural faculties as such can never suffice, any more than the faculty of sight can see truth.

We have to ask ourselves therefore what happens on the advent of grace. Does God destroy man's natural faculties and supplant them with others entirely new? This is, of course, possible. But is it conceivable that God should confer this perfection on man in a way incompatible with the natural faculties He has already given him? It would not appear so unless we are prepared to impugn the Divine Wisdom Itself. The alternative is that God must fortify the natural faculties of the soul so that whilst remaining the same in kind and in co-ordination they are given a surpassing excellence, and supernaturalized and perfected in quality to an almost infinite degree. This perfection which is absolutely necessary for the supernatural operation of the soul is to be found in the supernatural virtues.

These virtues differ, therefore, from the natural acquired virtues not only in quality, the degree of their perfection, and in their purpose but also in their origin; they are God-bestowed whereas the natural virtues are a perfection of man's natural faculties acquired through the repetition of acts. But however perfect these natural virtues may become through these human endeavours, they can never be the means of the supernatural operation of the soul. It follows then that whereas man can perform a good natural act without possessing the facility of the natural virtue, he cannot perform a supernatural act at all without the infusion of a supernatural virtue.

Again, as a supernatural virtue does not originate from a repetition of acts neither can it grow more perfect through such acts. As its origin must be by way of a divinely infused perfection, any increase in its supernatural perfection must be divinely bestowed. And as the measure of God's love of a soul increases that soul's capacity to love divinely, so the faculties through which it operates must by the grace of God be rendered more perfect by an increase of supernatural virtue, in the measure of its capacity to love.

The source of the perfection of supernatural virtues therefore is charity, the love of God, and the measure of their perfection is the intensity of charity. We possess the supernatural infused virtue of chastity, for example, in the degree of our love of God and not through the repetition of acts of chastity, or by any other human means. It is for this reason that the perfection and fruitfulness of virginal chastity is to be sought in the growth of charity through the divinely appointed means of grace—the sacraments and prayer.

But if supernatural virtue of its very nature must be infused, that is to say if neither its origin nor increase in the soul depend on our own acts or efforts, even if these be supernatural, how shall we explain the fact that facility in the practice of these virtues increases through the repetition of acts? Surely, it may be argued, God bestows His graces and increases our virtue in the measure of our fidelity to His will which can mean nothing else than the persevering practice of supernatural virtue. And again, although the natural acquired moral virtues can never be meritorious because they are not supernatural, have they no function at all in the spiritual life? Is it not possible that the supernatural moral virtues and the acquired virtues exist in one and the same person at the same time and have some complementary function in relation one to another?

These are not purely speculative questions; they must be answered satisfactorily if we are to understand the nature of chastity, and to cope with the practical difficulties we shall discuss later.

To answer them we must return once again to the specific and essential difference between the natural and supernatural moral virtues. Let us first of all take the example of a pagan who by the help of God's natural concurrence has led a good moral life. We would say of such a man that he has acquired natural virtue, that is, natural habits perfecting the faculties of his soul through his consistent efforts to live in accordance with the natural law. These habits of their very nature are primarily modifications of the active principles of operation of his soul, just as habits in the angels though fewer in number are perfections and modifications of their powers of operation.

But man is not immaterial like an angel but a creature composed of body and soul and whose soul is united to his body as its substantial form. In the case of the man in question, therefore, his good moral life has not only perfected the faculties of his soul, but has also affected his body by bringing about certain psycho-

physical changes or modifications.[1] Every organism grows to the
mode in which it is exercised and so the acquired moral
perfection of the man we are considering has brought about a
complementary facility and co-ordination in his physiological and
mental functions.[2] The more firmly his moral habits are established the more determinate becomes this complementary disposition which helps to restore order in the passions through a
continued and uniform control of their biological and emotional
causes. In other words, through the acquisition of moral virtue
his whole body and indeed his person has become organized and
self-adjusted for virtue with corresponding mental associations of
every kind. That is why the practice of virtue becomes increasingly
easy, and joyful, because virtue perfects the whole organism, which
functions the more easily and joyfully in the measure it functions
aright. Contrariwise in the case of the habitual sinner not only
is there disorder in the faculties of his soul but in some degree his
whole person becomes organized for sin. If he is converted he has
not only to alter the purpose of his life, but also to re-educate his
mind and body to correspond to this new attitude. This, fundamentally, was the difficulty of Nicodemus, as it is of everyone else
who has made up his mind to begin afresh. It is a comparatively
simple thing to bring over the helm, but it is not quite so easy to
bring round the ship, as St. Augustine found.

Again, a moment's thought will reveal that here we are at the
root principle which should guide us in the education of young
children, that they may be inspired to organize their persons for
Christ before they are called upon at the age of reason to practise
the virtues of the Christian life. But it would be a great mistake
to confuse these natural habits and the cognate psycho-physical
dispositions we have referred to with virtue. These natural predispositions which govern the good behaviour of the child are
not virtuous but they will make the way to virtue easier when the
child arrives at the age of reason. Even the order and determinacy
brought about in the faculties of its soul by early training are not
virtuous. Training predisposes for virtue. When a child arrives
at the age of reason its first act is an act of supernatural virtue, if
it chooses to act virtuously and is already baptized. But the point
is, that through early training many obstacles to the growth of

---

[1] See Note 11, p. 225.
[2] 'Ex similibus actibus similes relinquuntur dispositiones et habitus.'—S.T., 3,
Supp., 42, 3 ad 4.

supernatural virtue have been removed. . . . We had better return to this later.

Secondly, having taken the example of the good pagan let us now take that of the exemplary Catholic who has grown in supernatural virtue and from the motive of charity has persevered in the Christian life. God has perfected the faculties of such a soul; but in his response to the divine love which is the cause of this supernatural perfection in his faculties he has of necessity to practise virtue. In other words, God's supernatural activity is increased in his soul through the sacraments but he himself is a kind of dispositive cause of this increase insofar as he co-operates through the practice of virtue, that is, through the repetition of good acts which are supernatural and meritorious.

Our Lord could not have made this clearer: 'If you love Me, keep My commandments'; and again, 'It is not those who say Lord Lord who enter the kingdom of heaven, but those who do the will of My Father who is in heaven,' and again, in the words of St. John,[1] 'This is the Charity of God, that we keep His commandments'; and again, 'He who perseveres to the end will be saved.'

Such good works are man's response to the Divine Love and are meritorious of an increase of this Love. But they also have a purely natural influence upon the faculties of his soul, confirming them in their respective acquired natural habits, and also disposing the cognate physiological and psychological functions complementary to such habits, all of which make the practice of supernatural virtue easier, more prompt, stable and joyful. But these acquired natural habits and the complementary natural dispositions of the human organism are not virtues, even natural virtues; because if habits become virtues when they are directed to the 'good life' of the person possessing them, this has already been brought about by the infusion of divine grace which directs the soul to its ultimate supernatural purpose through the supernatural virtues.

Clearly, then, these natural acquired habits and dispositions cannot directly promote the supernatural purpose of our life but indirectly they can make its attainment easier by removing many obstacles to it. The distinction, however, between natural habits and dispositions must be kept in mind. A habit is a modification of a spiritual faculty; a disposition is a tendency in the bodily

[1] 1 John 5. 3.

functions which may be inherited, due to early training and environment or the result of a habit acquired through repeated acts.[1] (Thus a man may have acquired a sober disposition through cultivating the habit of sobriety.) Habits are fixed and lost with difficulty; but dispositions are less stable, particularly those acquired through the habit of chastity due both to the more extensive psycho-physical co-ordination of the sex impulse, to its intensity and to its nature. Sex-desire of its nature gathers the entire human organism into a unity of purpose which is to love another, body and soul. Sex-activity is the love activity of the whole person; it drives down to the organic, generative and biological functions of the human body over which the will has little or no control; these bring forth the emotion of sex-love and this in turn involves the will which is the spiritual faculty of love. But such is the vehemence of this love-surge that any lack of control over the emotions draws the whole person into a vortex of desire in which the will, a blind faculty, becomes immediately involved of its very nature. For this reason any indulgence in the emotion of sex-love in a refusal to avoid the emotional causes of sex-desire can fire the love-potential of the entire human organism. It requires only a small detonator to release the latent energies of the most explosive material and for this reason we should protect our chastity behind prudent and circumspect behaviour so that our emotional life may always be under reasonable control. Of all our dispositions, that of chastity, therefore, is the most easily disturbed.

[1] Cf. Appendix 3, p. 209.

Chapter 4

PRINCIPLES IN PRACTICE

AS we have seen in the foregoing pages we grow in the virtue of supernatural chastity in the degree of our love of God. On the other hand the natural habit and disposition of chastity depends upon the repetition of chaste acts through our firm intention to live chastely. The growth of supernatural chastity is thus determined as far as we are concerned by the degree of our love of God as expressed in our efforts to keep chaste.

I

The immediate difficulties to be considered derive from two sources: first, the mistaken idea that the growth of this supernatural virtue depends solely or disproportionately on our efforts to love God (as, for instance, by multiplying our prayers and devotions), making us indiscreet, careless and even reckless in the presence of temptation; and secondly, that the repetition of chaste acts and the formation of the natural habit and disposition necessarily implies a corresponding increase in the love of God and therefore in the supernatural virtue of chastity. The motive for these chaste acts may be largely natural, and therefore in due proportion unmeritorious of an increase in the supernatural virtue of chastity.

During the air-raids on London, a certain Dominican Father, feeling more panic-stricken than usual, went to the late Father Vincent McNabb and asked his prayers. His reply was shattering:

'My dear Father', he said, 'there is only one way of acquiring courage and that is by being courageous. Be off with you! Get into the middle of it!'

What this holy man obviously meant was this: the habit of fortitude can be formed only through living courageously—by actually and repeatedly 'facing up' to things which make us afraid. If we refuse or neglect to do this, long prayers, penances, novenas and so forth will not help us. We have to do it ourselves.

Similarly, our status as religious does not of itself give us a natural leaning towards chastity even though we have such an abundance of spiritual help. We have to be vigilant—on our guard in this matter like everyone else. Apostles sometimes expect a certain immunity especially from gross temptations partly from the nature of their vocation and partly from the attitude of the faithful, either expressed or implied, that religious are not quite like other men and women. It is not difficult for a religious sister, for instance, to judge herself by a peculiar and personal law of dispensation in regard to her affections. What may be dangerous for others, she might think, can hardly disturb one who is dedicated heart and soul to Christ, and with so many spiritual helps and safeguards, to say nothing of the example of her own sisters.

But this is a very dangerous self-deception; and it can be disastrous in the case of a sister who is emotional by temperament and who finds a stimulus and outlet for her emotional condition in time of prayer. This to some extent cannot be avoided. But such a person is too inclined to look upon prayer as an end in itself. She may even find the indiscreet affections which increase her emotional tensions are also transferred to Christ in prayer, not deliberately but in the very nature of things. The more she loves others the more she tends to exonerate herself at least for a time, because her prayer seems to go much better.

The one safeguard, therefore, both for ourselves and those under our care is to realize that there is only one way of freeing our souls for the growth of supernatural chastity and that is by living chastely and by removing as far as we can the causes of inordinate emotion. It is the constant effort to keep pure no matter what temptations beset us which gives us the natural habit and disposition of chastity. By all means let us pray and pray well; we must love God with our whole mind, soul and strength, for His love is the cause of our chastity. But we have to let Him love us in the measure He wills by removing all natural obstacles to this divine activity. The religious woman should be particularly on her guard against any emotionalism in prayer which may seem to make prayer, naturally speaking, more congenial. Such emotion should be controlled, not by suppressing it, but by making every effort to remove its causes.

II

Again, there is a tendency in the thought of religious to confuse chastity with charity. This may be due in part to the difficulty we have been discussing. Many religious rightly condemn what they would call a negative chastity—the tendency to look upon this virtue as a kind of necessary discipline or at least too much on the level of an acquired and therefore natural virtue. This attitude can be aggravated by any inclination to misprize the function of marriage and of sex as things good in themselves and God-given.

The prevalence of negative chastity is considered by some to be due to lack of prayer, that is, the true surrender of contemplative prayer. The remedy then is to love God more and seek a more intimate union with Him. But this again lends itself to a certain distortion, because religious so easily begin to confuse the supernatural virtue of chastity with chastity metaphorically so-called. This state of mind can be encouraged quite accidentally by the language of the saints and exalted souls who speak about the love of God anthropomorphically, as they must, in their attempts to transcribe the raptures of mystical union under the symbols of human love, and who look upon all sin as the betrayal of a lover, an infidelity which is unclean, impure, unchaste. Even in the Old Testament this refusal to give God His due in a total surrender to His will is described as 'fornication'.

But the use of such words in these contexts does not refer specifically to the virtue of chastity at all, but to chastity metaphorically speaking. The difference between this and the infused virtue of supernatural chastity must be clearly understood. St. Thomas explains:

The term *chastity* has both a proper and a metaphorical sense. Technically, it is a special virtue, a part of temperance, occupied with the special matter of desire for sexual pleasure. This is centred on physical intercourse, into which enters chastity properly-so-called, and also the contrasting vice of lust. The terms may be extended to our spiritual intercourse with things. This also provides delight. By a figure of speech, accordingly, spiritual chastity is engaged when our spirit enjoys God with whom it should be joined and refrains from enjoying things God does not mean us to mingle with: '*I have espoused you to one husband, that I may present you as a chaste virgin to Christ.*'[1] Similarly, spiritual fornication when our spirit delights in embracing things against God's fair order: '*Thou hast played the harlot with*

[1] 2 Cor. 11. 2.

many lovers.'[1] In this sense, chastity is a characteristic of every virtue, each of which holds us back from contracting illicit unions, though its heart lies in charity and the other theological virtues, through which the spirit is immediately united with God.[2]

III

But we must not go to the other extreme and measure any increase in the supernatural virtue of chastity in terms only of our personal struggles to keep chaste. The quality of a supernatural virtue derives from the quality of the love of God inspiring it. This capacity to love God is God-given but its measure depends not only on our striving but on the degree of love God wills to bestow upon us. In our Father's house are many mansions.[3]

It is important to get our thinking right on this point. One sometimes hears the remark that many holy people have little emotional life and seem somehow or other to have been preserved from temptations against chastity. Quite apart from the fact that God has many other ways of proving the spirit, this relative immunity has to be seen in due proportion. Let us take one or two typical examples.

Some adolescents who enter religion show every sign of having a chaste disposition; but the plain truth is that they are immature, often retarded, and suffer from a kind of holy stupidity; they are timid, bewildered, helpless in emergencies and tend to cling to others for protection. And as helplessness of any kind pulls at the heart-strings of a woman, they usually do not appeal in vain.

A story is told in the life of St. Teresa of Avila which illustrates this point. A priest once brought a penitent to her of whose piety he had a great regard. The saint looked at the child rather doubtfully and then shook her head. 'You see, Father,' she explained later, 'even though Our Lord has given this child such great devotion and perhaps will afterwards lead her to contemplation, as she has so little sense now she will never come to have any. Such people are useless in our communities and end by becoming a burden.'[4]

But this kind of immaturity should never be confused with the disposition of many other girls whose chaste and transparent

[1] Jer. 3. 1. [2] *S.T.*, 2–2, 151, 2.
[3] This is the spiritual meaning of St. Matt. 20. 1–15.
[4] *Life of St. Teresa*, Bollandists, II:408.

innocence enshrines great firmness of purpose and a practical recognition of moral danger. One often finds that such young people have been under the special protection of Our Lord and have been steered by His grace through at least one critical period of their lives. There can be little doubt that if their supernatural chastity is of the rarest quality it has been hardly won. Something very similar happened to the young Aquinas when he drove the evil woman from his room with a firebrand seized from the hearth. It is well to remember that the very ferocity of this attack was a kind of symbol of the dreadful power which he felt threatening his soul.

Perhaps the religious least to be envied are those who appear temperamentally immune from the difficulties we are considering. This apparent immunity is usually offset by a noticeable lack of other womanly qualities needed in the apostolate. Such religious have little natural sympathy with the trials of others in this matter.

St. Thomas asks whether frigidity or insensibility can be a sin; and he answers:

> Whatever is contrary to the natural order is vicious, but as nature has introduced pleasure into the operations necessary for man's life, the natural order requires that man should make use of these pleasures, insofar as they are necessary for man's well-being both regarding the preservation of the individual or the species. If anyone, then, were to reject pleasure to the extent of omitting whatever is necessary for nature's preservation he would sin, because he is running counter to the order of nature. This is what is meant by the vice of insensibility.
>
> Even so it is sometimes praiseworthy, and even necessary for the sake of some purpose to refrain from these pleasures. Certain persons may, for instance, refrain from pleasures of the table and of sex, for the sake of their health, or like athletes and soldiers forgo many pleasures the better to fulfil their duties. Others again, like penitents, abstain from pleasure as a kind of discipline for the good of their souls; and others must refrain from carnal desires if they are to give themselves up to contemplation and to divine things. None of this has anything to do with the vice of insensibility. Such people are acting reasonably.[1]

What we have called frigidity is therefore not sinful, but rather a natural disposition. Just as the psycho-physical economy of some gives rise to many temptations of the flesh, it is not surprising

[1] *S.T.*, 2–2, 142, 1.

that the reverse should happen with others. It is important to bring home to such people the need for cultivating a truly Christian sympathy; and that in their case it is not so much a question of being more chaste than others or less, but merely of being made differently.

How far such differences are due to inherited tendencies or purely environmental factors is difficult to tell. In some cases it is an act of God, purely and simply, as when girls lose their parents in early childhood. But the characteristic of most of these insensitive souls is a poverty of love and affection; the feeling of not being wanted which often tends to make them forthright, unyielding, ambitious and domineering. They appear to have little emotional life until we remember there is more than one kind of emotion.

Such natural frigidity should not be an impediment to the attainment of high charity, but in the early stages of divine union it can have a crippling effect on the apostolate insofar as it restrains the outflow of human love. Such people need self-confidence, a great trust in God through a life of prayer and self-dedication. In the novitiate they should be given a prudent care especially when sick or inwardly troubled; inspired to open their hearts to a new world of love and affection in God. These religious can do great work in the apostolate. Often they are born leaders and a great stand-by in emergencies. But self-criticism does not come easily to them; nor, naturally speaking, does the surrender of obedience. But how unwise it is to match their chill and sometimes forbidding exterior with an over-severity which can only aggravate their trouble.

When such religious meet temptations against chastity, as they are bound to do sooner or later, they can be driven almost to despair. A natural disposition to this virtue is delicately poised and easily disturbed, as we have said. Insensitive souls may have been naturally disposed to chastity for many years, until some physical illness or change or the altered metabolism of the human organism brings about an emotional condition which can rock the very foundations of their moral life. Only those who have conducted such souls through this crisis can realize how little they are to be envied their years of comparative immunity.

IV

Perhaps the most ineffective and spiritually sterile of all apostles

is the proud virgin; that is to say the religious who cherishes *pride*
virgin chastity as a personal excellence rather than as an offering
to Christ. Virginity is the fruit of our love of God but its primary
cause is God's love for us expressed in His gift of the supernatural
infused virtue of virginity. Our only capacity as creatures is to
return the love whereby God loves us; we love in the degree we
are loved, no more, no less. We are virgins because God has called
us and uplifted us by His love to be virgins; it is not an excellence
we have of ourselves. The gift is His, the acceptance ours.

It is this surrender which must always be central and pivotal in
our spiritual lives. Pride therefore and the supernatural gift of
virginity are mutually exclusive. The latter is the reward of our
abandonment to God's will; of humility. The saints never tire of
emphasizing this great truth, which is in fact merely one application of the principles laid down in this chapter. Let their words
speak for themselves.

St. Bernard (Hom. I, on *Missus est*, No. 7, 8. Breviary: Feast
of the Holy Family):

> 'And was subject to them.' Which shall we more marvel at:
> the Son's most benign condescension or the Mother's most
> excellent dignity? That God should submit to a woman, un-
> precedented humility: That a woman should rule God,
> unparalleled sublimity. In special praise of virgins it is sung
> that they follow the Lamb wherever He goeth. What praises,
> think you, befit her who even precedes?
>
> Learn here, O man, to obey. Learn, O earth, to be down-
> trodden. Learn, O dust, to submit. Blush, ye proud ashes! God
> subjects Himself to men, and dost thou, desiring to lord it over
> men, place thyself above thy Creator? If ever I think of such a
> thing, may God rebuke me as He did His Apostle: Get thee
> behind Me, Satan, because thou savourest not the things of
> God. For whenever I desire others to defer to me, I strive to
> place myself above God, and then truly I do not savour the
> things that are of God. For of Him it is written: 'And He was
> subject to them.'
>
> Perchance thou disdainest, O man, to follow the example of a
> man; surely it is not unworthy of thee, to follow thy Creator?
> If thou find it too high a matter to follow Him wherever He
> goeth, at least do not think it beneath thee to follow Him where
> He condescends to thee. If thou canst not walk the sublime way
> of virginity, at least follow God in the most sure way of humility.
> And even virgins, if they swerve from the straightness of this

way, not even they follow the Lamb wherever He goeth. He follows indeed who is unchaste but humble; and the virgin follows who is proud; but neither follows Him wherever He goeth. For the one cannot rise to the purity of the Lamb, Who is without spot; and the other disdains to descend to His meekness, who was silent not only before the shearer but even before the slayer. Nevertheless the sinner has chosen in humility the more wholesome way than in virginity the proud one; for the first purges his uncleanness in humble expiation, while the pride of the second defiles his purity.

St. Augustine (*Serm.* 354, iv, 9, *Aug. Syn.*, pp. 412–3; also, *de Scta Virg.*, XLIV, 45):

Holy virginity is preferable even to chaste marriage. Yet let not any particular virgin, who obeys and fears God, dare to set herself before this or that woman who is also obedient and God-fearing, otherwise she will not be humble, and God resisteth the proud.[1] What therefore shall she have in her thoughts? Assuredly the hidden gifts of God, which nothing but the questioning of trial makes known to each even in himself. For, to pass over the rest, whence doth a virgin, however solicitous for the things that belong to the Lord, know how she may please the Lord?[2] but that perchance, by reason of some weakness of mind unknown to herself, she be not as yet ripe for martyrdom, whereas that woman to whom she rejoiced to prefer herself, may already be able to drink the chalice of the Lord's humiliation, which He set before His disciples who had shown themselves enamoured of high places.[3]

I venture to say that it is good for those who observe continence and are proud of it to fall, that they may be humbled in that very thing for which they extol themselves. For what benefit is it to any one in whom is the virtue of continence, if pride holds sway in him? He is but despising that whereby man is born, and striving after that which led to Satan's fall ... Holy Virginity is a better thing than conjugal chastity ... But if we add two other things, pride and humility ... I have no doubt that a humble married woman is to be preferred to a proud virgin ... A mother will hold a lesser place in the kingdom of heaven, because she has been married, than the daughter who is a virgin ... but if the mother has been humble and thou proud, she will have some sort of a place, but thou none.

---

[1] James 4. 6.　　　　[2] 1 Cor. 7. 32.　　　　[3] Matt. 20. 22.

Part Three

SPIRITUAL MOTHERHOOD

Chapter 1

THE RELEASE OF LOVE

ANY serious consideration of virginal chastity brings to light the strangest contrasts and apparent contradictions. Indeed one is tempted to say that the exaltation of virginity in the literature and life of the Church altogether exceeds its theological significance. Theologically speaking it is one of the subsidiaries of temperance, in the general catalogue of the virtues. St. Thomas asks himself, for instance, whether virginity is the greatest of the virtues, and after explaining that it is the most perfect form of chastity goes on to say, that in itself, simply, in relation to the other virtues, it is not the most perfect virtue; and that the theological virtues and the virtue of religion are to be preferred to virginity. He also says that martyrs who are willing to sacrifice their very lives in God's service as well as those who surrender their own will and possessions in religion cleave more powerfully to the divine will than virgins, who as such renounce venereal pleasure for the same purpose.[1]

By contrast the vow of virginity is spoken of by spiritual writers and invariably by the Church when approving the rules of religious orders of women, as a 'spiritual wedlock with Christ'. The same is implicit in the Apocalypse.[2]

Again the Church insists that the greatest prerogative of Mary is her Virgin-Motherhood; but when the woman in the crowd called out: 'Blessed be the womb that bore thee and the breasts that suckled Thee', Our Lord replied: 'Yea rather, blessed are they who hear the word of God and keep it.' And this is re-echoed by St. Thomas,[3] following St. Augustine, when he says that the supernatural obedience of the religious is preferable to virginity.

Again, it is a theological truism that the sins of the flesh as such are less grievous than spiritual sins, as, for example, spiritual pride; yet in the popular estimation of the faithful immorality is synonymous with sensual sin. The reason for this is not easily explained, as it cannot be due solely to the sense of shame attaching to these sins.

[1] S.T., 2–2, 152, 5.   [2] 14. 1–4.   [3] Loc. cit.

Somewhere the key to all these questions must be found. But where? We find the answer more easily by starting, not with chastity, but the contrary vice. St. Thomas insists again and again that an excess of venereal pleasure plays havoc with the human mind. But venereal pleasure is not wrong or harmful in itself. Quite the contrary; it is essential for the preservation of the human species, and it is only fitting that God should attach to it the greatest and most vehement pleasure. But though this pleasure as such is attached to the individual, its very purpose requires that it should be experienced only by being shared. A man enjoys the use of his bodily senses—the food he eats, the music he hears, for instance, but these are related to self-preservation and his natural individual drive towards completeness and fulfilment. But sexual pleasure has not this individual purpose. It is ordained to the well-being and perfection of the race, something which selfishness can pervert and by so doing bring disorder and frustration into human society. That is why lust—the inordinate enjoyment of venereal pleasure—can have such terrifying consequences. These are listed by St. Thomas under the general heading of *Filiae Luxuriae*—the Daughters of Lust; they are a darkening of the mind, thoughtlessness, rashness, inconstancy, self-love, hatred of God, love of this world and abhorrence of the next. He concludes this article by saying that man through this sin is in despair of a future world; being held captive by carnal pleasures he has little heart for spiritual delights, as these become distasteful to him.

We should never forget, therefore, that just as a man can bring harm, even ruin, upon himself by the over-indulgence of his appetites, so he can let loose the forces of disruption upon society through his lust, precisely because his sexual appetite and the pleasure pertaining thereto are intended of their nature to be used by being shared in the name of the race.

Sex in this sense is a social responsibility; its primary purpose can never be merely self-gratification or personal well-being. Sexual pleasure is intended by God to be the incentive, reward and biological expression of the mutual love of the sexes in and through which each loves and serves the race. When this natural pleasure-principle is perverted to become the incentive to, the reward and biological expression of self-love, the consequence must be that the race is made subservient to the individual; the whole serves the part, the race attending as menial in the ritual service of self-love.

More even than this. The sexual pleasure-principle is powerful and intense by reason of the paramount and overriding needs of the race, in the conservation of society, and the expansion of Christ's Mystical Body, through mutual love and understanding. Through lust all this tremendous dynamism is packed into a single soul, and narrowed down, canalized like the waters of some great dam, to become the expression of that soul's love of itself. When this perversion is multiplied and spreads through society in the habitual misuse of marriage, it is inevitable that it should become socially accepted and legislated for, bringing about a general repudiation of the restraints of religion, the depreciation of spiritual values, and the degradation of the national character and culture. It is unreasonable for modern psychologists to pretend that fear alone (which they often trace to the 'Christian bogey of hell-fire') prevents a natural, uninhibited and healthy sex-function, or on the other hand that the social nature of this union for the secondary ends of marriage is a sufficient reason for artificial birth-control, when the real problem is man's innate tendency to concupiscence and lust. A psychology which refuses to admit the reality of the Fall is a social death-trap, because the only means of unmasking its basic errors in a faithless world is social and moral catastrophe. By denying the reality of sin we would deny men power to live. In this matter it takes very little to break down all personal and social restraint.[1]

We see then the forces of evil over which chastity can triumph. This virtue is the guardian of the creative might of marriage, and the saviour of the home where human love is born, and from which it radiates into the life of society and of nations. Chastity preserves that normal extraversion by which men perceive what is good, true and beautiful in the real world around them and fortifies their minds and hearts against a dangerous subjectivism. If, therefore, it is by no means the greatest virtue, theologically speaking, accidentally it brings forth greater benefits to man than any other moral virtue, sociologically, anthropologically and even cosmologically speaking, for it controls and safeguards that dynamic and primordial urge which elicits the means by which man passes himself on, gives himself to all by confiding himself to the flow of God's creative providence, which has its ultimate purpose in the honour and glory of God.

We begin to see, then, why sex is sacred. Apart from revelation,

[1] See Note 12, p. 226.

in the hypothetical order of pure nature,[1] it would have been—as expressed in the fusion of two human lives and in the mutual self-giving of marriage, that is, 'in the wider sense as an intimate communion, association and companionship in all life'[2]—the 'normal condition under which man would learn to love God in his creatures most ardently, in the way most suited to human nature.'[3]

Even in the state of original justice, had man not fallen, a chaste and fruitful marital love would have been preferable to virginity, for then man's whole sensitive and imaginative life and activity would have been completely under the sway of reason, with an absence of all concupiscence.[4]

And it is clear from the reasons already given in this and the preceding chapter that even after the Fall the natural chaste love of marriage is to be preferred to virginity when the motive for the latter is selfish and sinful; for virginity would then be a natural habit without being a virtue, in the sense we have already explained, whilst the natural chaste love of marriage would be both a habit and a virtue.

If this is true then *a fortiori* those who are united in the chaste love of Christian marriage have chosen a state of life preferable to that of natural virginity. The latter may be a virtue but it can never be meritorious, whereas the chastity of a Christian marriage is a supernatural and infused virtue. The sex-love of such a marriage if exercised to bring up children for God's honour and glory is an act of the supernatural virtue of religion. 'Since no act proceeding deliberately from the will is indifferent,' writes St. Thomas,[5] 'the matrimonial act is always either sinful or meri-

---

1 The state of pure nature is the condition in which man would be had God never given him any gifts beyond those due to human nature; enjoying his natural powers of soul and body, intellect, free-will, subject to the moral law, guided by conscience: but without original sin and sanctifying grace, destined neither to Heaven nor Hell, but to an eternity of natural happiness or natural misery. Adam was gratuitously given the relatively supernatural gifts of integrity, immortality and impassibility, which together with sanctifying grace gratuitously bestowed constituted him in a state of original justice, his state before the Fall.

2 Cf. *Casti Connubii*.

3 Cf. *Love, Marriage and Chastity*, by E. Mersch, S. J., p. 58.

4 'There would have been honourable marriages in Paradise', writes St. Thomas, 'because in that state, marriages, as such, would have been more honourable than virginity because as the integrity of the mind would have been unimpaired, the fruitfulness of the flesh in marriage would have been preferable to the sterility of virginity.'

'Sed potuerunt in paradiso esse nuptiae honorabiles, quia in statu illo, nuptiae simpliciter virginitate honorabiliores fuissent, eo quod in nullo integritate mentis laesa, fecunditas carnis in matrimonio, sterilitati virginitatis praevaluisset.'—In 2 *Lib. Sent.*, D.20, Q.2, a.3. Cf. also *S.T.*, 1, 98, 2 ad 3.

5 *S.T.*, 3 Suppl., 41, 4.

torious in one possessing grace. For, if one is led to perform the marriage act, either by the virtue of justice, in order to render the debt, or by the virtue of religion, that children may be procreated for the worship of God, the act is meritorious.'

We begin to see then that the vow of virginal chastity, especially as far as religious are concerned, can only be defended because its purpose is social, whatever the motive may be of those who take it.[1] The chaste life of the religious is commanded by the virtue of religion which is essentially social in character, for in ordering the individual to the end or purpose of the whole creation this virtue of its nature promotes the good of the race which is part of that whole.

Further, as sex-love of its nature is ordained to the perfection of the race, and the love of Christian marriage to the growth and perfection of the Mystical Body, so the virginal chastity of the religious is ordained to a similar social and redemptive purpose. First, because those who renounce the natural delights of marriage can give themselves more easily to a total service of Christ. As St. Paul says: 'The unmarried woman and the virgin thinketh on the things of the Lord, that she may be holy both in body and spirit; but she that is married thinketh of the things of the world, how she shall please her husband.' And secondly, as sex is a creative instinct ordered to the well-being of the race, it can only be renounced by way of consecration. God in His wisdom never withdraws His natural gifts, as we saw in the case of the virtues, but must use and uplift them by His grace to a cognate and transcendent purpose. Virginity, therefore, is the supernatural flowering of sex-love and not its repudiation and for this reason must be ordained to the perfection of the race. Our Lady's Virginity at the conception and birth of Christ was an attribute of her divine Motherhood. Far from being the suppression of her womanhood her virginity was its crowning in the highest expression of her feminine qualities and endowments through motherhood; and through a Motherhood which was fruitful in begetting the Word made Flesh and the new race in Christ.

This is a matter of some importance to the life of the religious. For as lust is sinful because it is using the pleasurable drive ordained to race-preservation in the interest of self-love, so supernatural chastity of its very nature is ordained primarily to the well-being of the new race in Christ. Not even the virginal chastity

[1] See Note 13, p. 228.

of the religious can be defended unless it is, at least implicitly, a creative collaboration with the Incarnate Word in bringing forth members of Christ's Mystical Body through the supernatural union of charity. On the other hand, in the degree the purpose of religious chastity is self-regarding, however exalted this may appear, the more sterile must it become.

II

Let us restate this argument in a slightly different form. We are said to love someone when we desire his well-being; if this is for our own sake we call that the love of concupiscence, if for his, the love of benevolence.[1] The meaning of the latter kind of love may be amplified thus: it is a love which is not only benevolent but also beneficent; it is to desire the well-being of another and to have the firm intention of doing all we can to help him to a personal completeness and happiness for his sake. So we say that two people are united in friendship when they are drawn to one another by the love of benevolence. In the words of the Angelic Doctor:

> Not every love has the quality of friendship. In the first place it is reserved to that love for another which wills his well-being. When what we will is not the other's good for his sake, but the desire of it as it affects us, then that is not friendship, but self-regarding love and some sort of concupiscence. Neither does the love of benevolence suffice for friendship: in addition a mutual loving is required for friend is friend to friend. This interplay of well-wishing is founded on companionship.[2]

The condition or foundation of such a love of friendship is sympathy—a certain like-mindedness and similarity of temperament, outlook, faith. True friends always tend to be united in a joyful companionship and common life, and this not only because each is drawn naturally to the reflection of himself in the other, but because in addition there is the added joy of a mutual creative collaboration. People who are too much like us or who acquiesce too readily in our views are boring and colourless because they deny us the joy of mental contrast. True friendship requires some kind of vital interplay.

---

[1] A more exact statement would be:
    Velle bonum sibi = *amor concupiscentiae.*
    Velle bonum alteri = *amor benevolentiae.*
    Mutuus amor benevolentiae cum communicatione vitae = *amor amicitiae.*
[2] *S.T.*, 2–2, 23, 1.

We perceive a new idea with joy when we can integrate it with what we already know. In our association with others who are like-minded this joy is shared and increased by reason of a mutual collaboration. We build up our thought and experience together and this deepens our sympathy. Each makes his contribution to this psychic begetting; each gains clarity of vision in explaining his mental content to the other and the other receives it according to his own contrasted mental mode, and gives a point of view or outlines a new approach which adds depth and perspective, as the use of two eyes, for instance, adds a new dimension to our sense of vision or our two ears to our sense of hearing.

If we are what we have lived and every experience is written deep in our memory and modifies our mind and character, we can understand how, through companionship, friends must grow together into one form. For everything has been shared, life's joys, disappointments, sorrows, the beauty of created things, truth itself and the discipline of a common purpose. It is a story, but not a story retold as it were in its own echo, but one which is richer for each because it has been told together. To share life with a true friend is to find an added reality in life itself. What each cherishes in the inner recesses of memory can never be mine nor his; it is ours—a new creation. That is why the betrayal of a friend wounds so deeply; it is a kind of death, a tearing asunder.

Now the most fruitful mode of this collaboration is to be found in the contrasted experience of sex-association whereby men and women, as complementary co-principles in society, see and fashion life wholly as in one form. And the highest expression of this association is married friendship.

> Marriage is the fusion of two *human* lives [wrote Cardinal Mercier]; it is the union of bodies, frail to be sure, and destined soon to fade and perish, but above and beyond all this, it is the union of two *souls* whose minds act together for the completion of their thoughts, whose hearts are united that their joys and consolations may be doubled by exchange, whose wills become as one will, that each may furnish the other with help, strength and energy to support their personal trials and fulfil their part in the grand work of bringing up a family to serve God.'[1]

The union of marriage, then, not only brings a new and richer

[1] *Lenten Pastoral*, 1909.

experience to which the sexes contribute diversely, but also the highest expression of such creative friendship which is the child.

If the fruitfulness of ordinary friendship unites us in a fusion of mind and experience, what shall we say of the bonding of husband and wife in the making of a child? Neither can say—it is mine; each must say—it is ours; or in words now sacred in Christian countries, 'God has blessed us with a child'. For the child belongs primarily to God through whose activity, as perfective Cause, its soul is created and infused, and only secondarily to its parents as the dispositive cause. That is why parents as custodians of the child have to redeem their responsibility to God, through His Church. But we must never think of the Church as assuming the responsibility of the child only on its birth. Our Lord as God Incarnate is not only the cause of the child but also of the love that begot the child. He is the heart of all true friendship especially in the creative union of marriage. That is the inner meaning of the Christian marriage and the Nuptial Mass. It is the union of bride and bridegroom in the friendship of Christ. St. Thomas writes:

> Inasmuch as matrimony is contracted in the faith of Christ is it able to confer the grace enabling us to be faithful to our matrimonial duties. And this is more probable because when God gives man the faculty to do something, He also confers the help whereby he can make becoming use of this faculty. . . . Therefore as man receives through matrimony by divine institution the faculty to beget children he also receives the grace without which he cannot becomingly do so.[1]

The Christian husband and wife therefore love Christ through their chaste love of one another. But Our Lord calls us not only to love Him but to love Him as He loves us through an undivided and virgin heart. It is a great privilege to love Him creatively in the love of one another, but it is the greatest privilege to love Him creatively in the love of Him alone, to bring forth souls in Him as members of His Mystical Body, and to serve His human Heart in the purifying and perfecting of all human love. In other words, if the chaste love of husband and wife serve a Christian purpose in the begetting of the child, and through their love of Christ introduce new members to the saving grace of His Mystical Body that they might be spiritually reborn, it is the virgin apostle who participates with the virgin Church in this spiritual rebirth and

[1] *S.T.*, 3 Suppl., 42, 3.

through this divine dedication strengthens and purifies the human love which begets the child.

III

The virgin apostle then not only participates with the Church in the spiritual begetting of God's children, but also in a sense in the very natural fruitfulness of marriage. And the reason is this. Apostles dedicated to Christ love Him as He loves them with a love that is at once divine and human; and as His human love, because He is divine, embraces the whole world and its needs, so in the measure His virgin apostles participate in His divine love do their human hearts expand to love all in Him. Christ therefore calls for their help and collaboration not only in bringing forth new members of His Mystical Body by participating as apostles in the fecundity of the Church but also in replenishing the natural fruitfulness of marriage through their radiation of a chaste human love, free of all taint of concupiscence.

We begin to see then as our thoughts unfold, first, that as in true human friendship the union of sympathy is creative in its own order, and as in the contract of marriage the fruitfulness of friendship expressed in the common life and companionship of the sexes is the begetting of the child, so in the supernatural order, the union of Christ and His spouse, through the Church, is creative of the children of God and even, in the natural order, of the children of men. There is a sense then in which Christ can say to the spouse, 'These spiritual children begotten of our divine and loving union and community of life are not My children nor yet yours—but ours.' We begin to see also why this should be true of all children born in wedlock; first, insofar as the virgin apostle participates in the apostolate of the Church in disposing souls for sacramental grace and therefore *a fortiori* for the infusion of the supernatural virtue of chastity which increases the natural fecundity of the Christian marriage; and, secondly, insofar as the example and ideal of the chaste human love and devotion of the virgin apostle is a moral cause of marital chastity, replenishing the fruitfulness of marriage and stemming the destructive tide of lust which claims so tragically the unborn child. When we recall once again what St. Thomas calls the Daughters of Lust—blindness of mind, thoughtlessness, rashness, inconstancy, self-love, hatred of God,

love of this world, and an abhorrence of the next—we begin to see
still more clearly the cleansing power of virginal chastity.

IV

To love Christ totally then we must surrender not only to His
divine but to His human love. In comparison with this complete
offering of self, marriage is constricting, dividing the human will
which loves better in the measure it loves simply. To love Christ
totally we must love as He loves, love what He loves, for to Him
there is neither Jew nor Gentile, bond or free. To 'put on the Lord
Jesus' is to show forth His Heart, it is to find in God a Father and
to see all men as our kith and kin. His appeal is incomparably more
compelling than that of any human lover. He won our hearts and
loyalty by His death; and He is present with us in His Church, by
our side, asking for our help. When we give a drink to the thirsty,
feed the hungry, clothe the naked, visit the imprisoned, bury the
dead—we do all this for Him. He who loved His own when on
earth and loved them to the end, who served the poor, the disabled, the outcast and the sinner, asks for our collaboration. No,
we do not renounce marriage because of our refusal to love
humanly but because we are compelled to love still more humanly
when we recall the love and tenderness of the Heart of Christ.

It is only to be expected that when such a Lover appears above
the horizon of our lives we should want to give Him all, and
want this giving to be for ever and ever. Nothing must stand in
our way. 'Who then shall separate us from the love of Christ?'
cried St. Paul. 'Shall tribulation? or distress? or famine? or naked-
ness? or danger? or persecution? or the sword? (As it is written:
For thy sake, we are put to death all the day long. We are
accounted as sheep for the slaughter.) But in all these things we
overcome, because of Him that hath loved us. For I am sure
that neither death, nor life, nor angels, nor principalities, nor
powers, nor things present, nor things to come, nor might, nor
height, nor depth, nor any other creature, shall be able to separate
us from the love of God, which is in Christ Jesus Our Lord.'[1]

That then is our inspiration. The whole defence of virginal
chastity is that through it we can return to Christ an undivided
heart, and put ourselves at the service of the new race which
potentially embraces all mankind. It is most emphatically not

[1] Romans 8. 35–9.

that we wish to avoid the duties of married love, its responsibilities and sacrifices, or that we regard married love and tenderness as frailties against which our human heart must be steeled. If indeed chastity does not deepen our charity and liberate our human hearts and natural affections for the extension of Christ's work amongst men then our dedication, whatever be its romantic overtones in our literature and even our prayer, is bogus—a thing of shame and utterly despicable. For if the apostolate is the continuation of Christ's redemptive activity expressed in, with and through the Church, then we may say that her apostolate of virginal chastity is the manifestation to the world of the human Heart of Christ.

For the Church is human as Christ is human, and her first contact with fallen man, as was that of Christ, is a human contact. She walks the earth, envisaging the human scene. She is drawn first by human need wherever this may be found, to the physical needs of the poor, the sick, the hungry, the dying, the ignorant, the oppressed, the hoboes—life's off-scourings. This showing forth of the Heart of Christ through His Church is universal. With her as with Him there is 'neither Jew nor Greek; there is neither bond nor free; there is neither male nor female';[1] with her as with Him, there are no home ties: 'For whosoever shall do the will of My Father, that is in heaven, he is my brother, and sister, and mother.'[2]

Christ indeed came as one 'ministering'. The people knew He belonged to them, without discrimination or distinction. He was at their service. But His miracles were not means, nor only symbols; they were wrung from His human Heart in compassion. At the tomb of the dead Lazarus He saw Mary and the Jews weeping, and He 'also wept'. He had compassion on the multitude as 'sheep without a shepherd'. They were indeed His; and they knew they were His. They jostled Him in their crowds; and 'He could not be hid.' 'And running through that whole country, they began to carry about in beds those that were sick, where they heard He was. And whithersoever He entered, into towns, or into villages or cities, they laid the sick in the streets and besought Him that they might touch but the hem of His garment. And as many as touched Him were made whole.'[3] They wanted to make Him King, and He fled from them. And when finally they rejected Him, He never ceased to love them. He

[1] Gal. 3. 28.   [2] Cf. Matt. 12. 50.   [3] Mark 6. 55–6.

came to His own, but His own received Him not; yet at the very end in that final tragic scene on Calvary He was making excuses for them: 'Father, forgive them, for they know not what they do.'

So too with His Church. She is bidden to go forth and to teach all nations, to recall men once again to the family of God, healing and uplifting their souls by the grace she dispenses. But like her Lord she must first give a sacramental service to men's bodies through a truly Christian compassion. It is for this reason that she calls her apostles to share her virginity that they might release into the world the human love of Christ. This is the first step in leading men back to God. The world begins to ask why Christians do these things forgetful of material recompense. Why young people, their life's work before them, leave home and family, reject the appeal of marriage and human love, and do this even gladly. These young apostles are normal, talented, promising. But why this waste? 'He came when he was wanted,' men said of a great religious, 'but when he was no longer wanted, he stayed because he was needed.' And people again asked, why? The answer would be simple enough if these men and women were not ordinary folk. The worldly wise would look and shrug and pass them by if they saw the fires of an abnormal fanaticism burning in their eyes. Whence, then, this extraordinary devotedness, to those who often seem the least worth-while? When those around us are puzzled and are asking these and similar questions, we know that virginal chastity has indeed released the love and compassion of Christ upon the world. Then only, and not through our books or sermons or propaganda, will men know that the old standards are gone, the 'old man' in Adam cast off, the 'new man' born in Christ.

Finally. Through this manifestation of Christian love the world will begin to realize that human love and affection has little stability unless it is rooted in Christ. As He was perfect Man because He was God, so man finds his characteristic perfection in the degree he belongs through Him to the family of God, sharing as a son in the divine nature. This manifestation of true manhood and womanhood has an intuitive appeal for all of us. We see in it the perfection of our own image—the human ideal, however imperfectly realized; the balanced mind and heart; discrimination in all things good, true and beautiful; control of passion; the ability to love and a capacity for human friendship. The work and activities of the virgin apostle are radiant with the divine love and life of Christ, which informs his soul; and if his gifts are at the service of others through a Christian compassion, he stands before the world as a new human type, a Christian, a 'Christened' man, who is all things to his fellow-men in the measure of their need.

Thus virginal chastity is the means both of the outpouring of the human compassion of Emmanuel, God with us, and of the human portrayal of man, the child of God. To sin against this virtue is not only a personal degradation but the restriction of Christ's redemptive activities in the world and the disfiguration of His image.

Chapter 2

THE HEART OF WOMAN

IT is sometimes thought that Our Lord was moved by a compassion He did not feel. Earthly trials are an evil infinitely less grave than the spiritual evil of sin, and it seems reasonable to believe that One who saw all things from the viewpoint of eternity should regard our human miseries as comparatively trivial annoyances. Was the compassion of Christ, then, more of a divine method than a human emotion? Or to put it another way, does not Christian compassion become a thing of the will the nearer we get to God and free ourselves from the drag of the flesh, so that it gradually resolves itself into a technique, a means of getting Christ a hearing or of enlisting popular support that we might minister to souls?

That may seem a crude way of putting it; but there is an ominous undercurrent of truth hidden in the foregoing remarks. Otherwise, when we reflect for a moment, why should so many people fail to understand the significance of virginal chastity?

Many evils follow upon the supposition, however vaguely or subconsciously conceived, that man's body at best is perhaps a little unworthy of him as a child of God or that human love is a sign of weakness hardly to be tolerated in the Christian; especially in the modern young apostle who should match the 'toughness' of Christ's enemies with the 'toughness' of the Christian ascetic.

Charity is the most resplendent of God's gifts, and the Triune Godhead, the principle of this divine love indwells our souls, but we still remain human as Christ Himself was human. It may be difficult to fathom the infinite love and mercy of a God who took to Himself the crudities of a nature like ours, but we cease to be Christians if we refuse to believe He did so. It would be much easier, humanly speaking, to fall in with the teaching of the ancient Docetae, and believe that the human nature of Christ was merely an illusion, a kind of cloak, or mask or means of expressing Himself humanly; but that is heresy. And it is heresy not because it was an attempt to safeguard the majesty of God as it falsely pretended, but precisely because it set limits to His love, affronting the divine Goodness through human pride. Such a doctrine, or the similar teaching of the Gnostics and the Manichees, would provide an easy way out of our human embarrassment by toning down our indebtedness to such a divine Lover. For if God took a human nature that nature in itself must be good; and if it is good then our misuse of it is evil and we are sinners. But on the other hand if Christ's human nature is merely an illusion because our body is evil then the door is wide open to every excess in our escape from guilt.

'The woman, whom thou gavest me to be my companion,' said Adam to God, 'gave me of the tree, and I did eat.' And the Lord God said to the woman: 'Why hast thou done this?' And she answered: 'The serpent deceived me, and I did eat.'[1]

But the truth is, however it may affright our human standards, that the Word was made Flesh and dwelt amongst us, and that both the Word and that Flesh are co-eternal.[2] Our bodies are sacred, and our human love, affections and passions sacred functions. Any attempt to think otherwise is rooted in pride. Man has fallen, but he remains an organism in the supernatural order even in his sin; his nature may be disordered, but it is not irretrievably ruined.

Only by charity, God's loving us as His children, can the tangled skein of our destiny be unravelled; and only in the degree we return that love may we dare to love humanly. It is simply not true to say that the nearer we grow to God through charity the more alien the flesh becomes to our higher spiritual interests. The very reverse is the case. We are as God has made us; and we shall never find harmony and integrity by pretending we are different. Nothing is better calculated to introduce the rift of spiritual pride into the depths of our souls than a refusal to accept ourselves and to wage the war of the spirit on God's terms and not our own. God has made us human, 'a little less than the angels';[3] but not even Our Lord, the Word made flesh, was an angel, though of course as a divine Person He is infinitely above the angels. We struggle that we may be Christ-like, not angelic.

[1] Genesis 3. 12–13.
[2] This is not true of course in the same technical sense of eternity. Eternity is a property of God and is said of other things only in a participated way. Christ's human body had a beginning in time.
[3] Psalm 8. 6.

We are all rather like children learning to walk. They fall, pick themselves up again, their mother's arms around them; they walk again trustingly in full view of those arms, and that loving invitation gives them courage to try again. So too in the way of the spirit. We walk best and safest, true to our God-given nature, when we look up and out and forward, remembering that as God's children we find our true selves in His love. We see then why it should be that those who have plighted their troth to Christ should find in Him who is the Word made Flesh the power to love humanly in His service; and why this love can never become merely a masquerade or even the mere outward sign of charity, but must also be its fruit. To 'put on the Lord Jesus' is to partake in His Sacred Humanity, and to function freely and harmoniously according to our nature.

It follows, then, that the natural endowments of the religious sister must be released into the Christian apostolate by reason of her very supernatural dedication. God who 'reacheth from end to end mightily and ordereth all things sweetly',[1] and with whom all make-shift readjustments are unworthy, must use His apostles through the natural gifts He has already bestowed on them, elevating and supernaturalizing them, if need be, for His own supernatural and divine purpose. It is only to be expected therefore that as God has endowed the woman with the maternal instinct to safeguard the continuance of the human race, He should use this same natural quality for the well-being and the perfecting of Christ's Mystical Body. If this is so, then the rôle of woman in the apostolate should be conceived according to her nature, and differ in some way because of her sex in the mode of its use. For this reason we look for some kind of association between the apostolic activities of our sisters and the apostolate of Our Lady, the mother of Christ's Mystical Body.

II

Before we examine this association, however, let us remind ourselves more formally of the relationship between married love and the maternal instinct. The efficient cause of the exercise of married love is the human will; its formal cause is its definition; its material cause is the psycho-physical differentiation of the sexes; and its final cause, that is, its purpose or reason why, is both the child—

[1] Wisdom 8. 1.

the continuance and perfection of the race—and the mutual love
of the married partners.

Now, although the efficient cause of married love is the human
will, clearly this causal drive must differ qualitatively according
to sex. The chaste functioning of marriage calls many basic
instincts into play, but two of these, the maternal and paternal
instincts, have an obvious importance in the present context.
These instincts are natural and complementary tendencies
directed towards the preservation of the race. Though they may
often differ relatively in intensity there can be little doubt that
the woman's instinctive attraction to the purpose of sex-love which
is the child, that is, the race, is more potent and dynamic. The
maternal instinct may be described as the characteristic and the
accidental efficient cause of sex-love and function proper to the
woman. If this is true, then this instinct must dispose her more
than her partner to the purpose (final cause) in the functioning of
sex-love, which is the child. In other words, the creative impulse
in the woman relative to that of the man is directed, naturally
speaking, more powerfully to the primary fruit of marriage which
is the child. She is in this sense, naturally speaking, more chaste,
finding in the virtue of chastity a control which is more connatural
to her. For this reason the effects of any misuse of the marriage
function which of its nature denies the woman her offspring is
immeasurably more harmful to her than to her partner, making
her restless and frustrated, and bringing the deepest instincts of
her nature into grievous conflict.

The social consequences of this conflict are even more harmful.
We should remember that the preservation and growth of the
maternal instinct depends on the right-functioning of sex, because
like every other instinct it becomes more potent with use. Further,
as this instinct is the only altruistic tendency throughout nature,
its social and racial significance can hardly be overrated. But once
woman loses her meaning as in modern society the balance of
nature is disturbed. It would be an over-simplification to say that
man, by nature, is concerned with the survival of the strong and
fittest, and woman with the survival of the weak; but in fact this
comes very near the truth. How unwise and short-sighted it can
be to think of the well-being of society in terms of the virility
of the race, and to try to strain out and eliminate the unfit!
Apart from the higher moral implications such genetic plan-
ning is self-destructive. The unfortunate people it is proposed to

eliminate through such policies—the mentally defective, the aged, the disabled, the incurable and so on—are all presumed to have little or no social purpose even in the natural order of things. This is obviously false. For what keeps the useless and unproductive members of society alive and gives them a real significance? On the purely biological level it is the maternal instinct which, throughout nature, is the counterpoise of the heartless struggle for survival. And it is this instinct, fostered, but never satisfied, in the natural functioning of the home and which is a natural potential awaiting release in the hearts of millions of unmarried women, which overflows into the general life of society, seeking to fortify itself through the very helpless folk we would discard.

We are sometimes told by modern eugenists that the Christian attitude towards suffering is sentimental and unrealistic, when, in one sense, it is the logical outcome of our insistence on the moral obligations of married life. It is these which strengthen and uplift the natural qualities of the woman. God promised that the devil's influence would be crushed under the heel of woman; and it is here once again we catch a further glimpse of the social significance of the virgin-chastity of our sisters. Chastity, and chastity alone, it would seem, can preserve this saving sense of motherhood amongst us in an age overshadowed by the spectre of human power.

III

How then shall we measure the spiritual and social influence of the maternal love of the religious sister? To begin with, her maternal instinct cannot diminish through the practice of virginal chastity. On the contrary there is every reason to believe that, even naturally and biologically speaking, it becomes the more imperious in the degree the sex instincts are unconsciously transformed and redirected under the influence of supernatural chastity.

Experience, however, would seem to testify beyond question through their labours in countless schools, orphanages, nurseries, hospitals, mission-fields, in the care of the poor, the aged and the dying, that the sense of motherhood among religious sisters thrives and grows ever stronger under the impulse of grace. And most noticeably perhaps in contemplative communities, where many would hardly expect to find it. The maternal love, for instance, of a great saint like St. Thérèse of Lisieux can never be dissociated from her natural endowments as a woman. Indeed it is the highest manifestation, the crowning, of her womanhood under the influence of her love of Christ. Her yearning to make a vicarious satisfaction for sinners springs from the very roots of her being in her one desire to be the mother of souls in Christ.

'*Offrons bien nos souffrances à Jésus pour sauver des âmes; pauvres âmes!*' she exclaimed. That is the cry of mother-love, purely and simply. And again: '*Les âmes ont moins de grâces que nous et Jésus veut bien faire dépendre leur salut d'un soupir de notre cœur. Quel mystère; si un soupir peut sauver* une âme, *que ne peuvent faire des souffrances comme les nôtres. Ne refusons rien à Jésus.*'[1]

IV

But the risks inseparable from such a rewarding vocation have to be faced; especially where our sisters are recruited from a modern, self-conscious society. One of the tragedies of our day is the frustrated woman, and it is little use pretending that a similar fate cannot befall the religious sister. She is dedicated to a life of self-sacrifice in the outpouring of her heart. Grace uplifts and consecrates her natural mother-love. But if chastity ceases to function as a liberating influence in the sense that it is debased by fear or any other natural motive, her stupendous love-potential as a woman tends to find an outlet in self-love. The most deadly conflict conceivable in a woman is to be found in the heart of the religious sister who is so to say victimized by her own chastity. That is why we have castigated any tendency to a negative chastity in the foregoing pages of this book; it is a blight—a corrosion of the heart which is responsible for many a barren apostolate; for by it, especially when it is the outcome of a wrong and too subjective approach to spiritual perfection, the woman, who is made by God to give, is induced by her very vocation to give to no one but herself. This negative chastity can creep upon the soul like a paralysis in a niggardly and piecemeal sneaking back of our self-offering to Christ by every subtlety of self-regarding and self-love. No one can be as embittered and self-absorbed as the wife who refuses to face the sacrifice of love, with the possible exception of the religious sister. Religious men being human, selfish and sinful are capable of the grossest self-pity, but never, even at their worst, can they be accused of mothering themselves,

[1] Lettre 61.

for that is beyond their natural capacity; just as even at their best they are rarely moved by that spontaneous, generous and self-forgetful service of others characteristic of the overwhelming majority of religious women.

It is essential, therefore, that the instinct or sense of motherhood should be released into the apostolate of our sisters, by a positive and supernatural chastity. Whether they are aware of it or not, it is inherent in and inseparable from their labours for souls and must develop and grow stronger through right use. Nothing in fact is so connatural to the religious sister and brings forth her finest qualities of mind and heart as the call to a fruitful virginity. Contrariwise nothing so disturbs her as the prospect, one might almost say threat, of a sterile womanhood.

Many of us have little conception of the power of this subconscious drive latent in the heart of the woman. Occasionally we become aware of it in more matriarchal Catholic countries like Ireland or the old Catholic communities of the Scottish Highlands; and, in religion, amongst sisters dedicated to maternity work. The apostolate of the latter, so generously blessed by the Church, gives great scope to the religious woman, provided it is rooted in a truly contemplative spirit; but whatever danger is to be found in this particular work is occasioned not so much by sex in the ordinary meaning of the word, as by the natural appeal of the child, especially to a woman who has had a sane and religious upbringing and whose impulses are healthy and uninhibited.

Chapter 3

STRAYING AFFECTIONS

I

MUCH is being said and written at the present time on the natural means of sublimating the instinctive life of religious women to readjust their minds to the demands of the modern apostolate. We are told that natural instincts should be treated with the greatest respect. They should never be suppressed, that is to say, unaccepted, because we regard them as abhorrent even though they are recognized; neither should they be repressed by an unconscious process which refuses to give them any conscious recognition at all. Our instinctive life, in other words, has to be acknowledged and accepted, and whenever necessary redirected; otherwise it inevitably finds its own release through abnormal channels. Fear and anxiety in any form halt this natural development of the human mind and personality, particularly in childhood when it becomes responsible for all kinds of repressed complexes which harass us in later life.

Now, whilst admitting the truth of all this, we must not lose our sense of proportion. From the nature of things a good deal happens in childhood over which children have no control. Their parents often fail them during the impressionable years. Their home environment, for instance, may be a place of unutterable gloom owing to the conduct of an erring father; or the child may be over-petted, or starved of affection, or be an only child, or a sickly child; and who can foretell the shattering effect of the premature death of its mother? As this kind of unforeseeable past threatens every child it is hardly surprising that most religious feel pretty certain that they themselves set out on life's pilgrimage encumbered by rather more baggage than was reasonably safe.

What then is to be done to remedy this state of affairs? Should it be remedied at all? Are we to encourage Catholic parents to consult the experts who only too rarely have any children of their own. The sins of parents will be visited upon their children till the end of time, but such divine retribution is surely brought to good purpose in the Christian economy of redemption. But what guarantee have we, as Christians, that God will deal in like manner with the indiscretions of modern practitioners who more or less claim to be redeemers in their own right?[1] This is a matter of grave importance, as we have already mentioned in a former chapter, especially when those in charge of our novitiates are wondering how to eliminate difficult types which find their way into religious life.

We can only repeat our conviction that for the most part there is nothing wrong with religious life in our own day that cannot be set right by God's grace and our co-operation *ex opere operantis*, in cultivating a greater freedom of spirit, together with the resolve to face our problems with courage and above all with common-sense. Psychologically speaking, the central feature of all of us, including our saints, is that we are not quite normal. One has always the suspicion that God prefers us to be that way, that we may glorify Him through our very abnormalities. A characteristic feature of God's providence seems to be a certain preference for doing the best work with the most imperfect human instruments. But there can be little doubt that when we, as religious, grow accustomed to the idea of being a little odd like everyone else we can do a great deal to prevent things from getting out of control. The cause of all our trouble is sin, and the radical cure for sin is God's grace which drives deeper into the human unconscious than many would have us believe. Of course, now and again, exceptional cases call for special treatment; but even the troubles of these people can usually be traced to an outrageous lack of discretion on the part of those who received them into religion. Too often in our modern religious life the unfailing intuition of the woman seems to desert her through senseless fears of every kind. What she needs more than anything else is freedom of function, to be the woman God made her; and this, as we have tried to show in another place, is not a challenge to supernatural obedience but its very fruit.[2]

When therefore religious sisters read about or are told about the need for using, redirecting or sublimating the maternal instinct it would be imprudent for them to try and bring this about consciously in their own lives. The less they worry about sublimation the better. The same advice would be tendered to all superiors and

1 See Note 14, p. 228.
2 Cf. *Religious Obedience* (Burns Oates and Washbourne).

spiritual directors. Sublimation in the life of the religious is not something consciously brought about as the result of specific advice but something which happens when religious confide themselves in the spirit of faith to the rule and customs of their order as an expression of the whole life in Christ.

II

In speaking of these matters, as the reader may already have gathered, we are not only warning sisters against all forms of scientific self-readjustment by way of sublimation but also against a habit of mind which urges them to argue their way out of some inner conflict, without quite realizing what they are doing. Let us take one or two examples.

As a woman it is almost impossible for the religious sister not to feel a loving compassion for those who appeal for her help and sympathy. The object of her maternal solicitude may be a child, a younger sister in distress, an older person who is ill or helpless; but as time goes on she may gradually become conscious that her affections are beginning to focus perhaps a little dangerously. What is she to do? She may try to convince herself there is nothing wrong in her affection, which is most probably true. She may go on to tell herself that her affection can be used to lead the person she loves to God. Nothing wrong in this either, but it is dangerous precisely because it is tending to become a false readjustment. If, for instance, she is fond of a child, she may try to convince herself that as this particular girl has a bad home influence, then a discreet love and affection may confirm her in the faith, and possibly even inspire a religious vocation. She prays for the child, especially when her image comes before her in time of prayer; she will encourage her to pray, lend her spiritual books, talk to her about our divine Lord. After all, she argues, what can be wrong with this? 'I cannot help being affectionate by nature, and it is surely our duty as apostles to use our natural gifts to lead souls to Christ.'

But all this time both the child and the sister are getting more and more emotionally involved, both in Christ and in one another. Still, the sister makes every effort to convince herself that the friendship is entirely spiritual, deriving from her own dedication to Christ. She tries to stifle her growing uneasiness by recalling the example of Our Lord and St. John, and the close friendships of many of the saints. 'And hasn't Sister So-and-So been the bosom

friend of Mother So-and-So for years.' But unfortunately the sister
in her distress does not pause to enquire whether she could
imagine Our Lord or St. John or the saints arguing with themselves in this way. Their friendships were found in God and they
were not always wondering whether or not God was in their
friendships. The question would have had no meaning. Similarly
in religion: we find friendships, not through an attempt to reconcile
our feelings with what God wants, by some kind of subterfuge,
but by delivering ourselves to a whole life in Christ, clinging to
Him at every moment and loving to be with Him in prayer.
We find our human love in the courageous sacrifice of it. If we
refuse to remain Christ-centred in this way, faithful to our consecration, we shall find ourselves at every emotional crisis trying to
reconcile what of its nature is irreconcilable, and even heading
for some kind of neurosis which may last a lifetime.

The situation we are trying to clarify can be seen in due proportion by comparing it with the love of the mother of a large
family. What is at once evident about such a mother is that she is
everything to each. There is a kind of matriarchal aloofness about
her which would never allow her to starve the affections of one
child by spoiling or petting another. She loves each more by loving
all according to their individual needs. The paradox of chastity is
similar. In our apostolate our love for others can rarely be selec-
tive and this applies particularly to women. But many of these
perplexities would never arise if we had the courage to trust God
and to put ourselves at the disposal of all in Christ, graduating
our services, not in terms of our affection for others, but according
to their need. The heart of the religious sister grows like the heart
of a mother of many children to meet all the demands made upon
it if she is a woman of prayer, and belongs first and foremost and
in all things to Christ. On the other hand, if she outpours her
affections on one or two she reduces her very capacity to love even
the one or two humanly.

III

The test of a true friendship, therefore, is whether it increases
our love of God and so even increases our natural capacity
to love others in Him. In the words of St. John of the Cross:

Some of these persons make friendships of a spiritual kind
with others, which oftentimes arise from luxury and not from

spirituality; this may be known to be the case when the remembrance of that friendship causes not the remembrance and love of God to grow, but occasions remorse of conscience. For, when the friendship is purely spiritual, the love of God grows with it; and the more the soul remembers it, the more it remembers the love of God, and the greater the desire it has for God; so that, as the one grows, the other grows also. For the spirit of God has this property, that it increases good by adding to it more good, inasmuch as there is likeness and conformity between them. But, when this love arises from the vice of sensuality aforementioned, it has the contrary effects; for the more the one grows, the more the other decreases, and the remembrance of it likewise. If that sensual love grows, it will at once be observed that the soul's love of God is becoming colder, and that it is forgetting Him as it remembers that love; there comes to it, too, a certain remorse of conscience. And, on the other hand, if the love of God grows in the soul, that other love becomes cold and is forgotten; for, as the two are contrary to one another, not only does the one not aid the other, but the one which predominates quenches and confounds the other, and becomes strengthened in itself, as the philosophers say. Wherefore Our Saviour said in the Gospel: That which is born of the flesh is flesh, and that which is born of the spirit is spirit.

That is to say, the love which is born of sensuality ends in sensuality, and that which is of the spirit ends in the spirit of God and causes it to grow. This is the difference that exists between these two kinds of love, whereby we may know them.[1]

We must, therefore, steel our minds against the subtle and dangerous suggestion that to confirm the habit of supernatural chastity we should work as it were upwards instead of letting God work downwards. Both activities are necessary in the sense that we have to dispose ourselves for the divine activity in our souls, but a good deal depends on precisely where the emphasis falls. On coming into religion we deliver ourselves to a mode of life which is pre-eminently sane, worthy, noble, and above all livable —what we have called 'the whole life', that is to say, not an ill-balanced or over-astringent version of human existence, conducive to every kind of conflict and inhibition, making life humanly speaking tolerable only in the thought of eternity, but a life of balanced tensions in which supernatural man can find an integral freedom of function and that degree of happiness possible in this

1 *Works*, Peers' trans., Vol. I, pp. 362–3.

world. If things go wrong as they are apt to in our fallen state we should not only take whatever practical precautions may be necessary, but keep the quality of our surrender to the divine will constantly under review. The religious sister is much safer and spared many trials if she gives her heart to the loving service of Christ alone, than if she is perpetually haunted by the need of reconciling loyalties. We grow far too self-regarding in the restrictive environment of religious life if we are always seeking outlets for our natural impulses. God builds the edifice of the Spirit upon a natural foundation; He expects us to give Him reasonable service, but Our Lord reminds us again and again that His help will be forthcoming in the degree of our surrender to the needs of the Kingdom. He could not have been more uncompromising. He will not share our heart, and this applies particularly to those bound to Him by virginal chastity. Neither will He be outdone in generosity even in this world. Faith in Him, if strong enough, will move mountains; He will restore to us the hundredfold; He will return to us the love of father and mother and brothers and sisters the world over, but only on condition we leave all and follow Him. That is the beginning and the end of the Christian life-synthesis, and the *Todo-Nada* of St. John of the Cross was but the distant and feeble echo of the call of the divine Lover: 'If any man come to Me, and hate not his father and mother and wife and children and brethren and sisters, yea and his own life also, he cannot be My disciple'.[1]

Yes, indeed, if we seek our life we shall lose it; and if we seek our love we shall lose it. If chastity is the liberation of human love in our hearts, and even an added capacity to love humanly, the measure of our love of God is the measure of this liberation. In other words this freedom and ability to cherish the well-being of all creatures without transgression by concupiscence is the natural reward of the supernatural infused gift of virginal chastity. Blessed Marie Thérèse de Soubiran writes:

> One must be fully convinced that it is impossible to work usefully for the sanctification of one's neighbour, until one is quite detached from creatures and from oneself by a complete control of the affections. A natural result of purity of heart is an intensification of charity: far from destroying our affection for our fellow-creatures whom it is our duty to love, the love of God alone develops in us a true devotedness; the soul then understands

[1] Luke 14. 26–7.

better that it is for God and in God that creatures must be loved, that it is God Who is loved in them, and they are loved because God wills and how He wills; thus the soul does not rest in creatures but in God, using them to draw nearer to God, to glorify Him in them, fulfilling the purpose for which they were created, seeing in them the likeness they bear to God, the imprint He has left of His perfections, and referring to Him as to the Author of all good, all that they may have of goodness, of loveliness and usefulness.[1]

The nearer the religious sister draws to Christ the more she looks upon herself as serving in His name. He uses her hands to tend the sick, the aged, leprous and dying. He speaks through her in all she says, to teach and to console. In Mary, she is Christ's hand-maiden. The same maternal tenderness should characterize her service of her own community. A religious family can be drawn together naturally by a common experience, life and tradition. But more is needed. The religious must give herself to Christ at home as much as she does abroad. He is her Lord and Spouse; and her one desire should be to do His slightest behest.

This applies most particularly to the enclosed sister. Humanly speaking, the family for her is everything—the vast world in the small bare home of Christ—in the midst of those who have been her companions for years, whose faults she knows, whose needs are ever apparent. But from that home her heart must radiate. Every true contemplative is at heart a missionary; and it is no anomaly, but merely a timely emphasis of a great truth that has led the Church to choose a contemplative religious saint as Patroness of the Missions. The contemplative who is not the mother of souls in association with the spiritual maternity of Mary, and who does not exercise her maternal heart in the welfare of her community in response to every need, and undertake vicarious expiation for sinners in union with Christ crucified, is hardly worthy of her great vocation. Contemplation is a disease of the mind if what the soul is habitually looking at is not outside the self, and in the case of the religious is not a self-forgetfulness in the loving presence and service of the Incarnate Word. Owing to her environment the contemplative sister is tempted to return in many subtle and devious ways to undue self-interest and self-exaltation; but if she bears always in mind that she is, as woman and as apostle, under a twofold obligation to give, she will of all religious

[1] *Life*, p. 51.

be the most balanced and normal. Through her prayer and sacrifice her maternal heart, love and tenderness will embrace the world.

We see, then, the need for a right understanding of the apostolate of the religious woman. Her vow of virginal chastity is not an asceticism which restrains and represses her natural gifts as woman and mother, but rather their spiritual elevation and fulfilment through her wedlock with Christ. In Mary she will bear the children of His Mystical Body.

IV

There is a noticeable tendency nowadays, due to a false conception of chastity, to look upon this wedlock of the soul with Christ at profession as merely analogous to the union between bride and bridegroom in matrimony. This is not true. When a religious sister chooses Christ as her Spouse, this spiritual and mystical union is not only real, but one compared with which earthly marriage is merely analogous, in the sense, for instance, that the rational life of the soul is analogous to that of grace.

This can be seen quite clearly by recalling the blessings of matrimony. First, there is *Fides* or fidelity to the loving contract undertaken. Bride and bridegroom belong in love and in justice to one another, 'to have and to hold from this day forward' . . . and in the mutual and exclusive rights over one another's bodies as dispositive causes of God's creative activity. 'The wife hath not power of her own body: but the husband', writes St. Paul. 'And in like manner the husband hath not power of his own body: but the wife'.[1] Conjugal love admits no rivals.

So, too, the religious sister plights her troth in fidelity to Christ. She belongs to Him alone; and He to her. And this love also admits no rivals. But this belonging is total, and not partial and restricted as in matrimony. For the wife does not belong to her husband body and soul. In marriage there is a limit to mutual possession, as each belongs to God, and this not only insofar as they must exercise their mutual rights according to His law, but also in the sense that He alone possesses each in the intimate and exclusive embrace of His creative power. There are deeps in the souls of married partners which are the preserve of the divine Lover and of Him alone and wherein even married love dare not

[1] 1 Cor. 7. 4. Cf. Eph. 5. 25.

trespass. But in the loving union of religious chastity there is no such division. It is the simple total dedication of virginity, which participates in the mystical and virginal union of Christ and His Church.

The second blessing of matrimony is *proles*, offspring. And once again human love and possession is limited in its power. The parents do not create the child through their mutual love of one another, but only dispose the conditions of God's immediate activity. The child is His; He alone as perfective cause brings a fresh and unique person into being which is the image of His thought. For God is Father of all. So also the second blessing of religious espousals is offspring. The total union of the spouse and Christ through the Church is fruitful in the order of grace conditioned by the degree of supernatural love and surrender. In union with the maternal activity of the Mystical Body, there is a begetting, not by the infusion of natural life, but of the supernatural life of grace, by the direct and perfective activity of Christ operative through the instrumental causality of the sacraments. The offspring of the virginal espousals of the apostle is therefore not the child of human parents but the child of God, participating in the life of its divine Father.

The third blessing of matrimony is *sacramentum*, the unbreakable bond of marriage. 'The Lord commanded that the wife depart not from the husband, and if she depart that she remain unmarried, or be reconciled to her husband. And let not the husband put away his wife.'[1] Marriage, therefore, imposes the duties of a domestic society in which the spouses dwell permanently together; and each has special functions in caring for the other. So, too, the vows of religion are permanent; and the love of Christ and His spouse is expressed in mutual service, a living together, one in mind and heart in a life of mutual sacrifice, communion and prayer.

[1] 1 Cor. 7. 10.

Chapter 4

THE RELIGIOUS SISTER, HEART OF THE PRIESTHOOD

I

THE consecration and elevation of Christian womanhood through virginal chastity is given a quasi-liturgical expression in the traditional ceremonials of religious profession. These are not only more elaborate in the case of religious women, as one would expect for other reasons, but strikingly different.

There is, for instance, the symbolism of the veil, ring and crown. Judging from the prayers conferring these sacred symbols it would almost seem as if this union—the mystical wedlock of chastity—were something essentially different in the case of the religious sister in view of her sex. This is of course not so. But can there be any doubt that as those united in this mystical union differ in sex, the language and terminology used in expressing such a union must be coloured by this sex differentiation; and further that the fruits of such a union must differ by reason of the qualitative differences of the human instrument? In other words, the outward ceremonial and signs of the religious profession of women must mean what they signify, so that this mystical and divine union of charity confers on the woman a characteristic function consonant with her nature, as helpmeet of Christ in His Mystical Body, insofar as this is the special prerogative of virginal chastity.

If this is true, can we say that the apostolate of the religious sister has certain qualitative features and even prerogatives in common with the apostolate of Our Lady, which are denied to religious men who for the most part are the appointed instruments and ministers of Christ in the priesthood? The answer to this question, as we shall see later, is both yes and no. But for the moment it is legitimate to point out that if both sexes brought about our ruin it seems only fitting that they should be used by God, each according to its natural endowments, in our deliverance and reinstatement. It would not be too much to say, then, that this characteristic function of the religious woman should bring with it not only privileged duties and obligations, but also corresponding graces and fruits in the supernatural order. This, at any rate, would seem to be so from the spirit, tradition and actual wording of the ritual. The praise and emphasis there given to the virginity of the woman could never have had the same significance but for her natural fruitfulness as woman. In this ritual it is the woman from whom through marriage would spring life eternal, the child of whose womb would never die, whose care and tenderness would preserve it from harm, and whose influence and example would introduce it to religious and social life, who is exalted. She gives herself, not to a human spouse, but to Christ, Incarnate God; and her surrender of love is accepted:

'*Veni Sponsa Christi, accipe coronam quam tibi Dominus praeparavit in aeternum.*'

Her fruitfulness thereafter will be no natural thing, but a real and mystical childbearing, nevertheless. The reality of such fruitful virginity alone can give meaning to the ritual of her profession. In marriage her body is sacred as the temple of natural life; in the mystical nuptials with Christ the crowning glory of that body is her virgin chastity. This is the sign of her dedication, and it derives its apostolic significance from the fruitfulness of her spiritual motherhood.

All the external rites of the Church are sensible signs of spiritual things [writes St. Thomas], but sometimes when the external sign does not adequately express the meaning of the spiritual thing signified, several sensible signs must be used to convey that meaning. The spiritual marriage of Christ and His Church is both fruitful since it begets the children of God, and absolutely pure and free of all corruption, for Christ chose for Himself a Church 'not having spot or wrinkle or any such things', as St. Paul says;[1] and that is why the same apostle says to the Corinthians:[2] 'I have espoused you to one husband, that I may present you as a chaste virgin to Christ.' But the fecundity of the flesh is not compatible with the integrity of the flesh, and therefore the spiritual marriage of Christ with the Church must be expressed through different signs; one expressing fecundity and the other integrity. The rite of marriage therefore is a symbol of spiritual marriage in respect of its fecundity; but another symbol is needed for spiritual marriage in respect of its integrity; and this symbol is the giving

[1] Eph. 5. 27. [2] 2 Cor. 11. 2.

of the veil together with the words and ceremonial accompanying it. That is why only a bishop to whom is committed the welfare of the Church can give the veil and so espouse virgins to Christ and he does this as the chosen friend of the Bridegroom.[1]

The more ancient liturgies surrounding the sacrament of marriage bear a striking resemblance to the religious profession. The modern ceremonial in the *Rituale Romanum*, approved by the Council of Trent, restricts the symbolism or external signs of marriage to the joining of hands (the ancient 'hand-fast') and the blessing of the ring conferred on the bride by the bridegroom.[2] But the more ancient ceremonials, which still persist in some countries, include the blessing and conferring of the veil and ring on the bride and the crowning of the bride and bridegroom. According to Tertullian, the ring is a symbol of fidelity; according to Clement of Alexandria, it is a seal, and the bride who wears it is queen and mistress of the house, having the right to affix her seal. The old form of the blessing of the ring was as follows:

Bless, O Lord, this ring which we bless in Thy holy name, that she who wears it in marriage as a token of faith may abide in Thy peace; and may she remain faithful in the integrity of the faith; may she ever live in Thy love and grow old in the same; and may her days be multiplied. Amen.[3]

Similarly when conferring the ring at religious profession following the *Pontificale Romanum*, the bishop says:

I espouse you with Jesus Christ, the Son of the eternal Father. . . . Receive this ring as the symbol of the Holy Ghost so that, remaining faithful to your heavenly Spouse, you may receive the eternal crown.

The sisters taking their vows then sing:

I am espoused to Him Whom the angels serve . . . My Lord Jesus Christ has given me His ring as a pledge of His love and with His crown has adorned me as His spouse.

And when taking the veil, the symbol of spiritual fecundity, they sing:

It is Christ I love, and into Whose bridal
    chamber I will go to Him

[1] 3 *Sent.*, D.38, Q.1, ad 5.
[2] The Council expressly permitted local marriage rites and customs.
[3] Cf. *Liturgical Prayer* by Abbot Fernand Cabrol, O.S.B., pp. 290 seq.

Whose Mother was a Virgin, and
Whose Father knew not woman. . . .
Whom when I shall love I am chaste,
And when I shall touch I am clean,
And when I shall take to my own I am a Virgin.
He has plighted His troth with His ring,
And encircled my neck with most precious jewels.[1]

The reason for the sacredness and esteem in which our sisters are held in the eyes of the Church is therefore to be found in their dignity as women, *par excellence*, insofar as they are invited to participate in the virginity and fecundity of the Church, in her unique espousals to the Incarnate Word, according to their proper and characteristic mode as women.[2]

II

The organic structure of the Mystical Body of Christ not only incorporates on the natural plane the divergent and complementary functions of the sexes as coadjutors in the apostolate, but also both in the natural and supernatural spheres, male and female co-principles. The one, the female co-principle, disposes the souls of men, for instance, through the corporal and spiritual works of mercy, such as the care of the sick, destitute, orphaned children and aged, and by teaching, preaching, the forgiveness of injuries, prayer, vicarious merit and satisfaction. The other, the male co-principle of spiritual fecundity, becomes operative through the Holy Sacrifice of the Mass and the administration of the sacraments.

These co-principles in the apostolate do not follow the division of sex-differentiation, but they are undoubtedly influenced by it. The priest is Father, through whom new members are born into the Mystical Body of Christ; for Christ as Head equips His Body with instruments to whom He commits full power to bring forth new members. This supernatural Fatherhood is conferred by the Sacrament of Order. The priesthood has such power, that through it the Eucharistic Christ as Head, Sacrifice, and spiritual Food of members is born, as it were, anew in the womb of the Mystical Body.[3] The priest acts in the person of Christ, participating in

---

[1] *Amo Christum in cujus thalamum introibo, cujus Mater Virgo est, cujus Pater feminam nescit, cujus mihi organa modulatis vocibus cantant : Quem cum amavero casta sum : cum tetigero munda sum : cum accepero virgo sum. Anulo subarrhavit me, et immensis monilibus ornavit me.*
[2] See Note 15, p. 229.   [3] See Note 16, p. 229.

His priesthood in the sense that in him as priest is invested the instrumental power to summon forth the Eucharistic presence of Christ and 'to make' the Holy Sacrifice of the Mass, from which flows the redeeming grace of the sacraments, thus consummating the holy wedlock between Christ and His Church.

But the Incarnate Word Himself is the principal cause of grace; the priest merely the recipient of Christ's power, but one who as a human instrument is shaped and enabled freely to use it through the habitual character and sacramental grace of Holy Order. Christ acts and works through His priest and he as an instrument is acted upon by Christ, the spiritual Father of souls. The priest has therefore a paternal function in the use of the power of Christ.

But in order that the life of grace so engendered may be shared by the faithful and souls reborn spiritually into the Mystical Body, it is not only necessary that the priest should be the cause of grace as the instrument of Christ, but that through his duties as pastor—by his work, prayer, merit, satisfaction and expiation— he should prepare souls for its acceptance, as one participating in the maternal activity of the Church. And it is in this maternal function, which disposes souls for grace, that every apostle and indeed every member of the Mystical Body in some measure participates—parents, teachers, lay institutes, non-clerical religious congregations of men and so on; but particularly, in the present context, the orders and congregations of religious sisters and nuns.

This influence of religious sisters is immeasurably greater than is generally supposed. By reason of their womanhood and sense of motherhood expressed in the care of the sick, needy and helpless, they are, as women, fitting consorts and helpmeets of the priesthood and indeed its inspiration insofar as they reflect the maternal heart of Mary. Their influence also tends to bring forth and to fortify the natural manly and resolute qualities of the true priest and to encourage him to appreciate still more the dignity of his priestly acts as one who wields the divine power of spiritual fecundation. It is in this sense that we should look upon and revere the religious sister as the heart of the priest. This relationship is the more fruitful because both participate in the virginity of the Mystical Body which releases into the apostolate a paternal and maternal love as dispositive and complementary endowments contributing to the salvation of souls.

Part Four

HANDMAIDENS OF MARY

Chapter 1

MARY MEDIATRIX

I

THE manner of Our Lady's intercession in heaven is sometimes distorted by a kind of pictorial error. We imagine that
to intercede in this sense is to plead, and entreat unwearyingly,
as for instance in the case of the Syrophoenician woman.[1] Our
Lady is invoked as Refuge of Sinners, but this does not mean that
she is the defender of lost causes in the sense that like a good
mother she is continually begging Our Lord to give us another
chance until, like the other woman in the Gospel,[2] she finally gets
her own way.

Our Lady's intercession is more noble, more effective and far-
reaching than this. Our Lord and His mother are as one united
in mind, love and purpose. She is His mother and ours. He sees
us all through the heart of His mother, as from all eternity He,
as God, had decreed; and through her He dispenses His own
mercy. In heaven we have as our advocate a human mother,
whose heart is the heart of Christ and whose intercession in Christ
before the throne of God is all-powerful. Her petitions never go
unheard or unanswered.

On January 12th, 1921, the Sacred Congregation of Rites
authorized the Office and Mass of Our Lady *Mediatrix Gratiarum*
—Mediatrix of Graces; the prayer is as follows:

> O Lord Jesus Christ, our Mediator with the Father, who hast
> vouchsafed to make Thy most blessed Virgin Mother our
> Mother also, and our Mediatrix with Thyself: grant, we
> beseech Thee, that whosoever shall beg Thy favour may be
> gladdened by obtaining the same through her prayers.[3]

Our Blessed Lady is, then, our mediatrix through her intercession. In ordinary human affairs we use the word mediator

---

[1] Mark 7. 24–30.
[2] Luke 18. 2–8.
[3] *Domine Jesu Christe, noster apud Patrem mediator, qui beatissimam Virginem matrem tuam,
matrem quoque nostram et apud te mediatricem constituere dignatus es: concede propitius; ut
quisquis ad te beneficia petiturus accesserit, cuncta se per eam impetrasse laetetur.*

to describe someone who is acceptable to both parties in a dispute and capable of reconciling them. Strictly speaking, the rôle of a mediator is to unite those between whom he mediates.

We can see then why Our Lord is the perfect mediator between God and men, who by their sins have offered the divine Majesty an infinite affront. No human creature however exalted and holy can reconcile man to God except the Incarnate Word, who, being divine, is both acceptable to God as His 'Beloved Son' and at the same time shares man's nature, mediating with the Father as our Brother and Head. The Incarnate Word alone can then unite men to God perfectively. As St. Paul says: 'God was in Christ reconciling the world to Himself.'[1]

But there is no reason why others should not be called mediators between God and men, in some respect, if they co-operate in uniting men to God dispositively or ministerially. The prophets and priests of the Old Law, for instance, were called mediators insofar as they foretold and foreshadowed the true and perfect Mediator, as, for example, by offering sacrifices which were types of the sacrifice of the Cross, what St. Paul called 'the shadow of the good things to come'.[2] In this sense the priests of the New Law also may be called mediators between God and man through their collaboration with the true Mediator in preaching the Gospel and administering the sacraments. We can see then that whilst in the words of St. Paul there is 'one mediator of God and men, the man Jesus Christ: who gave Himself for a redemption for all, a testimony in due times, others can and do assist in this mediation, dispositively and ministerially.

Does Our Lady co-operate in this way as mediatrix? Before answering this question we must be quite sure in our minds that there is one only perfect Mediator between God and man—the Incarnate Word of God. Every grace Our Lady received during her lifetime came to her through the merits of her Son as Mediator, even the graces of her Immaculate Conception, her divine maternity and her worthiness to be the cause of divine grace, and every grace she so causes. She is not the principal, but a subordinate cause of grace insofar as Christ wills her to assist in this way, and gives her the grace to do so. In the words of St. Grignon de Montfort:

I avow, with all the Church, that Mary, being but a mere creature issuing from the hands of the Most High, is, in com-

[1] 2 Cor. 5. 19.   [2] Heb. 10. 1.

parison with His Infinite Majesty, less than an atom; or rather she is nothing, because He only is 'He who is', and thus by consequence that great and noble Lord, always independent and self-sufficing, never had, and has not now, any absolute need of the Holy Virgin for the accomplishment of His will or the manifestation of His glory. He has but to will, in order to do everything. Nevertheless I say that . . . God having willed to begin and to complete His greatest works by the most holy Virgin, since He created her, we may well think that His conduct will remain unalterable throughout the ages; for He is God, and He changes not.[1]

Our Lady's office and function in the redemption as the universal mediatrix is therefore not strictly speaking necessary; it is God's good-pleasure that His bridal-mother should assist as the chief subordinate cause of divine grace in the hierarchy of causes through which the Incarnate Word, as the one and only Redeemer, operates. 'The work of redemption', writes Père Garrigou-Lagrange,

proceeds therefore entirely from God as First Cause of grace, entirely from Jesus as principal and perfect Mediator, and entirely from Mary as subordinate mediatrix. These three causes are not partial and co-ordinate, as are three men who drag the same load; but total and subordinated. The second acts under the influence of the first, the third under the influence of the second. An example which may make the point clear is that of the fruit which proceeds entirely from God the Author of nature, entirely from the tree, and entirely from the branch on which it grows. It does not proceed in its different parts from different causes; neither is our redemption the work in part of the Divinity, in part of the Humanity, and in part of Mary. It is worth noting how becoming it is that Mary who was redeemed by the Saviour in a most excellent manner and preserved from all sin, original and actual, should co-operate in this way in our justification and our final perseverance.

Mary's mediation is of a much higher order than that of the saints, for she alone has given us the Saviour, she alone was so intimately united to the sacrifice of the Cross, she alone is universal mediatrix for all mankind and for each and every grace—even for that grace which is of all the most particular, the grace of the present moment.[2]

[1] *True Devotion to the Blessed Virgin*, Part I (i).
[2] *The Mother of the Saviour*, Part II, Ch. 2.

II

Sometimes it is thought, even in Catholic circles, especially when reading such devotional literature as the *True Devotion* of St. Grignon de Montfort, that too much is being claimed for Our Lady out of love for her, as though our filial devotion had somehow got the better of our discretion and even of our commonsense. Such 'excessive devotion', as some would call it, will, we are told, crowd out all prayer to the saints and even obscure the redemptive majesty of Christ Himself.

But curiously enough, both in theory and in practice, freedom in all our prayers and devotions is only to be found by facing the truth and the whole truth regarding Our Lady's prerogatives, and not by shrinking from the imaginary consequences of such truth when it is only half assimilated. When we speak of Our Lady as the universal mediatrix in such phrases as 'All graces come through Mary', it is not suggested that she is merely an object of devotion as, for example, the saints or even St. Joseph. She is not an object of devotion: she is a *function*, and has been so honoured by Christ our principal Mediator before God. The central feature of our Catholic life has always been Christ and His mother; but it was He who placed her by His side at Nazareth and on Calvary; and at Bethlehem, it was He, the Word of God, who placed Himself in her arms. Whether we consciously think of Our Lady or not as a function in Christ's redemptive activity, her co-operating intercession will be at the service of our prayer and sacrifice, even when we turn to God in the highest prayer of union, or make our thanksgiving after Communion, or pray to any of our patron saints. In a word, Our Lord has ordained that we should work out our salvation in this way; it is an essential part of His plan of redemption, and only our deliberate will to eliminate her as a function can exclude her intercession. Is it not to be expected therefore that having been chosen for such a high dignity by Our Lord out of His love for her we, her children, should rejoice in her prerogatives and even become inquisitive, as is the way with children, to know more of the power and majesty of our own mother? The more Our Lord has done for her the greater should be our joy.

According to the order fixed by Our Lord Himself, therefore, His merits and intercession will be of no avail without Mary's

co-operating intercession, and accordingly every grace is granted
only as conjointly with her. But we must never be tempted to
think there could ever have been any disunion between the will
of Christ and His mother. Whilst on earth no union of love was
ever comparable to theirs; and now in the enjoyment of the Beatific Vision they are even more closely united, so united indeed
that the love of Mary for her spiritual children is virtually the
substantial mother-love for us radiating from the Sacred Heart of
Christ Himself. We cannot offend one without offending the other,
love one without loving the other; to cut oneself off from Mary is
to cut oneself off from Christ. For she is His mother, the maternal
expression of His love for us, eternally. But she remains subordinate to Him—as noble and loving as He has chosen her to be. The
more glorious and great we find her, and the more she radiates
His mother-love for us, the more readily and spontaneously
should we turn to Him in thanksgiving.

However profound the theology of Mary it is not difficult to
find a certain becomingness in her privilege as universal mediatrix, by reason of her intimate union with Incarnate God. God
so loved the world, that is to say, the human race, and the race as
represented by Mary; in other words, God so loved Mary that
He chose to be united to her in the most intimate manner by
inviting her to become His mother.

> In natural marriage the bride is taken up by the bridegroom
> through his will which she accepts and which the Creator sancti-
> fies [writes Father Scheeben in a striking passage]. This taking
> up is so intimate that she ideally and really grows together with
> him to one whole and, as though incorporated and united with
> him, forms with him one moral body, in which both physical
> persons belong to each other through mutual gift, in the most
> perfect manner. Thus the virgin mother is united through
> the will and power of the creating Word of God with His own
> person. Through the acceptance of the flesh of the mother in
> the physical unity of His purely spiritual person, He accepts her
> in a purely spiritual, but most real manner into a moral cor-
> porate unity of person and gives Himself to her just as He
> appropriates her to Himself.
> According to the expression of the Oriental languages,
> marriage is a mutual 'clothing' of the married persons through
> which the bride becomes the body and raiment of the bride-
> groom, and the bridegroom becomes the head and crown of the
> bride. Here also, as the Fathers frequently indicate, such a

mutual clothing takes place in an eminent degree and in a manner analogous to that in Christ Himself between His humanity and divinity. There as well as here, the marriage occurs between the 'flesh' and the 'spirit': the flesh clothes the spirit externally, and the spirit clothes the flesh interiorly. Moreover, it is a marriage between created flesh and creating spirit; the flesh, according to its entire being, belongs to the spirit and is subject to it; and on its side the spirit can dwell in the closest manner in the flesh and fill it with itself.

In a certain sense the pure union of grace with God also forms a marriage with Him, and indeed a marriage analogous to the hypostatic union. However, as it is not communicated through the hypostatic union, it has not the full specific strength of marriage. On the contrary, it bears only the character of a simple friendly relation.[1]

By the power of the Holy Spirit therefore, that is, under the impulse of God's love for Mary, the Person of the Son seeking to embrace her, His chosen bride, in the most intimate union, was conceived as a Child in her womb. This union is the most perfect possible, save only that between Christ's humanity and the Person of the Word. At the beginning of the old order God made woman from man; to inaugurate the new order God takes His human nature from a woman, that He might restore woman to man. Their life together was begun in the womb; each fully conscious of the other in a total and ineffable fusion of mind and heart from the first moment of the child's conception. The man-child within her womb, Flesh of her flesh, Blood of her blood, was God. And she a woman having co-operated with the vitalizing activity of the Holy Spirit, by her consent remains for ever as closely united to the Godhead as is possible whilst still remaining a creature.

Again; as Mary is the bride of the divine Person dwelling within her at His invitation and through her surrender to His will, He, as Bridegroom, takes up the mother unto Himself as His bride. The divine motherhood in this way resembles the hypostatic union since it is a union with a divine Person which embraces the mother's entire and most intimate being. This ennobles and sancti-fies her in the most perfect manner and forms the basis of the most complete participation in the life and possessions of the divine Person, as Bridegroom.[2]

[1] Scheeben, *Mariology*, Vol. I, pp. 164–5.
[2] Scheeben, *Loc. cit.*, pp. 166–7.

The Incarnate Word, born of Mary, was then the Head of the new race, and Mary, the New Eve, the helpmeet 'like unto Himself', had by her consent as chosen bride of the Word not only become His mother, but the mother of the new humanity He had inaugurated. It was the union of the perfect man and the perfect woman, both united to the Godhead—He hypostatically in the Person of the Word and she by reason of her bridal maternity. It is the perfect union of the sexes in the natural order ascending and made transcendent in the very life of God. The Word of God gives Himself manhood in assuming our human nature; and the Word made Flesh unites Himself to womanhood in His human and divine natures in an embrace to which the sacramental love of marriage bears merely a distant and reflected analogy. In this communion of perfect man and woman, the progenitors of the new race, there is a total, virtual union of mind and heart; they are one form in a reciprocity of complementary functions proper to the sexes which finds expression, each in due proportion, in the supernatural union of Jesus and Mary in the Godhead. And conversely, it is man and woman in their natural and supernatural union reflecting in the most perfect manner possible to them, as one whole and complete principle of the new humanity, the image of God. For there are activities and perfections in the Godhead analogous to those of the woman and mother, and perhaps the chief of these is mercy. And there are activities and perfections in the Godhead which are analogous to the human qualities of the man and father, and perhaps the most characteristic of these is the executive power of justice.

If we can say then that the blending and fusion of the sexes is the manifestation of a complete and complementary human attitude to life, then, that blending and fusion reaches its perfect expression in the union of Jesus and Mary. Can we not say, therefore, that this is the most perfect human analogy of the divine activities and perfections, and that when they are caught up into the transcendence of a divine union in the Word by the Incarnation, these qualities find themselves absorbed and transmuted, like shadows into the reality, in the Beatific Vision?

Jesus and Mary in heaven are therefore Founder and mother, Head and heart of the new race, which is the Mystical Body of Christ; and as man and woman they bring the sexes into their final and eternal complementary relationship in their return to God whence they came, gathering together and co-ordinating in themselves the diverse perfections of man and woman throughout the ages, and that similar complementary relationship of things throughout nature, which is the infinitely remote and vestigial expression of the divine power, wisdom and goodness. Mary is eternally woman and mother, and Jesus eternally Father, Leader, Lord, Saviour, Head; and towards the Church Militant it is fitting that both should exercise a similar complementary relationship as mediators between God and the new humanity of which they are the progenitors and co-principles.

Christ, indeed, sufficed in Himself [says St. Bernard], for even now all our sufficiency is from Him; but it was not good for man to be alone; and it is far more fitting that both the man and the woman should be joined together for our redemption, since both contributed to our fall. The Man, Christ Jesus, is beyond all doubt the faithful and almighty Mediator between God and man, yet in Him men worship with all reverence the Majesty of God. His Manhood seems absorbed in His Godhead; not that Its substance is changed, but that Its affections are deified. Not only is mercy sung of as His, but judgement also: 'Mercy and judgement will I sing to Thee, O Lord.' For although He learnt compassion through suffering, yet has He also the power of judgement. In a word, 'our God is a consuming fire'. How, then, shall not the sinner dread to approach Him, lest, even as wax melteth away before the fire, so also may he perish from before the face of God?

Thus, then, is it seen that the Woman herself, who is blessed among women, is not idle, since a place is found for her in the reconciliation of man with God. For we have need of a mediator to the great Mediator; nor can we have a better one than Mary. Cruel, indeed, was Eve when she stood between us and the serpent, and infused his deadly poison even into the man. But faithful is Mary, who drank the antidote of salvation both for men and women. Eve was the minister of seduction; Mary of propitiation. Eve, by her suggestion, wrought prevarication; Mary brought about redemption.

Why should human weakness tremble and fear to come to Mary? Nothing in her is austere, nothing terrible. She is all-loving, offering milk and honey unto all. Go over with care the whole course of the Gospel story, and if you can find one chiding or inconsiderate word, or the sign of the least anger, then you may have reason to mistrust her and fear to approach her.

But if, on the other hand, you find her full of tenderness, graciousness as indeed she is, and so gentle and merciful, then

be grateful to Him who, in His mercy, has given you a mediator
of whom you need never be afraid. . . . There is none who can
hide himself from the glow of her love.[1]

III

But this complementary mediation of Mary, however becoming
and however consonant with the hierarchic order of Divine
Wisdom as we have tried to show, is not strictly speaking necessary.
Our Lady's mediation as a creature is infinitely removed from
that of her divine Son and Saviour. Nevertheless she stands as the
most exalted of God's creatures between God and men, and especially between Christ and men. It is God's will she should so
mediate. But, we must repeat, it is not complementary to Christ's
mediation in the sense that without it His own would have been
imperfect. God could have reinstated fallen man in other ways
than by the Incarnation; but having willed to become the Founder
and Head of the new race and having loved and chosen Mary as
His bride and virgin mother He also makes her, in virtue of that
loving choice, His universal mediatrix.

Christ, the Incarnate Word and Saviour, is then the primary
and principal cause of merit and satisfaction through His mediation; Mary is the principal cause but in a secondary or subordinate order which is itself totally dependent on Christ as primary
Mediator. She does not therefore hold this dignity by right, but
as an honour lovingly conferred on her by her divine Bridegroom.
In other words, God so loved the sinless perfection of His own
mother that He chose to make her through her universal mediation the substantial and personified expression of the mercy and
compassion of the divine Heart of the Incarnate Word. And it is
most fitting that as Adam and Eve, man and woman, were co-
principles of our fall, Christ and Mary, man and woman, should
be co-principles in our justification, and that this complementary
activity should persist in the sacrifice of the whole Christ eternally
offered to the Father.

Mary in virtue of her bridal-motherhood belongs to all of us.
And it is this sense 'of belonging to a mother' that has moved the
Church, through the hearts of the simple faithful, to recognize the
power of her motherly intercession in their prayers and devotions.
It may seem at times to the cynic and those who fail to realize how

---

[1] *Sermon within Oct. of Assump.*   See also Note 24, p. 235.

deeply rooted in our nature is the Christian Faith, that the attitude of these quite ordinary folk towards Mary is too often a transference of natural mother-love, altogether too credulous, too pietistic or whatever such critics think may be responsible for the setting up of candles, the massing of flowers on her altar, the pilgrimages to her shrines, popular hymns in her honour and so on. But when all is said and done Mary is in fact a heavenly mother, and a human mother who knows the joys and sorrows of our life from experience, and who knows our needs, spiritual and temporal.[1] Her immaculate heart beats in heaven as it did in Nazareth. By all means let us sing her praises with liturgical perfection and show forth her majesty as Queen; but these quite ordinary people we have mentioned have the sense to see that we can only recognize her privileges as Queen of Heaven when we have accepted her literally and by right as the Queen of our domestic hearths and kitchens. In the words of St. Thérèse of Lisieux:

We all know quite well that Our Lady is the Queen of Heaven and earth, *but she is more Mother than Queen*; and it does not do to lead people to believe (as I have often heard done) that by reason of her prerogatives she eclipses the glory of the saints just as the stars fade away at the rising of the sun. That would indeed be an extraordinary thing! Fancy a mother diminishing the glory of her children in this way! I think, myself, it will be the other way about and that she will greatly increase the splendour of the elect. So by all means let us remember her prerogatives; but we must not stop there; we must show that she is *loving*.[2]

This sense of belonging to a heavenly mother expressed in the devotions of the Faithful, besides being essentially founded in her bridal-motherhood is in a special sense the reward of her virginity. The vow of virginal chastity frees the human heart to love all in loving Christ, to love as Christ loves, that we may draw all to the love of God, the cause and motive of our dedication. The human love of Our Lady being a mother-love of Christ through the physical fact of her maternity, this universality of love which rewarded her virginal chastity was the extension of the human love of her maternal heart to all men in every age. Further, if the virgin spouse loves humanly only in the degree she loves God, the final cause or motive of her dedication, how shall we measure the

[1] See Note 17, p. 230.
[2] *Novissima Verba*, p. 157.

outpouring of human love and affection from the heart of Mary, more especially as through her supernatural and divine love of the Word of God, she mystically conceived all men at the Incarnation and has a real spiritual relationship to them as mother? As the Sacred Heart of Christ loves each one of us divinely-humanly; so does the immaculate heart of Mary love each one of us in Christ with the total love of a divine Mother.

We can see then how unerring is the Catholic instinct which guides the Faithful in their love of Our Lady. When they grow up from childhood to look upon her as 'Mother Mary', this is not a devotional extravagance merely to be tolerated, but theologically correct, as it is a necessary counterpart in the Christian apostolate of the incomparable human love and compassion of Christ. When it is said, therefore, that the Catholic family should be brought up with the Holy Family, the human implications of this principle are theologically right and pedagogically flawless.

Chapter 2

CHRISTLIKE IN MARY

I

AS apostles we participate in the maternal activity of the Church in preparing souls for grace and the Christian life. How does Our Lady help us in this work? The answer to this question sheds great light on the virginal apostolate of the religious sister.

When we say that Our Lady is the cause of grace we are speaking in terms of final causality, in the sense that she is the cause of all graces whatsoever through her intercession. Subordinate to Our Lord she is the eminently active and influential mediatrix of salvation because she holds a unique and central position between Him and mankind by reason of her consent to become His mother. Our Lady's maternal co-operation in heaven converts the grace of redemption to the use of mankind; or, rather, she leads each individual person to a participation in the grace of redemption and thereby to union with God.[1]

(a) The Power of Mary's intercession

This has been fittingly described by St. Grignon de Montfort. He writes:

> Inasmuch as grace perfects nature, and glory perfects grace, it is certain that Our Lord is still, in heaven, as much the Son of Mary as He was on earth; and that, consequently, He has preserved the most perfect obedience and submission of all children towards the best of all mothers.

> But we must take great pains not to conceive of this dependence as any abasement or imperfection in Jesus Christ. Mary is infinitely below her Son, Who is God, and therefore she does not command Him, as a mother here below would command her child, who is inferior to her in dignity. Mary, being altogether transformed into God by grace, and by the glory which transforms all the saints into Him, asks nothing, wishes nothing, does nothing which is contrary to the Eternal and Immutable Will of God.

[1] Cf. Dublancy, *Dict. Theol. Cath.*—'Marie': and *Mariology*, Scheeben, Vol. 2, p. 263.

When we read, then, in the writings of the saints like St. Bernard, St. Bernardine and St. Bonaventure, that in heaven and on earth everything, even to God Himself, is subject to the Blessed Virgin, they mean to say that the authority which God has been well-pleased to give her is so great, that it seems as if she has the same power of God, and that her prayers and petitions are so powerful with God, that they always pass for commandments with His Majesty, Who never resists the prayer of his dear Mother, because she is always humble and conformed to His Will.[1]

(b) *The Universality of Mary's Intercession*

(i) Père Garrigou-Lagrange writes:

This is affirmed in the prayers of the Church . . . Graces of every kind, temporal and spiritual—and among these latter all those which lead to God, from the grace of conversion to that of final perseverance—are asked through Mary. She is prayed to also for the graces needed by apostolic workers, by martyrs in time of persecution, by confessors of the faith, by virgins that they may preserve their virginity intact. . . . The Litany of Loreto gives some idea of the many graces which the Church asks through her intercession. . . .

Among all the different graces, that which is the most peculiar to any particular wayfarer is the grace of the moment in which he finds himself. That, too, comes through Mary. We pray for it daily and many times when we say: 'Pray for us sinners, *now* and at the hour of our death.' By the word 'now' we ask for the grace required to fulfil the duty of the present moment, to practise this or that virtue asked of us, here and now. Even if we do not ourselves realize what grace we need, Mary in heaven knows, and through her intercession we obtain it. The succession of graces of the moment, varying from one moment to the next, is like a spiritual atmosphere which we inhale and which renews our souls as air replenishes our blood.[2]

(ii) Mgr. Canon George Smith writes:

As to the *graces* in the distribution of which Mary intervenes, there is no restriction. She has her part in distributing all graces. And by graces, it would seem, we must understand all that in any way helps us to gain eternal life; therefore not only the first infusion of sanctifying grace, by which we are made adopted sons of God and heirs to our heavenly kingdom, but also every

[1] *True Devotion to the Blessed Virgin*, Pt. I, No. i.
[2] *The Mother of the Saviour*, pp. 249-50.

increase of grace which makes us more pleasing in our Father's sight; also every actual grace, every supernatural enlightenment of the mind and every inspiration of the will which enables us to overcome temptation, to persevere in well-doing and to devote ourselves to God's service; above all, the grace of a holy death. Moreover, all the graces which are granted to sinners for their conversion and to unbelievers that they may find the faith. In addition to these supernatural graces which sanctify, or tend to sanctify, their recipients, we must include all those supernatural powers (*gratiae gratis datae*) which God gives to men that they may work more effectively for the salvation of their brethren: gifts of miracles, of prophecy, of knowledge. And not only these; even those providential 'accidents'—the hearing of a sermon, the making of a retreat, the good advice and, above all, the good example of our fellow-men—which may lead us to grace, confirm us in our good resolutions and make us better men; all these, intended as they are by God for our eternal weal, are due to the intercession of Mary. All this we owe to the merits of Christ; all this we owe to the subordinate merits of Our Lady; all this falls within the scope of her universal and maternal intercession.

But what of the grace which we receive through the sacraments? Is it not the teaching of the Church that the sacraments produce grace in us *ex opere operato*, by an intrinsic efficacy which they possess as the Christ-ordained instruments of our sanctification? And yet this grace, too, we receive through Mary's intercession. Of course, it must not be imagined that the efficacy of the sacraments is made conditional upon Mary's intervention; for if a sacrament is validly administered and duly and properly received nothing can prevent it from producing its effect in the soul. But we cannot receive the grace unless the sacrament is administered; and it is Mary's intercession which ensures that the sacrament is available. Moreover, the valid administration of the sacrament calls for the due rite to be used, as well as the requisite intention in the minister; and Mary is at hand to see that these conditions are not lacking. Above all, the fruitful reception of the sacrament requires the necessary dispositions; and Mary's prayer obtains that we do not frustrate the sanctifying virtue that flows from the Sacred Side of her Son.[1]

II

Through her consent at the Incarnation Our Lady freely

[1] *Mary's Part in Our Redemption*, pp. 164–5 (1954 edn., pp. 169–70).

associated herself with the redemption as the second Eve. In a subordinate manner she is a co-principle with Christ, Redeemer and Founder of the new race.

This association of Mary is total, not from absolute necessity, but by reason of the divine decree that Christ, the New Adam, should have a 'consort and helpmeet' like unto Himself in all He did by way of merit and satisfaction to redeem the world. For this reason Mary was immaculately conceived and shared increasingly in His grace, till on Calvary she merited as co-redemptrix to be made Christlike even unto His final self-immolation. Our Lady therefore whilst on earth merited for us congruously all that Christ, the Redeemer, merited in strict justice. Through these merits her intercession as our spiritual Mother is all-powerful in heaven.[1]

Let us now ask ourselves two questions: first, how does Our Lady help the Mystical Body? And, secondly, how do we in the Mystical Body help Our Lady?

The answer to our first question has already been given; Our Lady helps us by dispensing grace through her intercession. The final cause or 'reason why' of her intercession is her excellence and love-worthiness in God's sight as His mother and bride who reflects in the fullest measure possible to a mere creature the image and redemptive activity of the Incarnate Word.[2]

Secondly, how can we in the Mystical Body help Our Lady and increase her fruitfulness as the mother of souls? By striving to become Christlike in Mary. In other words, we must reproduce Christ in our lives—'put on the Lord Jesus'—and the more we do so, the more closely shall we be gathered into her spiritual family as the 'consorts and helpmeets' of Christ, in, with and through her.

But the mode of our congruous merits, however, is precisely that of Mary, though her merits are immeasurably greater because she loves God beyond the capacity of any other creature. By reason of this love she reflects the Christ-life as His chosen mother and the mother of souls, in the most perfect manner possible, whereas our reflection of it, however perfect it may be comparatively speaking, as, for instance, in St. Joseph, remains dim and remote. We can only love Christ and so become Christlike in the measure of our capacity; and this capacity is determined

1 See Note 18, p. 231.
2 See Note 19, p. 232.

for each of us by the divine Wisdom whatever be the degree of our surrender. The cup cannot hold more than a cupful, but Mary is the sea.

The function of Our Lady's apostolate is then to bring forth the likeness of Jesus her Son in the hearts of men. To that end does she intercede for us in heaven. Our function as her children and apostles is to help her in this work by reproducing Christ in our own souls, and through our participation in the Christ-life to bring forth His image in the souls of others.

Indeed Our Lord Himself tells us this again and again. The Christian way of life is not to live in our own image, but a surrender and self-effacement in allowing Christ to re-enact His life, passion and death in our particular circumstances,[1] in and through us. God regardeth our humility. Nothing is more characteristic of Our Lord's teaching, for instance, than the words 'follow Me' or the equivalent expression in word and figure. We are called upon to live Christ, by reproducing His merits and satisfaction congruously in our own lives. 'If any man will come after Me, let him deny himself and take up his cross daily and follow Me.'[2] Our apostolate is then a participation in the Christ-life and its radiation. 'I have called you friends. . . . You have not chosen Me: but I have chosen you; and have appointed you, that you should bring forth fruit.'[3]

We must conclude, therefore, that the whole family of Mary in the Mystical Body has a co-redeeming activity; we are all co-redeemers because such is the will of Christ, co-redeemers of ourselves and others, just as Our Lady is the co-redemptrix of herself and of all. Every grace we receive from her through her all-powerful intercession as our mother, is ordained to this specific purpose. It is her will that we should make her intercession as it were our own in our determination to become Christlike in our own merits and satisfaction, both for ourselves and for those in our apostolate.

The more perfectly our oblation and our sacrifice corresponds to the sacrifice of Christ [wrote Pope Pius XI] . . . the more abundant will be the fruits of propitiation and expiation which we shall receive for ourselves and for others. For a wonderful bond unites all the faithful with Christ, a bond similar to that

[1] See Note 20, p. 233.
[2] Luke 9. 26.
[3] John 15. 15–16.

which exists between the head and the other members of the body; and that mysterious communion of saints which our Catholic faith professes not only binds individuals and nations to one another, but also joins them all with the head.[1]

[1] *Miserentissimus Redemptor.*

Chapter 3

CHRIST-BEARERS

AS apostles we associate ourselves with the apostolic activity of Mary in bringing forth members of Christ's Mystical Body and in presiding over their spiritual growth. We cannot be the instrumental cause of grace unless we are chosen by the Church to participate in the Priesthood of Christ, her Spouse. But all priests and apostles can and do participate in the dispositive activity of our heavenly mother as exercised through the Church, principally in three ways: first as Christ-bearers; secondly by teaching the word of God; and thirdly by participating in Mary's self-oblation on Calvary. Let us consider these in order.

As apostles called upon to bear the image of Christ in our hearts we should ponder the words of Our Lord Himself:

> You are the salt of the earth [He told His disciples]. But if the salt lose its savour, wherewith shall it be salted? It is good for nothing any more but to be cast out and to be trodden on by men. You are the light of the world. A city seated on a mountain cannot be hid. Neither do men light a candle and put it under a bushel, but upon a candlestick, that it may shine to all that are in the house. So let your light shine before men that they may see your good works and glorify your Father who is in heaven. Do not think that I am come to destroy the law or the prophets. I am not come to destroy, but to fulfil. For amen I say unto you, till heaven and earth pass, one jot or one tittle shall not pass of the law, till all be fulfilled. He therefore that shall break one of these least commandments and shall so teach men shall be called the least in the kingdom of heaven. But he that shall do and teach, he shall be called great in the kingdom of heaven. For I tell you, that unless your justice abound more than that of the scribes and Pharisees, you shall not enter into the kingdom of heaven.[1]

Each of us radiates the life within him. And he manifests himself the more readily and faithfully in the degree of his surrender to the divine will. A truly God-centred and worshipful Christian soul is never likely to assume a mask or *persona* through some pretence

1 Matt. 5. 13–20.

or hypocrisy in its effort to show forth qualities of mind and heart which have no roots within and which conceal its unique natural gifts. When we attempt to be other than we are, we descend at once into the humdrum and commonplace of the merely superficial, like the man St. James tells us about who, having looked at himself in the mirror, went away and forgot what manner of man he was.[1] Living for Christ is to accept His rule—'the perfect law of liberty'—to work together with Him that we may be, love and live according to our predestined mode in Christ.

Each of us, then, is a unique portrayal of the Christ-life—one facet, as it were, of its sublime perfection which is expressed in the mode of his natural endowments. When we consider the Christ-life of Mary, His mother, for instance, we have not only to appraise it in terms of her participation in the grace of Christ, particularly the grace of her divine maternity, but to see manifested in her as a woman, the maternal Heart of Christ, that is, all the supernatural and natural gifts and qualities characteristic of her as the Second Eve, as of one issuing forth from Christ as a consort and 'a help like unto Himself'. If then the apostle is to dispose the souls of others for grace and the knowledge of Christ, he himself must be a Christ-bearer, according to his own characteristic mode.

'We must make the Gospel live and make it known, we must preach it', said Abbé Huvelin. 'Where is the Gospel written? Not only by the four evangelists. Our Lord and the Holy Spirit do not only write in inspired books. They write in souls. The Gospel, then, is not only set down in writing in a book, it lives in souls. We admire the written Gospel; but much finer and much greater is the sight of a living Gospel, the sight of one who has learnt to show forth in his life the virtues which the Gospel enjoins us.'[2]

To become Christ-bearers, and so carry His Gospel engraven on our hearts and lives we must, first, participate in His grace as Head of the Mystical Body; secondly, have an affective union with Him; and thirdly, seek a real union with Him in the Holy Eucharist.

(i) *The Union of Grace*

In the first place we are one with Christ through our participation in His grace. The source of all grace which men receive is

[1] James 1. 23.   [2] *Addresses to Women.*

the *gratia unionis,* the grace of union, which constitutes Christ the representative of mankind and the Head of the Church, His Mystical Body. On account of His nearness to God in the hypostatic union His grace is the *highest and first,* since all members receive grace by reason of His grace as Head. In the words of St. Paul: 'whom He foreknew, He also predestinated to be made conformable to the image of His Son; that He might be the first-born amongst many brethren.'[1] Again Christ has the *fulness of all grace,* in the words of St. John: 'We saw Him . . . full of grace and truth.'[2] He also has the *power to bestow* His grace on all members of the Mystical Body, for 'of His fulness we have all received'.[3]

Christ is also the Head of men's bodies as well as their souls on account of the natural relationship between body and soul, for the soul gives life to the body and the body serves the soul. We must say, therefore, that the whole manhood, body and soul, of Christ influences both our bodies and our souls; but principally our souls, and secondarily our bodies. As the interior influx of grace elevating the soul of each member of the Mystical Body is from Christ and from Christ alone in virtue of His Headship, we must say that each of us bears the Christ-life within himself in the measure of his grace, and that this grace also influences the body through its union with the soul, as its instrument.

(ii) *Affective Union with Christ*

By the grace of Christ we are made the friends of God and become Christlike. With the increase of grace through the sacraments the image of Christ becomes the more deeply engraven upon our hearts. Our Lord left us in no doubt that He, the Incarnate Word, seeks this union with each one of us.

> *Abide in me: and I in you. As the branch cannot bear fruit of itself, unless it abide in the vine, so neither can you, unless you abide in me.*
>
> *I am the vine: you the branches. He that abideth in me, and I in him, the same beareth much fruit: for without me you can do nothing. If any one abide not in me, he shall be cast forth as a branch and shall wither: and they shall gather him up and cast him into the fire: and he burneth.*
>
> *If you abide in me and my words abide in you, you shall ask whatever you will: and it shall be done unto you.*
>
> *In this is my Father glorified: that you bring forth very much fruit and become my disciples.*
>
> *As the Father hath loved me, I also have loved you. Abide in my love.*[4]

[1] Rom. 8. 29.   [2] John 1. 14.   [3] John 1. 16.   [4] John 15. 4-9.

And again:

And the glory which thou hast given me, I have given to them: that they may be one, as we also are one.

I in them, and thou in me: that they may be made perfect in one: and the world may know that thou hast sent me and hast loved them, as thou hast also loved me.

Father, I will that where I am, they also whom thou hast given me may be with me: that they may see my glory which thou hast given me, because thou hast loved me before the creation of the world.[1]

When St. John Chrysostom said 'the heart of Paul was the Heart of Christ', he meant that besides the intimate presence of Christ through grace there was also an affective union resulting from St. Paul's correspondence with this grace, in that he had 'one mind and heart in the Lord'. He became as it were another Christ, reaching out, and yearning to possess Him. He lived for nothing else; his interests were those of Jesus, his honour that of Jesus, his love that of Jesus. When he cried: 'I live and yet not I, but Christ liveth in me', he meant that, body and soul, he wished in all things to identify himself with Our Lord, to become one with Him.

Now the principles governing this affective union are as follows: The mutual union or indwelling of a lover and his beloved can be brought about in two ways: first by knowledge and secondly by affection. As regards the former, the beloved is in the lover in the sense of being 'in his thoughts'. We say, for instance, especially when writing to our friends: 'You are forever in my thoughts', or 'I am always thinking of you and wondering how you are', all of which signifies a kind of possession in the mind.

But the lover may also be said to be in the beloved when he is not content with a mere superficial knowledge but is ever striving for a more intimate discovery, and seeking to penetrate even his very soul. In this way a faithful religious, her mind enlivened by faith, will ponder the word of God or apply herself to spiritual reading that she may know more and more about the Lord she has espoused. Love makes us inquisitive for a deeper knowledge of those we love.

The next day again John stood and two of his disciples. And beholding Jesus walking, he saith: Behold the Lamb of God. And the two disciples heard him speak: and they followed Jesus. And Jesus turning and seeing them following Him, saith

[1] John 17. 22-4.

to them: What seek you? Who said to Him: Rabbi (which is
to say, being interpreted, Master), where dwellest Thou? He
saith to them: Come and see. They came and saw where He
abode: and they stayed with Him that day.[1]

Secondly, in regard to the movement of his will, the beloved is
also said to be in the lover, inasmuch as he is in the lover's affections in the sense that a complacency in the beloved is rooted in
his heart. That is why we speak of such a union of love as being
intimate. It is the union we have with a mother, who has gone to
God, as we take up her photograph, look at it for a while, and then
put it aside with a word of endearment.

But, on the other hand, the lover is said to be in the beloved
inasmuch as he esteems what is good or evil to his friend as being
so to him, and his friend's will as his own, so that it seems as though
he feels the good and suffers the evil in the person of his friend.
Insofar therefore as the lover considers what is done to his beloved
as done to himself, he seems to be in the beloved, as though he
were one with him. By such sympathy we share the joys and
sorrows of those we love, as if these things were happening to us.
We say we are 'with them in their grief'. But in this sense God
alone can become one with those in sorrow, and He did so by a
real as well as by an affective union when the Word was made
Flesh and dwelt amongst us. God enables us also to become like
unto God, and to unite ourselves with the joys, sorrows and purpose of the Incarnate Word, so that as lovers of the Redeemer
we regard what is done to Him as being done to us. By our union
first in the grace of Christ, and secondly of mind and heart in
true sympathy with Him, we are inspired with the right attitude
towards the apostolate, that is, to live and work in Him as the
lover in the Beloved.

(iii) *The Eucharistic Communion*[2]

As the lover longs for the presence of the beloved, so it is this
affective union, founded on grace, which draws the Christian to

---

[1] John 1. 35–9.

[2] The reader will understand that this summary is very inadequate as an explanation of the Christ-life within the Church and in the soul of every member of the
Mystical Body (Cf. *S.T.*, 3, 65, 1). The Holy Eucharist, nevertheless, is the greatest of
the sacraments and they are ordained to it as to their end or purpose, which is the
incorporation and unity of the Mystical Body with the Head. The explanation we
have given is adequate only in the sense that it is best suited to our purpose; this is
to show as clearly and briefly as possible lest the overall perspective be lost, the
function of the virgin apostle in disposing souls for grace, in, with, and through Mary.

Christ's eucharistic presence and to the real union with Him at the altar. At Communion Our Lord is present in our hearts—Body, Blood, Soul and Divinity; He gives us an increase of sanctifying grace, forgives us our sin and repairs its ravages, making our souls and even our bodily faculties resplendent with His life. And He has much to say. It would be strange indeed if He who longed to be with us had nothing to tell us when He came; not, of course, in audible or even interior words, but by a gentle, imperceptible reorientation of our minds and hearts that we may begin to see all things wisely and in due proportion through Him, and be less concerned with worldly values. Through this activity of the Incarnate Word in our hearts at Communion we grow in the knowledge of our own vileness and resolve at whatever cost to become more worthy of His friendship.

But how often, alas, we misconstrue the inner meaning of Communion, unmindful that it is the occasional trysting-place of friends. At these moments we feel the embarrassment of awe—'Lord, I am not worthy'—but also a delight in being so splendidly loved. We must learn to be still, to be receptive like Magdalene, and not too preoccupied in giving Him what we may think He wants, or too eagerly recounting our needs which in any case He knows. By giving Him ourselves we make our petitions in the best way possible in our self-effacement. This prayer of the soul in Communion should therefore be sufficient to keep it in worshipful attention to the divine Lover. The rest He will do imperceptibly in the deeps of our unconscious life, pervading and reordering it under the divinely-human influence of His grace.

Communion is not merely a rite, a feature of the Christian rule of life. We should think of it as a reunion which is the one desire of the Heart of Christ. 'With desire have I desired to eat this pasch with you', He announced to His disciples at the Last Supper. He longs for our Communion. At times we may not be well; or, poor creatures that we are, we may not be in the mood—'not feel like it'. But it helps us if we remember that He, Incarnate God, is expecting us. What a loving friend indeed whose Divine Heart will be pleased should we care to attend! But when He has come and gone He will leave us refreshed, uplifted by grace, more radiant of His life from His brief sojourn.

I am the bread of life. . . .
For My flesh is meat indeed:
and My blood is drink indeed.

He that eateth My flesh and drinketh My blood abideth
in Me, and I in him.

As the living Father hath sent Me and I live by the Father:
so he that eateth Me, the same also shall live by Me.[1]

It is this Christ-centred attitude of mind through our oneness
in His grace and our affective union with Him which is increased
at our communions, and which strengthens our resolve that at
whatever cost Christ Our Lord shall be exalted. Our life will then
be lived more and more in Him. His good-pleasure will be our
will. We shall strive in all things to be what He wants us to be,
laying aside all inordinate spiritual ambition, and false incentives
to spiritual progress, in the consuming desire to love Him more
by cleaving to His will, and to dispose others to love Him through
our apostolate. Only through such disinterestedness can we reveal
to the world the Christ-life within us. It is the sinful egocentric
tendencies of the apostle which hide the Christian ideal from the
world. The eyes of the lover should be for the Beloved, and they
should never stray to himself except insofar as his self-examination
is undertaken to please the One he loves.

Particularly is this true of the virgin apostle who has plighted
her troth to the Incarnate Word. The refuge of those who have
renounced marriage and family must be in some form of self-
love, unless Christ, the Incarnate Word, is ever in their thoughts
making their whole life a prayer, and unless Communion is seen
as the renewal of their plighted troth. When their lives are informed with the desire to please Him—and in the case of our
religious sisters to give Him the loving service of a woman through
whom shines forth the Christ-life of Mary—the world will meet in
Jesus of Nazareth One whom it must either accept or reject, but
whom it can no longer ignore.

This union of grace and affection with Christ is then one of the
principal means of disposing souls for the grace of God. It is a
detachment. Here we have no abiding city. The apostle is a pil-
grim. Many things along his way are a delight—alive with a
fresh and eternal meaning; but he must refuse to stifle life's joys
by possession. He belongs to One who fashioned all this loveliness
and in whom it abides resplendent as in its source.

This is especially manifest in the apostle's attitude to human
love. Love is a cosmic drive which man alone of all God's creatures
has little power to control. It captivates, enslaves, frustrates. Too

[1] John 6. 48, 56–8.

much is asked of it. The apostle lives in the midst of this nostalgia of God's children who (could they only realize) are seeking to possess Him in the possession of one another. They are incredulous of the aspirations of the Christian virgin. Only the reality can convince them that our Faith holds the power that can at once control and replenish the founts of human love. For is it not true that our virginal dedication restores all true love to every lover? The Christian virgin is not one who despises love, but one who has rediscovered its secret.

> *There cometh a woman of Samaria, to draw water. Jesus saith to her: Give me to drink.*
> *For His disciples were gone into the city to buy meats.*
> *Then that Samaritan woman saith to Him:*
> *How dost thou, being a Jew, ask of me to drink, who am a Samaritan woman? For the Jews do not communicate with the Samaritans.*
> *Jesus answered and said to her:*
> *If thou didst know the gift of God, and who he is that saith to thee: Give me to drink; thou perhaps wouldst have asked of him, and he would have given thee living water.*
> *The woman saith to Him:*
> *Sir, thou hast nothing wherein to draw, and the well is deep. From whence then hast thou living water? . . .*
> *Jesus answered and said to her:*
> *Whosoever drinketh of this water shall thirst again: but he that shall drink of the water that I will give him shall not thirst for ever. But the water that I will give him shall become in him a fountain of water, springing up into life everlasting.*
> *The woman saith to Him:*
> *Sir, give me this water, that I may not thirst, nor come hither to draw.*[1]

Therein, from the very lips of the divine Lover, is the innermost secret of love. Or in the words of that great woman—Mère Marie de Jésus—who so ardently returned His love:

> *Aimer c'est avoir une si ardente soif de voir aimer ce que l'on aime que rien ne coute pour l'obtenir; aimer c'est chercher partout mille vies, mille cœurs pour les sacrifier et les embrasser, et pour les jeter en trophée sous les pas du Bien-Aimé Vainqueur.*[2]

[1] John 4. 7–15.
[2] *La Sainte Messe et les Ecrits*, p. 142.

Chapter 4

TEACHING FROM THE CROSS

IN the foregoing pages we began by considering Our Lady's intercession—what is sometimes called her 'Suppliant Omnipotence'. All graces come to us through Mary, as it is fitting that one who was the 'consort and helpmeet' of the Redeemer on earth through her congruous merits and satisfaction, should exercise an all-powerful intercession in heaven as His Queen. This privilege is not due to her in strict justice, as Christ alone is Mediator, but by reason of the love uniting her and the Incarnate Word. The cause of all Mary's supernatural endowments and privileges is her love-worthiness in God's sight as His mother.[1]

But in virtue of her consent at the Annunciation Mary became our mother also; and all religious sisters participate in her maternal activity when they dispose souls for the Christ-life of grace through her intercession. This they do in a threefold manner:

First, as Christ-bearers, by themselves surrendering to the influence of the grace of Christ; and by Christ's affective presence in their souls chiefly through the grace of the Holy Eucharist, and prayer, thus becoming radiant of the Christ-life in the active apostolate; for the apostle is one who is *sent* and whose message should be inscribed upon his life if he is to win souls for Christ. That is a summary of the preceding pages. Now let us continue.

Secondly, apostles also dispose souls for grace, by teaching the Word of God.

And thirdly, by reparation, that is, by becoming Christlike in their voluntary and vicarious satisfaction.[2] These last two means are the subject of the present chapter.

But before continuing let us emphasize once again that when we speak of the apostle as one participating in the maternal activity of Mary we must be careful to understand this participation as referring to her motherhood as exercised in and through the Church. Our Lady by virtue of her divine maternity is mother both of the Church herself and of the Incarnate Word who espoused His

1 See Note 21, p. 233. 2 See Note 22, p. 234.

Church. Her maternal activity brings them together. Mary co-operated in a more fundamental way in effecting and obtaining the rebirth of all mankind, whereas the Church is active only in applying the fruits of redemption to individual souls.

The Teaching Apostolate

As apostles we dispose men's minds and hearts for grace by teaching the way of truth, in obedience to Christ's command:

> All power is given to Me in heaven and in earth. Go ye therefore, teach ye all nations: baptizing them in the name of the Father and of the Son and of the Holy Ghost: Teaching them to observe all things whatsoever I have commanded you. And behold I am with you all days, even to the consummation of the world.[1]

The blessing of Our Lord is therefore upon every word we utter in His name, whether it be through the apostolate of some lowly religious sister delegated by the Church to teach little ones, or the priesthood itself to whom especially Our Lord has promised His protection and guidance. Every apostle has His promise: 'Behold I am with you'.

One great difficulty, however, must always confront the Christian apostolate. If the purpose of preaching and teaching the Gospel is to pass on the Christ-life, we have to face the historic fact that when Christ, the Incarnate Truth, appeared among men He was rejected, and both He and His immediate followers were put to death. He revealed His divine message to the world, but in the event He had to win men to truth by sacrifice.

The same condition holds good for His Mystical Body. It is never sufficient to know the truth and to take every opportunity of disseminating it; nor even to bear Christ in our hearts. Still less does conversion to the Christ-life depend on the number we address or our facility as teachers, writers or orators, or on our learning as philosophers or theologians. The apostolate to-day is in fact so weighed down by apparatus of one kind or another that the Christian message, to say the least, is confused. No, the Christian teacher, in the last analysis, is not one well-versed in the pedagogic art or in modern techniques, but one who teaches from the Cross. He must bear not only Christ but Christ-crucified in his heart. 'When I am lifted up, I shall draw all things to Myself', said the Redeemer; and so it must be with His apostle.

[1] Matt. 28. 18–20.

The truth is that Satan is abroad to-day, as perhaps never before in the world's history since the tragedy of Eden. And how helpless we often feel when confronted by his power. This is not shown by any single temptation here or there, but in his ordered campaign to bring forth chaos, devised patiently and with consummate skill over decades and even centuries, and which in our own day seems to be gathering momentum for the final assault. Such a description may seem exaggerated, but it is pale rhetoric indeed compared with the utterances of recent Popes. Our common-sense therefore should drive us to the conclusion that if the forces of evil are engaging in no tactical move, but threatening Armageddon, then our resistance must be gathered round the Cross and our counter-offensive waged under Christ's leadership. This is surely the main reason why the Church is insisting more than at any other time in her history on the need for reparation.

It is against this background that the religious sister enters her classroom and the priest his pulpit. In their despondency they may try to persuade themselves of the urgent need of teaching and preaching better, whereas the real need is to teach and preach differently. By all means let us do our human best; but the difficulty is not in teaching the truth but in making it acceptable. And this implies a movement of the will we call conversion. No man can turn men to God. 'To prepare oneself for grace', says St. Thomas, 'is, as it were, to be turned to God; just as, whoever has his eyes turned away from the light of the sun, prepares himself to receive the sun's light, by turning towards the sun. It is obvious, therefore, that man cannot prepare himself to receive the light of grace except by the gratuitous help of God moving him inwardly.'[1] And the one and only infallible means of influencing the will of man to turn freely to the light of truth is the condign merit and satisfaction of the Incarnate Word made available to us through the prayer and reparation of the Mystical Body.

To help us see the need of this let us bear in mind that the very reasoning faculty of men is vitiated by a bias in the will. Our difficulty is to induce men to see Christ as He really is and not as they want Him to be. The city set on the hill cannot be hid; but men can turn their backs upon it. The bushel may be lifted from the light that all may see, but men can still shut their eyes and refuse to see what the light reveals. The world is full of

[1] *S.T.*, 1–2, 109, 6.

wishful-thinking and wishful-doubting. The effect of modern enlightenment is in a sense not ignorance but error.

> Men are most anxious to find truth, but very reluctant to accept it [writes Gilson]. We do not like to be cornered by rational evidence, and even when truth is there, in its impersonal and commanding objectivity, our greatest difficulty still remains; it is for me to bow to it in spite of the fact that it is not exclusively mine, for you to accept it though it cannot be exclusively yours. In short, finding out truth is not so hard; what is hard is not to run away from truth once we have found it. When it is not a 'Yes but', our 'Yes' is often enough a 'Yes, and . . .'; it applies much less to what we have just been told than to what we are about to say. The greatest philosophers are those who do not flinch in the presence of truth, but welcome it with the simple words; 'Yes. Amen.'[1]

Our most urgent modern need is humility. This applies particularly to men's attitude towards religion. Too many of us mean well and can influence others by what we are pleased to call our sincerity. But surely everything depends on what we are sincere about. Many sincere men are in padded cells. The trouble is that too few of us have good will; for this implies the firm intention of accepting and living by objective and reasonable standards; not merely living up to or being true to one's convictions, but having the courage to examine our own credentials, the source and foundation of the things we live by, even should this mean a change of mind and heart, the 'metanoya' of the Baptist. Christ alone can bring about this surrender of the human will by His grace. But to do this He needs our help; and we return once again to the need for reparation. Let us now examine it more carefully to see in more practical detail how it affects the apostolate of the religious sister.

[1] *The Unity of Philosophical Experience*, p. 60.

Chapter 5

REPARATION

I

AS we have already seen, nothing could be more explicitly stated in the Gospel than the need for participating in our own redemption. We must bear Christ crucified in our hearts, making satisfaction to the Father as in one fellowship of suffering with Him, the Incarnate Word; not viewing His sufferings from afar, feeling sorry; but being grateful that He has asked us to carry our cross for His sake. 'If any man will follow Me, let him deny himself, and take up his cross and follow Me.' And in the words of St. Paul to the Philippians, 'for unto you is given for Christ, not only to believe in Him, but also to suffer for Him.' The Apostle also reminds us that this fellowship of suffering with Christ is the condition whereby we in the apostolate of the Mystical Body help others to dispose themselves for the grace of Christ: 'I now rejoice in my suffering for you', he wrote to the Colossians,[1] 'and fill up those things that are wanting of the sufferings of Christ, in my flesh, for His body, which is the Church'. And as he lay a prisoner in chains, he wrote to Timothy:[2] 'I labour even unto bonds, as an evildoer. But the word of God is not bound. Therefore I endure all things for the sake of the elect, that they also may obtain the salvation which is in Christ Jesus.' From St. Paul onwards the whole Christian tradition bears witness that the Christian is in this sense the consort and helpmeet of Christ. For instance, St. Cyprian dared to affirm in the third century that 'the sacrifice of Our Lord is not complete as far as our sanctification is concerned unless our offerings and sacrifices correspond to His passion;'[3] and in the sixth century St. Benedict prays in the Prologue of his Rule that 'we may by patience share in the sufferings of Christ, that we may deserve to be partakers of His Kingdom'.

The call to Christian sacrifice is not however to inflict an unnatural burden on the spirit of man, as some outside the Church

[1] 1. 24. [2] 2 Tim. 2. 9. [3] *Ep.* 63, n. 381.

who see only the Cross stripped of the divine Victim, seem to
think; on the contrary it is a divine ennobling of man's natural
sympathy. Our Lord summons forth from the depths of our
nature qualities of mind and heart and elevates them to a redemptive purpose in the supernatural order. For if, as we have already
seen, when speaking of affective union, the lover dwells in the
beloved insofar as he esteems whatever is good or evil to his
friend as good or evil to him, so that it seems as though he feels
the good and suffers the evil in the person of his friend, it is only
to be expected even in the natural order of things that the lover
should long to go to the assistance of his beloved. This truth is
verified almost daily in the world around us; in the love of a
wife for her husband, for instance, or of a mother for her child.
What then are we to say of such a welling-forth of human sympathy when, in Jesus Christ, God Himself becomes our Beloved
and we stand by the crucified Redeemer on Calvary; when the
Beloved is suffering the tortures of world-expiation for our sins,
broken in body and agonized in mind and soul, calling for our
help? Even ordinary human decency should compel us to give
Him the help He asks; but when our natural vision is illumined
by Faith and our natural sympathy elevated by His love, what
then should hold us back? Nothing is more characteristic of the
great lovers of Christ than an insatiable desire to ease His sufferings, by their own voluntary satisfaction and expiation.

He appeared to me after Holy Communion under the figure
of an ECCE HOMO laden with His Cross, covered with wounds
and gashes [writes St. Margaret Mary Alacoque in her Auto-
biography], His Adorable Blood flowing on all sides. He said
in a sorrowful voice full of anguish: 'Is there no one to take
pity on Me, especially at the present time?' Prostrating myself
with tears and groans, at His Sacred Feet, I offered myself to
Him, and taking on my shoulders that heavy cross, all studded
with nails, I was overwhelmed with its weight. I then understood better the grievousness and malice of sin, for which I felt
such a horror, that I would have preferred a thousand times to
cast myself into hell than to commit a single one wilfully.
'O accursed sin', I exclaimed, 'how detestable thou art, since
thou dost inflict such injury on my Sovereign Good!' He then
gave me to understand that it was not enough to carry the cross,
but that I must fasten myself to it, with Him, in order to keep
Him faithful company by sharing in the sufferings, contempt,
opprobrium and other indignities of which He was the victim.

I forthwith abandoned myself to be fastened to the cross according to His good pleasure.

More lyrical, buoyant and joyful are the words of St. Thérèse of Lisieux, when she cries out:

O Jesus, my Love, my vocation is found at last—*my vocation is love!* . . . Thus shall I be all things and my dream will be fulfilled. . . . But how shall I show my love, since love proves itself by deeds? I, the little one, will strew flowers, perfuming the divine Throne with their fragrance, I will sing Love's means of proving my love, and these flowers will be each word and look, each little daily sacrifice. I wish to make profit out of the smallest actions and do them all for love. For love's sake I wish to suffer and to rejoice; so shall I strew my flowers. Not one that I see, but, singing all the while, I will scatter its petals before Thee. . . . But of what avail to Thee are my flowers and my songs, dear Jesus? . . . Of what avail? I know well that this fragrant shower, these petals of little price, these songs of love from a poor little heart like mine, will nevertheless be pleasing to Thee. They are but trifles, it is true, yet Thou wilt smile on them. The Church Triumphant, stooping down to her child, will gather up these scattered rose-leaves, and placing them in Thy divine hands that they may acquire an infinite value, will shower them on the Church Suffering to extinguish the flames, and on the Church Militant to make her triumph.[1]

II

This doctrine has in more recent years been re-stated with increasing emphasis in several encyclical letters, from two of which we quote the following:

Pope Pius XII writes:

What St. Paul says of the human organism is true also of this Mystical Body: 'The head cannot say . . . to the feet: you are not necessary to me' (1 Cor. 12. 21). That Christians stand in absolute need of the divine Redeemer's help is clear enough, since He Himself has said 'Without Me you can do nothing' (John 15. 5), and the Apostle tells us that all increase of this Mystical Body for the building up of itself is from Christ the Head (Eph. 4. 16: Col. 2. 19). And yet it is also certain, surprising though it may seem, that Christ needs His members . . . In His capacity of direct and invisible ruler of the Church

---

[1] *Autobiography.*

our Saviour wants to be helped by the members of His Mystical Body in carrying out the work of Redemption. This is not due to any need or insufficiency in Him, but rather because He has ordained it for the greater honour of His immaculate Bride.

Dying on the Cross, He bestowed upon His Church the boundless treasure of the Redemption without any co-operation on her part; but in the distribution of that treasure He not only shares this work of sanctification with His spotless Bride, but wills it to arise in a certain manner out of her labour. This is truly a tremendous mystery upon which we can never meditate enough: that the salvation of many souls depends upon the prayers and voluntary mortifications offered for that intention by the members of the Mystical Body of Jesus Christ, and upon the co-operation which pastors and the faithful, and specially parents, must afford to our divine Saviour.[1]

Pope Pius XI writes:

The more perfectly our oblation and our sacrifice corresponds to the sacrifice of Christ—in other words, the more we sacrifice our self-love and our passions, and crucify our flesh with that mystical crucifixion of which the Apostle speaks—the more abundant will be the fruits of propitiation and expiation that we shall receive for ourselves and for others. For a wonderful bond unites all the faithful with Christ—a bond similar to that existing between the head and the other members of the body. Likewise that mysterious Communion of Saints, which our Catholic Faith professes, not only unites individuals and nations together, but joins them to the 'Head, even Christ from Whom the whole body being compactly and fitly joined together, by what every joint supplieth, according to the operation in the measure of each part, maketh increase of the body, unto the edifying of itself in charity' (Eph. 4. 15–16). This was the prayer that Jesus Christ, the Mediator between God and men, made to His Father on the eve of His death: 'I in them and Thou in Me, that they may be made perfect in one' (John 17. 23). . . . But how can it be truly said that Christ reigns blessed in heaven if He can be consoled by such acts of reparation? We might answer in the words of St. Augustine: 'A loving soul will understand what I say'. Everyone that is truly inflamed with the love of God turns his mind to the past, and sees in meditation, Jesus suffering for mankind; he sees Him in the midst of the most grievous torments, 'for us men and for our salvation', afflicted by sorrow and anguish, weighed down with ignominy,

[1] *Mystici Corporis Christi.*

'bruised for our sins', healing us by His stripes. He will meditate with the greater truth if he considers that the sins and iniquities of men, at whatsover time committed, were the cause for which the Son of God was given up to death, and would, of themselves, even now, cause the death of Christ, and a death accompanied by the same pains and anguish, since every sin in some manner renews the Passion of Our Lord; 'crucifying again to themselves the Son of God, and making Him a mockery' (Heb. 6. 6). If, then, in foreseeing the sins of the future, the soul of Jesus became sorrowful unto death, it cannot be doubted that He already felt some comfort when He foresaw our reparation, when 'there appeared to Him an Angel from heaven' (Luke 22. 43) bearing consolation to His Heart overcome with sorrow and anguish. Hence, even now in a mysterious, but true manner we may, and should, comfort the Sacred Heart, continually wounded by the sins of ungrateful men; for Christ—as we also read in the sacred liturgy—complains by the mouth of the Psalmist that He is abandoned by His friends; 'My Heart hath expected reproach and misery. And I looked for one who would grieve together with Me, but there was none; and for one that would comfort Me, and I found none' (Ps. 68. 21).[1]

Why, we again ask ourselves, is the Church so insistent in our own day on the need for co-operating with Our Lord in His eucharistic Sacrifice? Have we not so little to give and has not He as God Incarnate already merited our justification by His condign satisfaction? This is of course perfectly true. But it is His will that if we are to share in His redemption we ourselves must become like unto Him in all things; love Him as He has loved us; carry our cross as He carried His—be Christlike even unto death. As he merited for others, so must we. Saint Thérèse writes very accurately when she reminds us that our sufferings and expiation are trifling things—like rose-petals fluttering to the ground, the tiniest sign of the most inconspicuous offering in the death of a flower. But as she says, addressing Our Lord: 'They are but trifles, it is true, yet Thou wilt smile on them. The Church Triumphant, stooping down to her child, will gather up these scattered rose-leaves, and placing them in Thy divine hands that they may acquire an infinite value, will shower them on the Church Suffering to extinguish the flames and on the Church Militant to make her triumph.'[2]

In other words, it is Our Lord's gracious will that we as apostles

---

[1] *Miserentissimus Redemptor.*   [2] *Loc. cit.*

should be the architects of our own redemption and that of mankind. We must redeem ourselves and others by our congruous merits and satisfaction in the sense that these are the key to the flood-gates of His redeeming grace. A key is a small thing, but in the hands of our heavenly mother, as she gathers the merits and satisfaction of her children into her own maternal intercession, it unleashes a power as compelling as God's omnipotence.

We begin to see then how our participation as co-redeemers with Christ in the Holy Sacrifice of the Mass is the key to all our problems in the modern apostolate. Only God's power can move the human will without violating its freedom. If men will not turn their faces to the light, neither learning, nor persuasiveness, nor any human influence whatever can make them if it does not acquire the power of the redeeming Christ in the Holy Sacrifice of the Mass, through the self-offering of the apostle.

When we ask ourselves therefore why the Church in our times should be so insistent on the need for personal satisfaction and expiation in the Mystical Body, the immediate answer is obvious enough: on account of the perilous state of the modern world. But there is also another reason which is far less obvious. A Godless world and the heresies of the past few centuries have infected the mental attitude of the faithful themselves towards the Christian life and spiritual perfection; and the insistence of the Church on the essential co-redeeming activity of the Mystical Body will help more than anything else to jolt them out of the rut of all self-conscious pieties.

There is a world of difference, as we have already pointed out in the earlier chapters of this book, between the mental attitude which looks upon religion as a means of self-improvement and that which finds in it a willingness as Christ's 'consorts and help-meets' to forget ourselves and our own troubles. When for love of Christ we offer Him a home in our hearts and invite Him to re-live His passion in the personal circumstances of our own lives, we have done a great deal to remove from our midst that kind of self-regarding religion which has been the curse of the past few generations.

No one in the world's history has ever been as uncompromising as Christ. For Him it is all or nothing. 'He who is not with Me is against Me, he who gathereth not with Me scattereth.' The modern humanist too easily forgets the age-long antagonisms between Christ and the prince of this world, between the wisdom of this world and the folly of the Cross. 'The weakness of God is stronger than men.' As Christians we must live for the Kingdom, for what is beyond. Let there be no doubt about that. Christ did not come to provide us with a world-saving sociology or to solve the riddles of modern philosophic and scientific thought or to preserve human dignity and sanity, not even primarily to enable us to 'become saints' in the sense often given to that term. Christianity is a surrender to a life in Christ, the purging of sin from our midst by a sacrifice which sweeps through time and eternity.

The trouble is that many of us no longer co-equate sacrifice and joy because the voluntary nature of true satisfaction has been lost. We are afraid of keeping the mind of the world centred on the Cross as though it has been taken down once and for all on Calvary. It has become the symbol of human misery because joy has fled from Christian hearts. The reason for this is not far to seek. We have grown into the habit of dramatizing our personal crosses, giving the impression there can be no laughter in this vale of tears and that the function of the Saviour is to ease our load instead of easing our mind by giving it a redemptive purpose. It is this kind of topsy-turvydom which scandalizes the modern world so prolific of human, social and spiritual tragedy. The answer is not to be found in a humanism which tries to explain the Cross away, but in a Christianity that, so to say, puts both arms round it, letting Our Lord work out our salvation for us, suffering and making satisfaction in, with and through us, to fulfil what is wanting of His suffering through the members of His Mystical Body. The symbol of such an attitude to the Christian life, is not tears but, in the words of St. Thérèse of Lisieux, a smile, a song and the offering of a flower. What He asks of us is a loving surrender that by making voluntary satisfaction we may join in this redemptive fellowship and undergo whatever He wills gladly for His sake.

III

Our co-offering with Christ is made in the Holy Sacrifice of the Mass,[1] and as religious apostles during the community Mass. There the sacrifice of self incorporated with that of the community is directed to the apostolate of the community in union with the offering of the Mystical Body. But it would be a mistake to suppose that this offering should be in any way a listing of our

[1] See Note 23, p. 235.

trials, pains and sorrows. Nothing withdraws our participation more effectively than that. The whole meaning of the Mass is to be found in an attitude of loving surrender to Our Lord which invites Him to live His satisfaction in our own lives; the greater our self-effacement the more fruitfully will He work through us in the apostolate. Our sole duty is to cling to His adorable will in faith and loving trust. We are safe only in self-forgetfulness.

When Our Lady stood by the Cross of Jesus, who can tell what agony racked her immaculate heart? What other creature has ever been so closely associated with the mysteries of Christ's passion? Her children can only stand in the plains and scan the clouds which conceal from us the inner secrets of this ineffable union of hearts. But of one thing we can be quite certain, that is the self-effacement and utter transparency of Mary. He that was mighty did great things in her on Calvary, because nothing of herself remained. Christ regarded the lowliness of His mother. Her heart was His; the heart of the lover rested in her Beloved, transfixed by His agony; and He wrought His own mystery in her to the limits of her creaturely capacity.

Those are the dispositions our heavenly mother asks us to share if we are to win grace for ourselves and for others. Should we ever be tempted to look upon ourselves as 'victims' let us remember this would have been the last thing Mary called herself on Calvary. Even though some trial in our life may be so grievous that we can with difficulty forget it, it is the effort to forget by *undergoing* whatsoever He wills that makes this cross acceptable to Our Lord. On the other hand if we dwell on it habitually it may easily grow into a phantasy-crucifixion or 'martyrdom' in which we become both the lover and beloved, the consoler and consoled. 'My yoke is sweet and My burden light', promised Our Lord. If either becomes otherwise, we ourselves make it so.

One day as I was in tears [says one of the novices of St. Thérèse] Sister Thérèse told me to avoid the habit of allowing others to see the trifles that worried me, adding that nothing made community life more trying than unevenness of temper. 'You are indeed right,' I answered, 'such was my own thought. Henceforth my tears will be for God alone. I shall confide my worries to One who will understand and console me.'

'Tears for God', she promptly replied, 'that must not be. Far less to Him than to creatures ought you to show a mournful face. Our divine Master has only our monasteries where He

may obtain some solace for His Heart. He comes to us in search
of rest—to forget the unceasing complaints of His friends in the
world who, instead of appreciating the value of the Cross,
receive it far more often with moans and tears. Would you then
be as the mediocre souls? Frankly this is not disinterested
love. . . . It is for us to console Our Lord, and not for Him to
console us. His heart is so tender that if you cry He will dry your
tears; but thereafter He will go away sad, since you did not
suffer Him to repose tranquilly within you. Our Lord loves the
glad heart, the children that greet Him with a smile. When will
you learn to hide your trouble from Him or to tell Him gaily
that you are glad to suffer for Him?'[1]

And again another great woman writing for women:

Empty yourself of self and of every care, apprehension,
weariness and fear of the duration of that state in which every
thing makes you fearful and causes you suffering. Your remedy
will be that of simply looking upon God and answering nothing.
I tell you this once more and in God's name. You look at yourself too much; trouble yourself no more about your trouble,
do not speak to God about it, nor to yourself; never look to
see what it is, to tell it or explain it to anybody, and never
make self-examination on it. Hide your trouble from yourself
and look at God as if you did not feel it. If you can speak to
Him let it be of Himself and not of your trouble.[2]

In this way only and in no other, can the religious sister hope
to release Christ's redeeming grace upon the world, in union
with His Mystical Body. She must 'stand' with her heavenly
mother; stand and be self-forgetful, her heart radiant with joy.
She will then be Christlike not only in His grace and in her affective union with Him, which is the fruit of grace accepted and lived
—the return of love for love—but she will also be one with Him in
sacrifice.

---

[1] *Soeur Thérèse of Lisieux*, 1917 ed., p. 236.
[2] *Works of St. Jane Frances de Chantal*, Vol. 3, p. 283.

Chapter 6

THE SACRIFICE OF MOTHERHOOD

IT was God's will that Mary should share in the whole mystery of redemption wrought by the death of her Son. Three things made His sacrifice perfect: first, His humanity was broken and crushed on the Cross—He was the victim of sin. Secondly, He offered this sacrifice voluntarily. And thirdly, He made a condign satisfaction for sin, bringing forth by His death a new race. In like manner Mary His mother through her congruous merits as the co-principal—'the help, like unto Himself'—of the Second Adam, also suffered, surrendered and brought forth. She was predestined to participate to the full extent of her capacity in His Christ-life and so on Calvary she was nearest to His Cross—like unto Him even to the death on the Cross.

As Bossuet remarks, other martyrs have their executioners and are done to death by every conceivable instrument of torture; but for the Queen of Martyrs 'one Cross suffices for her and her Beloved'. It is perhaps true to say that, humanly speaking, only a woman, or at least a mother, can appreciate the physical torture of Mary on Calvary as she looked upon the lacerated Body of her Son. No woman has ever loved as she loved Jesus, nor has any mother ever been so loved by her Son. But this natural love was as nothing compared with the bond uniting them in the supernatural order of grace, and it was this divine love which brought forth in Mary's body as woman and mother such physical pain that can only be described in terms of the Gospel narrative of the physical torture of her Son.

Our Lady asks the religious sister to share this offering of pain, and even to share it as a woman who is also the spouse of Christ. Religious sisters are called upon to suffer the greater and more searching physical pain, and for this reason are more generously equipped as women with a natural capacity to bear it. Can we question for a moment that this suffering is sent by God to be transmuted by the sister's love of Christ into a woman's redemptive offering for souls with the pain of Mary?

But if pain comes to us through some evil or hurt afflicting our bodily senses, particularly the sense of touch, sorrow, on the other hand, has its source in evil perceived by our interior faculties, that is, our reason, memory, imagination; as, for example, grief, distress of mind, remorse, temptation, fear of impending evil and so on. Our minds can also range over the past, re-opening old wounds, recalling injuries done to us or to those we love—such as ingratitude, betrayal, and injustice. All this helps us to understand the suffering of Our Lord, and especially to see why His bodily pain was insignificant compared with the dreadful agony afflicting His interior soul.

Our Lord voluntarily abandoned Himself to an infinite sorrow for all our crimes [writes Bossuet]. He was aware of each of them in particular and was distressed beyond measure as if He had committed them, because He was held guilty of them in the sight of God. Yes, our iniquities were heaped upon Him from all sides and He could well say with David: 'The sorrows of death surrounded me: and the torrents of iniquity troubled me'.[1] This was the cause of His distress when He said 'Now is My soul troubled'.[2] Hence the mysterious agony when from the depth of grief He uttered the words: 'My soul is sorrowful even unto death'. For the crushing burden of this sorrow would have killed Him had He not preserved His Soul to confront still greater evils and so to drink this chalice to the dregs.[3]

Now if sorrow is proportionate to our love of the person offended and to our knowledge of the offence committed, how great must have been the grief and compassion of Mary? Who shall measure the depth of her love? 'Behold, thou art fair, O my love, behold thou art fair', cries the Bridegroom in the Canticle of Canticles. 'How beautiful art thou . . . Thou art all fair, O my love, and there is not a spot in thee.' At her Immaculate Conception Our Lady received the fulness of grace, far exceeding that of the whole heavenly court. This initial grace grew unceasingly throughout her life by reason of her perfect conformity to God's adorable will. No sin, however small, had ever tarnished the splendour of her virgin soul, so that each meritorious act increased the intensity of her love, which brought forth a greater capacity to merit. This reciprocal interaction within her soul swept her into the inner life of God by a prodigious flight of the spirit unparalleled in the history of grace. No one has ever loved God as did Mary the mother of Jesus.

[1] Psalm 17. 5.   [2] John 12. 27.   [3] *Troisième pour le Vendredi-Saint.*

But the mother of the Redeemer could grieve only in proportion to the knowledge of the evil afflicting her divine Son.

Modern theologians would conclude [writes Father Scheeben] that, like Christ, Mary had on earth, as she now has in heaven, an intimate knowledge of all those to whom that activity (that is, her redemptive co-operation) is extended. This is a profound and beautiful thought, which in this form may perhaps appear equally as daring as it is novel. But it is not only probable but certain, if the idea to be conveyed is that beneath the Cross on Calvary Mary had not an indefinite and vague idea but, by supernatural enlightenment, a profound and vivid conception of every human soul involved in the great mystery of redemption. Something similar is also found in the life of many of the saints who, in a special manner, were called to co-operate by their prayers and sufferings in the salvation of their fellow-men.[1]

Let us remember then that Mary was the Second Eve, the mother of the new race in Christ. On Calvary she was our representative and our mystical virgin mother. She was sinless, but the sins of her children were known to her, their infidelities, betrayals, their lack of response to the self-immolation of the divine Lover which Mary saw enacted before her eyes.

So, too, the religious sister suffers through her love of the divine Spouse, and in the knowledge of her own sins and the sins of those within her apostolate. She grieves for the sins of the world, its infidelity, its scorn of Christ, the Redeemer. This was known to Mary as she stood by the Cross of Jesus; and in the measure the religious sister shares her love and knowledge she also shares her grief. 'Oh most holy Mother of God', writes St. John Eudes, 'remember that the pains which thou didst not suffer in the virgin birth of thy only Son, thou now dost suffer doubly at the foot of the Cross, in the spiritual birth whereby all sinners become thy children. I have cost thee so much, receive me as thy son.'[2]

In this subordinate sense Our Lady 'became sin' for us, and we, as apostles, in our turn 'become sin' for others. In other words, as Mary in virtue of her spiritual motherhood undertook a congruous and vicarious satisfaction on Calvary for the sins of her spiritual children, so we also are invited as apostles to share in her merits and satisfaction. Each member of the Mystical Body, in one sense, merits vicariously for every other member as we are all

[1] *Mariology*, Vol. 2, Chap. 1.   [2] *The Sacred Heart of Jesus*, p. 71.

organically One Body; but it is only fitting, as Our Lord has appointed each of us to a definite apostolate, that our ascetic life, the fervour of our community, or the suffering and sorrow which afflicts it, should be accepted by Him as vicarious merit and satisfaction both for the community and its apostolate. That is why the tradition persists amongst us that a suffering member of our community brings God's blessing upon its life and work.

But apart from this kind of organic satisfaction there is nothing to prevent the apostle (or anyone else) from making reparation for any supernatural purpose whatsoever, even though its application in that case would be at the disposal of Christ and in a sense hidden from us. But there is one way of making quite sure that such satisfaction, apart from the normal asceticism of the religious apostolate, is directed to the purpose we intend; that is by leaving the matter in the hands of Our Lord. We can then be confident that whatever He sends He will give us the grace to bear without injury to our spiritual life, and also that He would not send it unless in some way He were going to grant our request. But in any case, if we feel the need of making satisfaction for our own sins over and above what the rule prescribes, there is no reason why we should not undertake additional penances, provided we seek the advice of a discreet and experienced confessor or superior.

But one thing is quite certain, generally speaking. As Our Lady was crucified by reason of her redemptive function as God's mother, so will the religious sister be asked to make reparation as a woman chiefly through her sense of motherhood. One reason amongst others may be given for this. Our Lady is not a mother 'so-called'; she has a real, organic, living and substantial relationship to us as our spiritual mother.[1] For this reason her virgin-motherhood was on trial as she stood by the Cross on Calvary. Mary had all the human and instinctive endowments of every normal woman and mother. Before her eyes Jesus her Son was suffering. He was an only Son whom in the natural order she had brought up to her image. No other mother has ever been able to say with such depth of feeling—*this is my Son*.

But a woman's love is naturally ordained to the care of the child, and for this reason it is highly focused, and profound. The woman of her nature is drawn more to persons than to things; above all, to human helplessness and need. And on Calvary, Jesus, Mary's Son, was in dire and tragic need. Yet she stood—*stabat Mater*—

1 See Note 24, p. 235.

rooted, and unavailing by reason of her dignity and function as mother of the Incarnate Word.

This indeed was the triumph of her virginity.[1] Mary had to bring forth other children through her bridal relations with God and her heart was torn between the imperative demands of her nature as the mother of One and her supernatural vocation as the spiritual mother of many. Humanly she was stirred by a mother's devotion to a one and only Child, for the Word was made *flesh*; and yet the sacrifice asked of her was to forgo and consecrate this natural devotion that she might beget the children of God, knowing at the same time that the sins of this new family were crucifying her Son, and that as a redeemed mother and mother of the redeemed she was their representative.

'Now there stood by the cross of Jesus His Mother and His Mother's sister, Mary of Cleophas and Mary Magdalene.' The religious sister as a woman has a special relationship to the compassion of Mary. The offering she makes at Holy Mass is that of a woman, and of a woman vowed to virginity in association with the virgin-motherhood of Our Lady. Her love, like Mary's, is single-hearted and profound. By her vow of virginity she has renounced marriage and children of her own; but she remains a woman, drawn to human helplessness and to the *person* of those in need. The sacrifice asked of her by Our Lady is to forgo this yearning to possess by consecrating her mother-love to her many children in Christ's Mystical Body.

But the struggle does not end there. Virginal chastity crowns the womanhood of the religious sister. She is not less but immeasurably more patient, tender, gentle and loving as a woman precisely because her heart belongs to Christ. Those in her apostolate who see and appreciate this flowering of the woman's natural gifts do not always know and respect the supernatural dedication that has called them forth. The danger is obvious enough. The religious sister should always remember that she is the custodian of one more facet of the resplendent and eternal Woman who radiates from the Heart of Christ throughout the ages. The Mary-ideal is on trial in her life and all possessiveness is a betrayal of Mary in the refusal to stand with her by the Cross.

The crucifixion of the heart of the religious sister through her vow of virginity gives a redemptive meaning to the difficulties we have referred to in earlier chapters. If her human love is given to

1 See Note 25, p. 236.

one in an excessive surrender to natural affection she is refusing to be the mother of souls in Mary. The significance of this betrayal must not be seen in a refusal to love all humanly, but in the frustration of a spiritual and virgin motherhood which refuses to be co-redemptive of souls in Christ.

Finally, in the present chapter we have spoken at some length of the Mass and its meaning in relation to Our Lady and the vocation of the religious sister. Much has been left unsaid by way of practical application. When we ponder the nature of the crisis threatening the vocation of our sisters we are gradually driven to the conclusion that too many of them have lost their bearings in relation to the central sacrifice of the Mystical Body. When this happens and our sisters fail to realize that the Mass loses its meaning unless it is both 'His sacrifice and ours', and that it can never be merely a devotion however exalted, the repercussions on the religious life of the woman must be disastrous. And the chief of these is a dreadful perversion of her very nature.

We repeat the warning already given in this book. No one should ever be tempted to underrate the primordial forces latent in the heart of woman. This is one of the great lessons of our time. The woman is the very personification of the outgiving spirit of mankind, and indeed of all created things; and of the force that establishes all cosmic interdependence and thereby preservation. The Spirit of Love brooded over Mary at Nazareth to bring forth a new creation, and mankind was born afresh in Christ through sacrifice. If the heart of woman is not the altar of this sacrifice in, with and through Mary then she loses her meaning in the new dispensation; especially when we remember that by her very nature she is destined to bring forth life and that this new life is born by separation. But when sin perverts her heart the woman becomes the altar of self-love and therefore a source of disintegration and destruction. Holy Mass alone can preserve her and us from such a calamity; for the Mass is the very cause and safeguard of her fruitfulness. To live the Mass is to pass oneself on and back to God; it is the sealing of the creative cycle, disrupted at the Fall, in the mystic glory of Calvary where a mother offered her Son to the Father, and heaven's gates were opened. These and many other thoughts race through the mind within the context of this book; but we must leave the religious sister to work out these relationships for herself. We beg of her not to mistake symptoms for causes in diagnosing any difficulty she may have in the practice of supernatural chastity.

Chapter 7

THE OFFERTORY OF PRAYER

IN the foregoing pages we have spoken briefly of Our Lady's part in the Redemption, and of the manner in which we as apostles share in her redemptive activity as the all-powerful mediatrix before God. All apostles must reflect the image and likeness of Christ if they are to dispose men for grace through the intercession of Mary: first, by living spiritually in the grace of Christ themselves; secondly, through His affective presence in their hearts; and thirdly, by becoming Christlike in their voluntary satisfaction both for their own sins and those of others. The one sure way of winning souls is by participating in the redemptive oblation of the Mystical Body made one with the eternal sacrifice of Christ in the Mass. We have also explained in what sense self-forgetfulness is essential to our personal offering at the altar. This is seen more clearly when we examine the relationship between prayer and the Mass; for true prayer is nothing less than our participation in the offering of the Mystical Body. Our prayer is the Mass.

Such prayer, however, must be a supernatural turning to God in worship. Some of us are attracted to prayer from predominantly human motives. This can be a subtle temptation in which the inner dispositions of the heart are at variance with the spirit of Christian sacrifice. We are not necessarily devout when the early associations of our life leave us with a natural attraction for 'devotions' and ceremonial. We may 'love' the rosary or the stations or even the sacred liturgy; but only the supernatural content of such prayers is incorporated in the Mass.

Prayer is surrender. It is not only an exercise but the submission of all our personal affairs and relationships to the divine scrutiny. It must be obvious, therefore, that prayer can never become the means of self-indulgence. On the contrary, it must of its very nature be most difficult and uncongenial. The very act of turning to God is a challenge to our pride. In turning to Him we are self-immolated. It is what we turn *away from* in *turning-to* that makes us reluctant to pray, because what we turn away from is our self-esteem and self-sufficiency. We do not like to be found out, whereas prayer is merciless in discovering us to ourselves, even to the most secret recesses of the unconscious mind. Pride seeks the hidden places where it poisons our spiritual life like a foreign body in the human organism. Only Christ can make us humble by scouring the unknown and unknowable depths of our souls and uplifting us by His grace. But He will not come uninvited; we have to let Him in. 'Behold I stand at the door and knock.' He will not even lift the latch unless we invite Him in to be our host. That is what we mean by surrender in prayer. It is not easy to say 'Come, Lord Jesus' and mean it. They are the key words of life and we know it. But human pride is as subtle as the devil in Eden. We may think we want Christ and Him alone; and yet when we kneel down to pray during the half-hour or so before Holy Mass to garner our offertory for the sacrifice, we may have all kinds of subterfuges at our finger-tips, bolt-holes down which we can escape to safeguard our immoderate self-esteem. We may adopt a comfortable attitude for prayer and then complain how difficult it is to keep awake. Or we may pick up a book to avoid coming to conclusions with God. It is a holy book, and, after all, did not St. Teresa use one? But when it is explained that this was 'to start her off' as the motorist pulls the self-starter, one is asked to remember she was a saint. 'And, in any case, Father, isn't it better to read if the alternative is sleep? Better, surely, to give God holy reading than nothing at all.' If the example of a holy friar is then quoted who pinched himself on 'off-days' that he might offer his sleep to God, the answer will be 'You can hardly expect a woman to do that.' Perhaps the most popular bolt-hole, however, is the common belief that reading, punctuated with occasional acts, is the best way of preventing distractions in time of mental prayer. But is this being quite fair to these involuntary distractions? Are not distractions God's way of probing the inner recesses of the heart, of summoning our inner self into the arena of choice?

We often imagine we can pray better during the day—loving God in and through our work. But can we be too sure we are not loving our work for its own sake? Even if our particular job is uncongenial, it can so easily inspire self-pity. We may even rejoice in the martyrdom of such work as a kind of subtle and unconscious revenge on those who have commanded us to do it. Such a state of mind is quite compatible with the conviction that we are offering everything up in a spirit of true resignation. There are in fact

a thousand avenues to self during the day, however near God
may seem to be. But there is no avenue to self that remains
undiscovered during prayer.

How then can true prayer (and by this we mean any method
which leads us to simple attention to God) be our offertory for
the Mass? The answer is simply this: such prayer of its very nature
is the arena of choice. We do not take easily to worship, even in
the religious life. Two forces within us rend our souls for mastery—
the spirit of revolt and that of surrender. We know quite well
where our peace and integrity lie and yet we will not surrender.
There is a sense in which it is true to say that he who refuses to
surrender everything surrenders nothing, because such a resolve
is conditional and the inner conflict not only remains, but is
aggravated, like the soldier shooting it out at the last ditch. He
may know in his heart of hearts he is shooting it out against his
best friend, but he will not pause to think.

True prayer is just that 'pausing to think'. It is going aside from
the hubbub of life and the press of affairs and standing face to face
with the Friend. And how unpleasant that can be! He knows us
through and through, better than we know ourselves. He knows,
for instance, whether or how much, our 'willing' is merely
wanting.

In true prayer our loyalty is tested. We notice how all manner
of interests, anxieties, attachments and ambitions come flooding
into our consciousness, how seemingly trivial things (like the apple
in Eden) [1] assume a strange significance and tear at our minds
for admittance. Everything to which we have clung selfishly in
the past, to which we cling now, rises up in answer to this challenge
of the voluntary surrender of worship. The relentless will to persevere in this prayer stirs up so much opposition, waywardness and
even positive filth in the form of involuntary distractions from the
hidden depths of our unconscious mind that we cannot recognize
the self that prayer unmasks; and when we reflect afterwards on
what has happened during our prayer (though this should be
done rarely), we feel we are meeting a stranger. Far easier to
disown this secret self with its evil propensities and to blame the
devil. It can indeed be a shattering experience to discover one's
vileness during prayer, but how wonderfully merciful of the good
God to love us in spite of it! The saints tell us to look beyond these
slag-heaps of the soul (St. Paul calls it—'offal') and seek God

[1] See Note 26, p. 236.

whose love is purging our hearts unbeknown. But it is no use looking for these things ourselves as we tend to do once we become aware of their presence. The most searching self-scrutiny will never reveal them. So let us leave this process of self-purification to God; and then our secret self will come streaming to our consciousness in the form of involuntary distractions to be rejected one by one for Him.

It is very important, then, not to underrate our distractions, which—to repeat—are manifestations of our self-interest and rebellion. Every time we refuse to yield to these allurements and fears in time of prayer—fatigue, ill-health, affections, dislikes, anxieties, inquisitiveness, anticipations, ambitions, and all kinds of rooted unconscious desires—turning easily and gently back to God, we are positively choosing God. To turn to Him is to turn away from some declaration of our self-interest, self-love and rebellion. This kind of prayer of simple attention to God can be an agony at all stages of the spiritual life in the sense that we may seem to be striving and yet never arriving. But to worship God lovingly is to be *en route* for God; we would not in fact be seeking Him if we had not already found Him.

In this prayer is found self-oblation in our resolve to go forward, and self-immolation in what we leave to continue our journey. What we leave aside by our voluntary movement during prayer is from this very act the offering of these things in the Mass.

> Prayer [wrote Dom John Chapman], in the sense of union with God, is the most crucifying thing there is. One must do it for God's sake; but one will not get any satisfaction out of it, in the sense of feeling, 'I am good at prayer', 'I have an infallible method'. That would be disastrous, since what one wants to learn is precisely one's weakness, powerlessness, unworthiness. Nor ought one to expect 'a sense of the reality of the supernatural' . . . And one should wish no prayer, except precisely the prayer God gives us—probably very distracted and unsatisfactory in every way!—On the other hand, the only way to pray is to pray: and the only way to pray well is to pray much.[1]

It is in such prayer that we gather our offering for the Holy Sacrifice, not by counting our wounds and miseries, but by leaving self and cleaving positively to God. But the point to be remembered is this: everything that may be the beginning of a disloyalty

[1] *Spiritual Letters*, No. 12.

to Our Lord as our Spouse is declared in true prayer immediately it begins to challenge our privileged position as His virgin-spouse. We should bear no one in our hearts, but only Christ, and prayer declares our loyalty. We may love many people; but whether we love them as Christ wills or not is decided, not by argument, but by our prayer. There He must reign alone, and we must prefer Him to do so by keeping faithful to our prayer.

In this way then religious sisters share the apostolate of Mary; they win souls on their knees in union with the Sacrifice of the Mass. It is sometimes asked whether souls can be converted by prayer. If by this is meant the multiplication of prayers the answer is at least doubtful; but if we mean the *sacrifice* of prayer in the sense we have explained, then it is indeed a very precious truth because such prayer is the Mass.

How often we feel overwhelmed by the spiritual needs of our time! If only we could *do* more! But we cannot in fact do more unless we realize that souls are to be won by God's grace and not by our good works, however far-reaching these may be. We must have the courage to kneel as Mary 'stood', and submit to the divine method of saving the world. Our hearts might be torn by the needs of those under our care—children in school without any depth of faith and with a background which offers little hope. We would like to go out among them and do what we could to remove these temptations and scandals. Must these little ones be left to grow up like their parents? But there are so many of them. The task is beyond us even should we multiply our numbers a hundredfold. The maternal heart of the sister will often drive her to do too much in the wrong way; bring a personal influence to bear when she should be kneeling to win souls through God and the sacrifice of the Incarnate Word.

All our sisters, especially contemplatives, may feel that the flood of evil around them can only be stemmed by some extra-ordinary divine intervention. That intervention is in fact growing in momentum; but it is coming through the Sacrifice of the Mystical Body and our share in it. If our contemplative sisters are to win souls, they must bear the Sacrifice of Christ in their own hearts, for the heart of the woman is the altar of redemption. Too often these days, our sisters forget this power within their grasp. Their maternal hearts are tormented because like every true woman they want to be busy with people, especially those in need. But what more can they do when they have done their best except leave the rest to God, and learn to kneel as Mary stood that they may dispose the souls of men for grace through the Mass and the offertory of prayer? Is not this power to be still with the Mother of Sorrows in utter tranquillity of soul the one sure sign that their lives will bear fruit in, with, and through her, in sacrifice, penance, and expiation?

> In the great calamities and in the great tribulations of Christianity [wrote Pope Pius XI], when the need of God was most pressing, the faithful either of their own accord or more often following the lead and exhortation of their holy pastors, have taken up the two most mighty weapons of the spiritual life—prayer and penance.[1]

[1] *Caritate Christi Compulsi*, May 3rd, 1932.

Appendix 1

ON MENTAL PRAYER

A

**WHAT VARIOUS SPIRITUAL WRITERS SAY OF THE SIMPLE APPROACH TO
GOD**

I

Père de Caussade, S.J., says:

'On the proximate dispositions for recollection two rules are to be
observed.

Q. What is the first rule?

A. To go slowly, gently, word by word, whether vocally or interiorly.

Q. What is the second rule?

A. To interrupt our discourse at times for the presence of God, as
Bossuet says, following Fr. Baltazar: or as others say, to interrupt our discourse for attentive silence, to listen to God after
speaking to Him. . . .

Q. How long should these attentive pauses last?

A. For a longer or shorter time, according to the circumstances;
beginners, who have not yet acquired any skill in holding
themselves in peace and silence before God, should make them
short; but later they gradually become easier and longer,
either through their acquired dispositions, or by the beginning
of some sort of attraction towards recollection; from which we
should conclude on the whole that we should rest in silence and
listening every time, and for so long as we actually feel some
good disposition of the mind or the heart towards God.'
(*On Prayer*, Book 2, Dialogue 5.)

II

'St. Teresa, treating of *vocal* prayer (or rather of vocal prayer medi-
tated), and starting from the principle that God dwells in the just soul
as in a magnificent palace and a little paradise, highly praises what
she calls the prayer of active-recollection. We close our bodily eyes;
and the soul, collecting together all her powers, enters into herself with
God. She ceases not to look upon Him interiorly while the lips are
reciting some pious prayer, and, knowing for certain that He is quite

near, and that she has no need to cry out aloud, she speaks to Him lovingly and noiselessly as to her Father, her Brother, her Spouse, her Lord. Since God is ever within us the saint exhorts her daughters not to leave such an august companion alone; she wishes them to look at Him while speaking to Him; it is the means to excite attention, to inflame devotion, and to prepare the soul for a higher kind of prayer. She declares that she herself never knew what it was to pray with satisfaction until the day that God taught her to act in this way. This is a method which depends on our will, and though we had to spend six months or a whole year in acquiring it neither our time nor our trouble would be lost.' (*The Ways of Mental Prayer*, Lehodey, pp. 9–10. Cf. *The Way of Perfection*, by St. Teresa; read Chapters 19 and 20, very carefully, also 30, 7. Ref. re Pause *ibidem*, 17, 3.)

III

Father Baker says:

'The first excellency of internal affective prayer above all other is, that only by such prayer our union in spirit with God (in which our eternal happiness consists) is perfectly obtained. For therein the will with all the powers and affections of the soul are applied and fixed to the loving, adoring and glorifying the only beautifying Object, whereas in vocal prayer there is continual variety and succession of images of creatures suggested, the which do distract the souls of the imperfect from such an application. And meditation, in which discourse is employed, is, so far, little more than philosophical contemplation of God, delaying this fixing of the heart and affections on God, which are only acceptable to Him.'

(Try to read the Third Treatise of *Holy Wisdom*, Chapters 1, 2, 3. Cf. Internal, Acquired, Affective Prayer—*Holy Wisdom*, pp. 343 seq. Cf. also *Inner Life of Dame Gertrude More*, by Father Baker—*The Prayer of Immediate Acts*, Vol. I, p. 62; ed. by Weld-Blundell, O.S.B.).

IV

St. Ignatius teaches a manner of praying vocally which:

'consists in saying some prayer very slowly, leaving the space of a full breath between each word. Let us apply this method as follows to the prayer: Soul of Christ, sanctify me.

  '1. Recollect yourself and ask yourself: What is it I am going to do?
  '2. Beg the grace to derive much fruit from this exercise.
  '3. Commence the prayer:
    Soul of Christ . . . sanctify me . . . Body . . . of Christ . . . save me . . . Blood . . . of Christ . . . inebriate me . . . and so on.

'During this time we think on the sense of the word we have just pronounced, or on the dignity of Him to whom we pray, on our own baseness, on our miseries, on our needs.

'This method is suitable for every one, for any time in the day, and may be practised during almost every kind of manual work. It is very useful for such as may have contracted a bad habit of reciting their vocal prayers too quickly; but it is particularly recommended to religious.' (Lehodey, *Ibidem*, pp. 9–10. Cf. *The Exercises of St. Ignatius Loyola*, Rickaby, S.J., Second and Third Methods, pp. 216 seq.— especially the latter which the saint calls: *Prayer of Rhythmical Beats* or *Prayer of Rhythmical Breathing*.

V

St. Jane Frances says:

'I strongly recommend to you, my dear Daughters, prayer of the heart, that is, that which is not made with the understanding, but with the heart. It is made in this way: when we are humbled before God and placed in His presence, let us not force our brain to make considerations but use our affections, arousing them as much as possible; and if we cannot arouse them by interior words, we must use vocal, such as these: I give Thee thanks, O my God, for that Thy loving-kindness allows me to be here, before Thy face, I who am but naught. Or, at another time: O my Lord, grant me the grace to learn to speak to Thee, for I esteem this happiness above every other. Finally, we should set about prayer with much simplicity; but as for those who take Our Lord in the Garden of Olives and lead Him to Calvary, I advise them to pause, because they are covering a great deal of ground in a short time and are going too quickly'. (Conference 33 by St. Jane Frances. Also cf. *Inner Life of Dame Gertrude More*; Fr. Baker, *The Prayer of Sensible Affections*.)

VI

St. John Fisher says:

'It remaineth now that we treat whether prayer of the heart only, or prayer which is made with the heart and lips together be most profitable unto him that prayeth. I do protest here, that it is not my intention to affirm anything in derogation of vocal prayer, such as is either received by custom, or ordained by the constitution of the Church, or inflicted by way of penance, or assumed by vow or any other promise whatsoever. But my opinion is that whosoever is free from these bonds, and in possession of his absolute liberty, and desires to serve God after the best, purest, and most pleasing way unto Him: it is far more profitable for such a one to pray with his heart only than with his tongue and heart together.' (*A Treatise of Prayer*, Pt. 3, Ch. 4.)

B

SOME DIFFICULTIES

(i) *Is Prayer of Simple Attention Waste of Time?*

Père Poulain calls this the classic objection. He replies:

'Let us study a case where the objection appears to have more force: that of the prayer of loving attention to God. . . . Let us suppose that for some appreciable time—a quarter of an hour, for instance—this prayer is made without any difficulty or admixture of anything else, with the exception of a few distractions. We should then be content to love God without adding any other special acts, such as acts of humility, petitions, etc., and also without making any practical applications or receiving any light upon our conduct. This extreme case is probably not realizable, but we will imagine it. I say that, even then, it is not time lost, if, as I have supposed, we are sufficiently well-grounded in spiritual matters.

'In fact, in order to regulate our conduct satisfactorily outside the time of prayer, two things are necessary: to know what we ought to do in some particular case, and to have the will and the strength to carry it out. In the prayer of meditation we pursue both these ends simultaneously; but nothing hinders our separating the two operations; and this is just what occurs in the state we are now examining. We have, in part, relegated the instructions to some other time, and we are satisfied to give free play to the will by penetrating ourselves with the love of God, which must necessarily include general dispositions to devotion and sacrifice. . . .

'Since the above objection is unfounded, how can we explain its being so widespread, and why does it arise so readily to the mind? Here are some reasons.

'(1) It is the result of prejudice. We often imagine that work is identical with noise. But is the artist whose brush travels silently over the canvas less busy than the blacksmith who deafens us with his activity?

'We fancy that we are thinking and accomplishing a great deal when we are conscious of a wealth of words and of material images. But if this activity of the inferior order diminishes, as often happens when our prayer becomes higher, it is then more difficult to take note of our thoughts, and so we wrongly conclude that we have almost ceased to think and have sunk into a state of sloth. A certain void is indeed produced for particular things have diminished; but these are merely the gross auxiliaries of thought, the form that it has borrowed from the senses, and not thought itself. This latter has become more spiritual, but less easy of apprehension. . . .

'(2) Here is a second prejudice: It is supposed that, in order to act in a holy manner, it is absolutely necessary to formulate *very distinct resolutions* in prayer. But many persons do not feel the need of this. All that is necessary is that they should develop *general dispositions* to generosity. They continue for a long time under their influence, and then, at the proper moment, the general impulse of all their faculties carries them promptly and, as it were, instinctively to action. . . .' (*The Graces of Interior Prayer*, Part I, Ch. 2.)

(ii) *A Judgement on 'Easy Prayer'*

'One of the most common and deplorable illusions', writes Lehodey, 'consists in judging of our prayer by the consolation, or dryness we meet with therein; in thinking it good because accompanied by consolation, bad, if chilled by desolation. No, no, such is not the case. The best prayer, were it ever so dry, is that which leaves us more humble, more disposed to renounce ourselves, to practise obedience, to live the life of dependence which our state requires, to bear with our brethren, and never to be a burden to others; in a word, to do in all things the will of God. On the other hand, our prayer, were it an ocean of sweetness, is barren and even baneful when it leaves us more full of ourselves, more attached to our consolations; for our end here below is not enjoyment, but ever to tend to perfection.' (*The Ways of Mental Prayer*, Lehodey, Ch. IV. The entire chapter should be read. Cf. also de Caussade *On Prayer*, Book 2, Dialogue 9; *Imitation*, Book 2, Ch. 12; *The Way of Perfection*, St. Teresa, Ch. 32.)

(iii) *Dryness in Prayer*

'It is of great importance', writes St. Teresa, 'that no one should distress himself on account of aridities; or because his thoughts are restless or distracted; neither should he be afflicted thereat, if he would attain to liberty of spirit, and not be always in trouble. Let him begin by not being afraid of the Cross, and he will see how Our Lord will help him to carry it, how joyfully he will advance, and what profit he will derive from it all.' (*Life of St. Teresa*, Ch. XI; cf. also Ch. XV.)

C

(i) *Simple Prayer in Practice*

The presence of God in the soul is real, as real and substantial as the presence of the Sacred Humanity on the altar. St. John always insists: 'You *have* eternal life', using the present tense, not the future, *shall have*. And Our Lord (Luke 17. 21) says, 'The Kingdom of God is within you'. The only difference between a soul in grace and a soul glorified is that its state in heaven is fixed (i.e. it can never fall into sin) and it beholds the face of God, the splendours of the Beatific Vision. That is why Our Lord said, on that memorable occasion reported in St. John (Chapter 6), 'He who eats of this bread shall live for ever'. He is telling the people around Him that those who already possess God through the instrumentality of His Sacred Humanity cannot die; for them there can be no tragedy of death, not even a 'passing on', but simply the unveiling of the beauty and lovableness of God.

The first step then in personal sanctification is to realize the hidden treasure that we carry in an earthen vessel. 'The saints bear God with them, their souls are in heaven, for God inhabits them,' says St. Augustine.

We are God-bearers: Yet how few people realize it! God is waiting in our souls for some act of recognition which, alas! is so seldom given. Many, even when they pray, turn upwards to the heavens and not inwards to the heart. Only when they have come to the end of life's journey, like the disciples on the road to Emmaus, do they understand that He has been the inseparable companion by the way.

We are God-bearers: Let us try to bring this truth home to ourselves. In the first place, God is not merely present as an infinite being. He is *thinking* of me; and not in the group of creation, but as an individual; and His glance is focused on me eternally, without distraction.

All human consciousness or awareness is successive. We cannot think of two things at once; we pass from one thought to another. The 'thought-stream' is flowing, unceasing and varied through our minds. But to Almighty God everything is *tota simul*. He contemplates each of us individually but not exclusively; He is *my* God. He belongs to me more truly than I belong to myself.

So the first thought that helps me to realize the divine indwelling is God's consciousness of me in the depths of my own soul. He is thinking of me, as I go about my daily task, looking at me, embarrassingly if I have not completely surrendered, but with a caress if I am entirely His.

'You gave us, O eternal Trinity,' cries St. Catherine of Siena, 'not only Your Word through the Redemption and in the Eucharist, but Yourself in Your fullness of love for Your creatures. In very truth, the soul possesses You Who art Supreme Goodness.'

(ii) *Method of Mental Prayer*

1. Begin your mental prayer by putting yourself in the presence of God.

Act of the Presence of God
Eternal and merciful God, I believe that Thou art dwelling within

my heart, looking at me and loving me without distraction. I thank
Thee for this gracious gift of Thyself. Most loving Lord, I belong to
Thee, because I am Thy child, dependent upon Thee for my being
and for every grace. Thou belongest to me because Thou art my
Father and hast given Thyself to me from Thine infinite goodness and
mercy. Grant me grace, O Lord, to adore Thee, to love and thank
Thee during these few minutes of my prayer, so that I may be
strengthened to do Thy holy will in all things for Thy honour and
glory, and for that alone.

Holy Mary, Mother of God, pray for me.

2. Take your crucifix and hold it before you as you kneel in prayer;
or if you prefer, compose some picture in your imagination, one perhaps in keeping with the liturgical season. Generally speaking, a
crucifix is more helpful.

3. Speak to Our Lord, remembering the word: ACTS.
   A—Adoration
   C—Contrition
   T—Thanksgiving
   S—Supplication.

4. *Adoration*

Our Lord is your loving Friend, your King. Make very slowly, and
repeat to your crucifix, the following or similar acts of adoration.

O my dear Jesus, I adore Thy divine greatness from the depths of
my nothingness; Thou art so great and I am so small. Jesus, my
Friend, Son of the Eternal Father, I adore Thee.

Jesus, my Lord, my Redeemer, infinite in majesty, I humbly
prostrate myself at Thy feet. Give me strength to be utterly abandoned
to Thy holy will.

Then, after making these acts of adoration, close your eyes and turn
to God within your soul. Say slowly, and repeat, acts of adoration
with which you are familiar. Remember that these acts must be made
very, very slowly. Pause between each act in utter surrender to God.
You belong to Him; try to rest in Him easily and silently without using
your imagination. If you are distracted, don't worry; come back to
Him again; He is waiting for you. Kneel upright without support.
This will help you more than you think.

You may find the following acts of adoration helpful:

Glory be to the Father—and to the Son—and to the Holy Ghost.
Almighty God, my Creator—my Father—I worship Thee.

Heavenly Father—Thou art so great—and I am so small—Thou art everything and I am nothing.

O God my Father—I am utterly dependent on Thee—I am Thy child and belong to Thee—hallowed be Thy name.

Once again let me remind you to pause between these acts of worship. At first you may be able to do so for only a few moments. But persevere; and gradually you will begin to rest in total abandonment to God for a longer period. Help this silent adoration with an occasional word of worship or of love. If words distract you from His presence, then don't speak. If imagination distracts you from Him, then don't use it. Just stay with God. Forget yourself in Him. Prayer is kneeling down and belonging to God.

5. *Contrition and Love*

Return to the crucifix or the imagined picture if you find this helpful. If these distract you, then remain united to God truly present within your soul and make acts of contrition and love. It may help you, however, to return to the crucifix; if so, then kneel once more at Our Lord's feet and recall the incidents of His Passion and Death. Take in turn, and briefly, the Scourging, the Crowning with Thorns, the Carrying of the Cross, the Crucifixion. As you recall these events make an act of contrition. Or, if you prefer, kiss the sacred wounds in turn, repeating slowly, very slowly, such acts as the following:

O my dear Jesus, I am sorry for my sins. Please forgive me; teach me to love Thee with my whole heart and soul. Give me grace, dear Jesus, never to offend Thee again. Jesus, my Lord, my Redeemer, I love Thee, because Thou art so good.

Jesus, wounded and broken for me, I love Thee.

Then, once again, turn to God within your soul. He is really present, looking at you, loving you, awaiting you. Make slowly such acts as the following, relishing each word:

O my God, I love Thee with my whole heart—and with my whole mind—and with my whole soul—and with my whole strength—because Thou art so good and lovest me with an infinite and everlasting love. O my God, Thou madest me because Thou didst yearn to love me—I belong to Thee—I am Thy child, Thou art my loving Father. I love Thee with my whole heart and soul. My God and my All—I surrender myself completely to Thy loving care—teach me to do Thy holy will in all things. My God, I am sorry for my sins—because by them I have shown my ingratitude to Thee who art my loving Father—give me grace never to sin any more.

6. *Thanksgiving*

Return to your crucifix or imagined picture if this helps; if not, then turn to God in your heart. Thank Him for all that He has done for you; for the gift of faith, for Christ's Passion and Death by which you are redeemed; for the many favours both spiritual and temporal He has bestowed upon you.

7. *Supplication and Petition*

What do you need most in the spiritual life? Praying either to your crucifix or directly to God within you, ask for the necessary grace to do God's will in all things, pray for grace to overcome your one great spiritual weakness; and ask God to increase your love of Him and to help you to pray. If you need some temporal favour, then ask Him to grant you this, but always on condition: If it be Thy holy will.

Remember:

It is not always easy to pray, and sometimes we even feel a distaste for mental prayer. Don't be alarmed at this. It takes courage to plunge into a cold swimming bath, but when the shock is over we enjoy it. The first five minutes of mental prayer are often the most difficult. Have the courage to begin, whatever you feel like. It is seldom those who are emotionally drawn to prayer who pray best.

Don't get discouraged when you find yourself distracted. If you don't give way to these distractions, but return immediately to God, you are preferring God all the time, which is what He most desires. We should not pray because we love prayer, but because we love God.

Don't envy the facility other people seem to have in prayer. Prayer helps us to do God's will. Be satisfied with the prayer He gives you, provided you are trying whole-heartedly to serve Him.

Don't be tempted to think that mental prayer, such as we have described in these pages, leads nowhere, and is waste of time. There may be very little constructive thought in this simple prayer, but it leads to God—and what else matters? Leave the rest to Him.

Too much imagination in prayer can be more harmful than too little. Many find it very helpful to address the A.C.T.S. alternatively to their crucifix and to the indwelling God.

You may use only a small part of the A.C.T.S. during the time allotted for prayer, and may never finish them. Many people spend the whole time in adoration. So go slowly; the principal thing is to pray, and gradually to rest in God during the silences.

The A.C.T.S. are an aid to prayer, chiefly for beginners. Modify them to suit your own way of approach to God; but don't change the general structure, or the order of the acts. Adoration is most important. If you haven't time to ask God for anything, never mind. Give Him what He wants and He will look after you in His own way. He won't be outdone in generosity.

Spiritual reading, done slowly and with prayerful relish, will help your prayer.

Kneel upright for at least part of the time. Give yourself to God. Belong to God. Let your prayer overflow into your day by frequently turning inwardly to God in love and worship.

Appendix 2

DISCUSSIONS IN THE NOVITIATE

(See Part I, Chap. 4, p. 50)

A novice-mistress writes:

'When Discussions were introduced into a fairly large Novitiate (over forty) the Novices were divided into two groups to admit of (*a*) a less formal atmosphere with smaller numbers, (*b*) a difference of subject matter for the First and Second Year Novices. The Mistress chose the topics—events from St. Luke's Gospel, usually to fit in with the Liturgical Year. With the aid of Commentaries and *The Lord we Serve*,[1] she prepared her matter and so was ready to meet her group. The young people had been instructed in the purpose of these discussions—to find out more about Our Lord, by a true seeking into the literal meaning of the Scriptures and then by applying Our Lord's teaching to life in general and to the ideals and practice of the teaching congregation in particular.

'The group meetings followed a normal pattern—the Gospel scene was read, the Mistress usually supplying useful information and background to help fuller comprehension. Then followed a verse-by-verse examination and explanation. This care over the literal meaning is very important, particularly with successful candidates of religious examinations!—many have a general but not too correct understanding of the text. With the literal meaning clear, the application to the Christian and perfect Christian lives could be made—few Novices fully realize that religious life is essentially evangelical!

'This quest for information required a careful ordering and directing. As far as possible the young people themselves were urged to "dig out" the meanings. One helped another. The Mistress helped by asking leading questions, answering others, correcting, enlarging, stimulating further ideas. She learned, in short, that her main work was to inspire thought. How? First, by the creation of a happy, easy family atmosphere. In any normal Novitiate this is simple enough where the Mistress, if she is young, tries to be, under God, the elder sister with the heart of a mother. Unless the young people feel at home, real thinking cannot take place. She must, therefore, let her children see that she, too, wants to learn more, that she appreciates their findings and ideas. She must not fear to admit her own limitation of knowledge. If she sincerely seeks truth, then her Novices will follow her example.

[1] Blackfriars Publications, Blackfriars, Oxford.

'She must lead—draw on! Having prepared her facts, she helps the Novices to arrive at the truth they seek. This she will do by careful questioning, slowly leading to the important point: by suggesting analogies in everyday life: by referring to parallel passages in the Scriptures, Old and New Testaments. In short, knowing most of the answers, she must use every possible means of leading the Novices to arrive at these answers by their own labours. She must learn to listen to their replies, draw the good from them (even from the careless and partially incorrect) and so induce the Novice to think more deeply, choose her words more exactly. She encourages by her interest and desire to learn. Like a wise mother, she must not force her children further than they can go, just because she wants to get there. Perhaps one day she will provide a list of leading questions on the literal and spiritual meanings, in this way, directing thought—or again, she can invite them to subject her to an inquisition. The keynote of the meeting should be *to find out*, but surely there will be some lighter moments when the thinking is savoured with touches of wit and humour!

'The difficulties? Of course there are many. Some young people want to hold the floor, to advertise themselves—others prefer to be silent—yet others find difficulty in following a line of thought. These symptoms can easily be dealt with. The Mistress learns much about human nature from her Discussions! Perhaps the best corrective to these forms of self-love is the Mistress's own attitude of simplicity and sincerity. Then there are differences in age, education, social background, but these differences constitute little difficulty. We are all children of our Heavenly Father, part of the Catholic Church; we are "one". The Discussion unifies, unifies the person, unifies the group. In the teaching congregation, with sisters of one grade, where these groups have been functioning, these differences in age, education and social background have been marked. But they have helped the members to a mutual giving, to a further appreciation of other points of view. They have enlarged the horizon of each Novice and widened the scope of tolerance. The young person who leaves school at fifteen and finds that she can get as much from the Gospels as can a graduate, knows, surely, a true and lasting joy. She realizes that the things of the spirit are not merely the things of the intellect. This levelling "up" of the less well-educated members provides a source of strength in the whole life of the Novitiate. Would it not help in Professed communities? *Ut sint unum!*

'The time factor might raise another obstacle. The Mistress needs much time to prepare her material. Yes—but it is well worth the extra labour. She need not be learned—thank goodness! But she has to consult books, to be very sure of right doctrine—but is not this part of her work? Often a Novice can be entrusted to find out a right answer, and this "out-of-discussion-time" interest continually shows itself. Where problems arise for which no solution seems forthcoming then the Mistress would surely ask priestly advice. This question of time suggests another difficulty. Are these "scriptural discussions" part of the normal Novitiate instruction, or are they an extra? Quite definitely an extra—neither part of the special instruction on the spiritual life and constitutions, nor yet part of the courses in religion. They have had to be fitted into a time-table already well-filled. Because of the numbers (and it is necessary that the Mistress should always be present) these particular meetings could only be arranged twice a week for each group.

'The scripture discussion was at first something quite apart from the rest of the day's activities. But its influence did not rest there. Within a month, the same method had insinuated itself into the formal "instructions" enjoined by the rule and constitutions. And it is in to stay! Instead of listening to talks on silence, charity, the Vows, the constitutions, the Novices talk these out with the Mistress. They find for themselves the connection between silence, poverty and humility. They freely talk out the meaning and difficulties of certain articles of the constitutions. They connect their rule of life with the Gospels. They piece together all the information that they gather. Their minds are becoming more unified—please God their lives will become so too. There is little wool-gathering, all are alert, to give or to receive. The scriptural discussion has been the leaven! Is not this as it should be?

'Every Mistress must use the material suited to her own Novices, but in case any should be nervous of beginnings, as was the writer, perhaps an outline of the work done might be of use. It seems best to start these extra discussions with the New Testament. As has already been said, St. Luke was used by these groups. *Reading Between the Lines* (St. John) provides anyone with a clear straightforward method of using scriptural material. At the end of a year, when the young people had acquired a way of handling the text, a change was introduced into this supplementary discussion class. *Whatsoever He shall say*[1] was chosen as subject matter. The Novices had to learn how to make spiritual reading—how to assimilate and make it part of themselves. Those who know and appreciate the book will easily see the reason for its choice. Besides this, the study of such a book brings back, in another setting, the teaching of the First Year instructions. Each paragraph, each sentence was subjected to a careful scrutiny—the whys and wherefores being dealt with. Much doctrinal knowledge, well buried after exams, was drawn forth and correlated with life and prayer. After the text had been thrashed out, the Novices were enabled to record their findings by writing answers in their own notebooks to questions set.

[1] Blackfriars Publications, Blackfriars, Oxford.

This slow reading and sifting has made a great difference to spiritual reading in general. Sometimes one is amazed at the comparison of ideas, the weighing of judgements, the keen interest in refectory reading! It was considered, too, that a little of the Old Testament should be introduced—to lay a foundation for further spare-time study later on. A simple study of the Book of Ruth was embarked upon. The literal meaning was soon grasped, the spiritual teaching was rather more obscure than that of the New Testament (the Mistress herself needed, and was given, guidance). When the spiritual burden of the book was made clear—the story of God's calling and dealing with a soul—interest and enthusiasm soared high. Ruth became a companion, a predecessor, a model.

'That is all about the simple syllabus. First year a little of the New Testament, second year some reading and very little Old Testament. But, for those who try this method, one important fact must be faced. One moves very very slowly, none can run in the way of discussions. The amount of ground covered is woefully slight. This should not bother one. The Discussion is to teach the young soul how to use spiritual material, how to grow up in Christ—not to fill her mind with unrelated facts. Her Discussion notebook, for she should have one, will not have very much in it. She does not take notes during the time of argument! But she learns to record her own findings—they may be few, but they are her own and for her own perusal. For general interest, one keeps a record of the minutes of each meeting.

'This method is to help the Novice—incidentally it is of great use to the Mistress. It provides an opportunity for an all-round view of a person; her outlook; her dealings with others; her readiness to grapple with difficulties. Two unsatisfactory candidates first showed their inability to imbibe the community spirit at these meetings! The living interest aroused in doctrine, in the Christian life, is striking. There is no "pious" talk. The atmosphere has been markedly healthy—the whole urge has been to see the unifying factors in life—appreciating how things "hang together", Love, the Commandments, the Counsels.

'The young of to-day talk much, talk too much. Yes, but the only sane way of using this "power" is, surely, to discipline it, canalize it into the right channels. The Novices must learn to see the unity of the Christian life; to see all things fitting into place, so that all may be "restored in Christ". The discussion method supplies a powerful means of arriving at this goal. How did He, the Divine Novice-Master, train His apostles? "And His disciples asked Him what this parable might be" (Luke viii, 9). Speaking of scandals, He turned to His twelve, "What think you?" (Math. xviii, 12). Or again, "Lord, show us the Father and it is enough for us" (John xiv, 8). "I am the Good

Shepherd" (John x, 11). The shepherd does not feed his sheep—he leads to pastures.

'In the last burning prayer to His Father He asked "That they may all be one, as Thou, Father, in Me and I in Thee: that they also may be one in Us" (St. John xvii, 21). Dare we limit that "one", does it not also refer to the integration of the person? And they should be one "that the *world* may believe that Thou hast sent Me". Should we not use His method to do His work?'

A second-year Novice writes:

'When the general idea of Discussions was first explained, there was no hint that a whole new world was about to be opened to us. Yet this is exactly what Discussions did. It is only now after two years of them that one begins to realize this. For the first time the Gospels came alive; they ceased to be text books we had "studied" in school, whose historicity, authenticity and veracity we had learned to prove, whose style we had appraised and whose subject matter we had crammed, neatly ticketed and listed, for examination purposes. They became instead the life of Our Lord and His fascination held us.

'Discussion time became a time of enjoyment, eagerly looked forward to and not to be missed. It meant real work as the mentally casual soon realized, but the joy in finding out (and for ourselves) more about Our Lord was very real.

'The plan was to take a passage from Scripture and having worked out its literal meaning, extricate the spiritual meaning and its application to daily life. To do this so simple thing we had to learn anew how to read and how to think. Just establishing the literal meaning was often a problem, a vague general idea was not enough, clear accurate thought was essential. This was one of the big benefits of the Discussions and taught us to read slowly and more carefully. (We saw this very clearly in the "Book" type of discussion from *Whatsoever He shall say*.) With much prompting and help from one another, first literal and then spiritual meaning was forged. Here was all the joy of discovery from personal research. Of course some difficulties and technicalities needed expert help and too private interpretation had to be checked and here the Mistress helped by offering the fruits of her deeper and more prayerful study.

'In a large group, varied in age, experience and attainment, ideas, opinions and lights were plentiful. We were often amazed, and at least one converted "slick" reader, humbled at the amount of thought that lay in one tiny phrase of Scripture. The large diverse group had advantages of its nature for these differences contributed to the interest and enrichment of the discussion. Much was learned and assimilated from the mutual give and take of ideas that would never have been possible from mere book study. We learnt to apply information and experience, not just to store it. It was truly education in the liberal sense that Newman so urged—the mutual drawing out by interchange of ideas and experience.

'Another big advantage of Discussions was the help they gave in getting to know people. Listening to others trying to work out an idea, hearing different angles on the same theme, strengthened friendship, created a sense of solidarity and made for tolerance of thought and sympathy with others' difficulties.

'Outside of Discussion time further interest was stimulated. This came from the necessity of looking up information. Commentaries always considered too learned and dry were searched for help in solving difficulties. In this the Mistress was able to encourage by suggesting sources and possible helps. Fresh interest was added to reading in general. One became more alive and alert to collect information of use, such as, a description of a Jewish wedding, thus solving the mystery of why the Virgins fell asleep. A casual glance at an illustrated geography cleared up the meaning of "his fan in his hand", not an implement to cool the face seemingly!

'But all this has been largely about Scripture Discussions. As a prelude to more Doctrinal ones we were divided into small groups and discussed a chapter from *For Better, For Worse*. As an experiment this was enjoyed, but all agreed that the larger group under the leadership of the Mistress was preferable. This was due to lack of competent leadership and the tendency was to wander far from the point and get out of depth. This may have been because the doctrinal element of the discussions made the differences in attainment more manifest. With the Mistress there is a centre of unity and she is in a better position to hold the threads of the discussion. Less competent leaders try to run the discussion rather than guide it.

'Most of the benefits derived from these Discussions seem at first sight to be in the nature of by-products such as learning anew to read, think and express ideas. But their greatest value has been in making the Scriptures accessible. Discussions cannot go on for ever, but the technique being learnt, the door is open to further private adventure into the Gospels. It seems true to say that their help to prayer and the spiritual life has been very great. In looking at Our Lord's relationship with His Apostles in St. Luke, for example—the fact that it was not just Our Lord's dealings then with those simple men that we were appreciating, but that now He is treating with us in the same way, has made a very great difference to us. In this way the Gospel has become Someone and not some book and this must be the greatest benefit of discussions.'

Appendix 3

HABITS

(See Part II, Chap. 3, p. 96)

'Contrary to the popular conception is the modern scientific determination of habit evolved as the result of experimental tests. It is, unless I am mistaken, fundamentally that of William James, whose unsubstantiated theory of the essence of habit is the generally accepted basis of the treatment of habit in modern empirical and behaviourist psychology. Largely speaking he regards habit as a purely passive disposition in matter which renders it more patient of the passage of impulse, more readily reactive to stimulus. As a result of his observations of the plasticity of organic matter, and especially of nervous matter, he confidently enunciates the principle that "the phenomena of habit in living beings are due to the plasticity of the organic materials of which these bodies are composed". Habit becomes thus confined to the purely material order and represents a mere physical modification of a bodily organ. Because some habits are shown empirically to include physiological determinations it is concluded that such physiological determinations completely cover the whole question of habit. Herein we see an example of the possibility of grave error in the findings of empirical science. Experience, and even sense experience, is accepted as the ultimate and sole criterion of truth. The facts of the immaterial world, the world of soul, of intellect and will, ascertainable by equally cogent evidence of a different order, are disregarded or frankly denied, or at least entirely segregated from the observable facts of the material world, the world of the body.

'We do not, of course, for a moment deny either the truth or the value of the facts discovered in empirical psychology. On the contrary our doctrine of the unity of the individual man and the hylomorphic relation of body and soul prepares us to expect in the body effects commensurate with the operation of the soul insofar as the soul makes use of bodily organs in its operation. It is a matter of intense interest to learn that habitual action produces physical modifications, grooves, as it were, in the brain and nerves; or contrariwise that the presence, for example, of a more than normal amount of adrenalin produces a tendency to anger. But we do not, therefore, conclude that this adequately accounts for our habits, for our virtues or our vices, because (besides the authority of supernatural religious teaching) the metaphysical principles of our speculative psychology safeguard us from error of concluding that bodily dispositions are the only source ⟨f habitual action. They represent, in fact, no more than the material or passive side which attains its significance only from the form or active principle that brings it into actual being. Otherwise we might just as well say that a piece of sculpture is explained entirely by the dispositions of the marble out of which it is made. Of their very nature habits are primarily modifications of the active principles of operation, and these active principles in a man are not his bodily dispositions, but his soul and the powers inherent in the soul. Undoubtedly there are purely corporeal functions in man, like digestion and growth, which are to a large extent mere automatic physical reflexes, and no one supposes that these are qualified in themselves by habit. We should never think of saying that a man has a habit of growing or of digesting food. But we might well say that he digests his food because he has a habit of eating deliberately, or has indigestion due to a habit of bolting his food. In other words a habit pertains to those operations over which a man can have and ought to have control, and to the faculties of the soul which, being of their nature undetermined, can be determined at will, by the person possessing them, to this or that habitual mode of operation. Even modern psychologists are compelled to recognize non-material principles of action, though some, like James and McDougal, tend to reduce them to sensation or instinct. They shirk, for certain perhaps valid reasons, the use of the word faculty, and speak for example of "psychical mechanisms"; but we are concerned with things and not with names. We are thus brought to the conclusion that habit properly so-called is a quality inherent in the soul and its faculties, but may connote a corresponding material and purely passive modification of the body. Further it is already clear that the pertinent aspect of habit as the psychological basis of natural virtue is implied in the fundamental notion of control by the will. Virtue is, indeed, nothing more than the ethical quality of this control. But in order to appreciate this fundamental point, it is necessary to treat briefly of the possible influence of bodily dispositions in the acquisition and exercise of habits and the volitional activity implied therein.

'Speaking of moral virtues, Aristotle says: "The virtues come to be in us neither by nature nor in despite of nature, but we are furnished by nature with a capacity for receiving them, and are perfected in them through custom (or habit)." This capacity includes both the faculties of the soul and the bodily dispositions. We say of a certain man that he is naturally mild or naturally abstemious, or of another that he is naturally choleric or naturally intemperate. Or again, we say that so-and-so is a natural linguist or a born musician. Such statements mean that a man has a natural predisposition to art or virtue which will make one line of action easier to him than another line, or easier

to him than to another man. It is possible that this predisposition may
be reducible in each case to the physical structure of the body. But is
that bodily disposition to be taken as a principle of action? If so, the
resulting habits of virtue, of vice, of learning and so on, will in no sense
be under the control of the man in question; there is no place for his
reason or his will. Granting such a hypothesis, we should have to conclude that a man's character and attainments must necessarily develop
entirely and only upon lines dictated by corporeal infirmities or ex-
cellences over which he has no control. If he has a physical conforma-
tion which inclines him to excessive consumption of alcoholic liquor,
he will necessarily become a confirmed drunkard. Or if he has physical
predispositions which lend themselves to musical ability, he will necessarily become an accomplished musician. Such a position is, of course,
utterly untenable and preposterous. It is true that these conditions,
insofar as they are purely corporeal, cannot be directly controlled by
the will; it is equally true that the passions, incited and aided by these
conditions, may conceivably prove strong enough on occasion to over-
whelm reason. But in spite of this, it is certain that a man can control
his passions and can act in accordance with or diametrically opposite
to his bodily predispositions. If a man follows the corporeal or purely
sensitive bent in his nature, he does so of his own choice, and he is
himself responsible for the actions thus performed and for the habits
which are thus generated in the faculties immediately productive of
those actions. Again, habitual action in a specified direction will produce a corresponding modification of the bodily organ or member
concerned. But that aptitude and prompt obedience in the bodily
member, though undoubtedly an important concomitant, is not the
habit nor even necessarily conjoined to the habit. A musician, for
instance, who is able to play the violin well, has developed a permanent
habit of being able to play. It is true that in order to play he must have
supple wrist and obedient fingers, but if these physical qualities be lost,
or in temporary abeyance, he does not forthwith lose the habit, any
more than it disappears when the violin is no longer in his hands. The
fingers are only the material instruments of the soul's operation.
Trilby sang superbly, but she could not be said to have the habit of
song. The habit belonged to Svengali, who controlled her by his will,
yet who was himself utterly incapable of using his own voice in song.'—
Moral Principles and Practice, Chap. 6: 'The Natural Virtues,' by Hilary
Carpenter, O.P., pp. 112–117; cf. also Additional Notes Nos. 9 and 11,
pp. 224, 225.

Appendix 4

A NOTE ON THE TITLE 'CO-REDEMPTRIX'

(See Part IV, Chap. 2)

Immediately after the publication of the second Encyclical letter on the Sacred Heart,[1] of Pope Pius XI, two noteworthy petitions were laid before the Holy See. First, the Bishop of Autun, together with many Cardinals, Bishops and Superiors of Religious Orders and Congregations, and the whole family of the Visitation nuns appealed to the Holy Father that the feast of St. Margaret Mary should be extended to the Universal Church. This was granted on 26th June, 1929.[2]

Secondly, the publication of this Encyclical was followed by a stream of petitions to the Holy See to authorize a new office and feast of Our Lady as Co-Redemptrix. The reasons for this were its closing words: 'May the most gracious Mother of God be propitious to these Our wishes and to these Our commands; she who gave us Christ the Redeemer, who watched over Him, and, at the foot of the Cross, offered Him a victim for our sins. She, too, by reason of her wondrous union with Him, and of a most singular grace of God, became and is piously known as the Mother of Reparation. Confiding in her intercession with Jesus "the one mediator of God and men"[3] who wished to associate His own Mother with Himself as the advocate of sinners, as the dispenser and mediatrix of grace. . . .'

Previously Pope Pius X (January 22nd, 1914) had granted indulgences to an Italian prayer in which Mary is called *Corredentrice del genere umano*.[4] And in his Apostolic Letter, *Inter Sodalicia*, published on 22nd March, 1918, Pope Benedict XV had written, 'Thus, when her Son suffered and died, so Mary suffered with Him and almost died, renouncing her maternal rights over her Son in order to placate the justice of God, according to her capacity, so that it may be truly said that together with Christ, she redeemed the human race.'

Again, we read in the prayer at the closing of the Jubilee year in 1935: 'O Mother of piety and mercy, who when thy most beloved Son was consummating the Redemption of the human race on the altar of the Cross, didst stand there both compassionating Him as

---

[1] *Miserentissimus Redemptor.*
[2] *Acta Apostolicae Sedis*, 1 Oct. 1929, p. 606.
[3] 1 Tim. 2. 5.
[4] *A.A.S.*, VI (1914), 108.

Co-redemptrix . . . preserve in us we beseech thee, and increase day by day, the precious fruits of His Redemption and of thy compassion.'[1]

This then is the mind of the Church. But many are still doubtful whether or not the term Co-redemptrix should be used in speaking of the participation of Mary in the passion of Christ. Father M. J. Scheeben, one of the greatest Mariologists, who lived in the latter half of the last century wrote: 'The expression "*adjutrix*" (helpmate) or "*adjutorium*" (help) of the Redeemer in the redemption is less objectionable and in itself more fitting, even more in accordance with the Sacred Scripture. It was used for the first time by Albert the Great, and indeed repeatedly. This help must not be understood as a support in the ordinary sense, that is, as the strengthening by another of a power which of itself is insufficient. It is used in a more general sense as the only help admissible on the part of the creature in reference to God, namely, as a service conducive to an end, or as a helpful co-operation working in its own way. Thus it is a help in the very sense of a co-operating partner, as "we are God's coadjutors" in the Vulgate. . . . So understood, the expression is all the more justified because, according to the idea of the Church, Eve, as "a help like unto himself"(Adam), is the prototype of Mary in her relation to Christ'. Father Scheeben's attitude, however, was influenced by a warning issued to all his clergy in 1882 by Francis Joseph, Bishop of Linz, who disapproved of the use of the term '*co-redemptrix*'.[2]

On the other hand the learned Père Dublanchy writes: 'The word co-redemptrix of itself means nothing more than a co-operation in the redemption, and it has been given the precise meaning of a secondary and dependent co-operation by the theological usage of centuries. There can be no serious objection therefore against its use provided some indication is given that Mary's part in this co-operation is that of a secondary and dependent cause.'[3]

Whatever be the value of these arguments for and against the use of the term 'co-redemptrix', there can be little doubt that it is not only permitted by the Church, but is actually used in her official documents. The reason for this would seem to be twofold; first, if the term 'co-redemptrix' seems to demand too much, Mary's influence even after the most careful and judicious theological scrutiny is much greater than even many of the faithful generally suppose. And secondly: it is only by insisting upon all Mary's prerogatives that she becomes comprehensible, even to those outside the Church. If the growth of

[1] *Osservatore Romano*, April 29–30, 1935. Cf. also: *O.R.*, Dec. 22–3, 1923; Dec. 1, March 25, 1934 and *A.A.S.*, 1928, pp. 170 seq.; also Leo XIII, Encycl. *Jucunda semper*, Sept. 8, 1894 ('Consors cum Christo existit laboriosae pro humano genere expiationis').
[2] *Mariology*, Vol. 2, pp. 196–7.
[3] *Dict. Theol. Cath.*—'Marie', p. 2,396.

Mariology has been retarded by the Protestant schism of the past few centuries, now surely is the time for a vigorous re-statement of her function in the divine plan of redemption. It might well prove a cause of scandal to act otherwise.

ADDITIONAL NOTES

(Illustrating points in the text)

1. (p. 9). 'The basic principle which should regulate a spiritual director's counselling of one who is firmly resolved to become a religious is that little or no counsel is required. Protracted deliberation and counselling are called for in matters of great doubt; this case, however, is stamped with the marks of certitude, and "certain things do not need discussion".

'First of all, it is certain that entrance into religion is the greater good, and to doubt or deny this fact is to call into question the veracity of Christ Himself. Secondly, there can be no doubt that the power required to carry out the resolution to become a religious will be made available by God. Finally, one who has resolved to enter religion, certainly knows his own intention, and has no valid reason to doubt that it comes from God. That this resolution must be traced ultimately to God hinges on the fact that it bears upon something good, and consequently, regardless of its proximate causes, it has its source in God the cause of all good. God alone can, and must, move the human will to freely move itself in making a choice. In this regard, St. Thomas considers the objection that, since the devil often suggests good things to man with the intention of deceiving him, consequently counsel and deliberation are required to escape the danger of deception. In his response the Angelic Doctor insists that the peril to religion vanishes when one recalls the limited field in which the devil can influence a man: he may suggest through the senses or even deceive them; he cannot move the mind or will from the intention of leading a good life. Hence, even if the devil were to suggest entrance into religion, there would be no danger involved in assenting to this suggestion, for it is good. God alone can move the mind and will of man to assent to this suggestion, and it is solely through God's internal motion that the suggestion becomes efficacious. Consequently "the intention to enter religion, regardless of who suggests it, is from God".

'*Since an act of an infused virtue is involved in religious vocation, which presupposes the existence of grace in the soul, a fact which cannot be known with absolute certainty, the certitude that the resolution to become a religious comes from God is no guarantee that a supernatural vocation has been given.* [Italics not in original.] In this matter the general theological norms concerned with proving the possession of grace must be applied. Thus, short of a special revelation of God, one cannot be absolutely certain of having sanctifying grace. Only that imperfect knowledge based on signs (the preference of divine things to temporal ones, joy and peace in making the choice, non-consciousness of mortal sin, and so on) is possible.

'What, then, does this certitude guarantee? Only this, the fact that God has called. How He has actually extended His invitation, through grace, through natural causes, through angels, both good and bad, eludes man's knowledge.

'Perhaps, too, the fact that a person can be certain with objective certitude that he really desires to be a religious will be called into question. Is there not a possibility of self-deception here? The answer is simply, that a man knows that he knows; he knows his own mind, his own intentions.

'These facts must be accepted by the director as certain and serve as his basis for giving whatever counsel may be needed. It is not his duty to question one well disposed in an attempt to "prove the spirit"; this is the exclusive duty of those in the religious institute who are charged with testing a vocation. A fundamental principle is involved here: a spiritual director is not a novice-master and should not act as one.

'If the candidate, then, is well disposed, i.e. firmly resolved to become a religious and gives evidence of relying upon God's power to sustain him in this new life, no questions should be raised about the existence of a divine vocation. Nor should the possibility that natural motives have entered into the decision of the individual cause undue concern. Human motives are not necessarily a sign of a false vocation but only a sign that a man has been called. Accordingly, if the aspirant's motives are mixed, the director should attempt to ensure by his counsel that the supernatural ones are given the primacy. But if, on the other hand, it becomes obvious—a somewhat unlikely eventuality— that a purely human motive, e.g. human affection for the brother or sister who taught the aspirant in the seventh grade, desire to make parents happy, the attempt to shroud some disappointment in life in a religious garb, holds first position, then the director ought to advise the aspirant not to enter religion until his motives have been purified. In general, however, the confessor or director should keep in mind that the period of probation and the canonical novitiate which all candidates must undergo are designed to test and discover the shaky foundations of improper motivation. It is here that they will be bolstered or will collapse entirely.'—*The Theology of Religious Vocation*, by Edward Farrell, O.P., pp. 195–9 (B. Herder Book Co.).

2. (p. 24). 'From the fact that artificiality is an essential component of neurotic behaviour, it follows that *the only person who can be entirely free from neurosis is the man whose life is spent in genuine devotion to the natural and supernatural obligations of life*, and who has steadfastly accepted and

affirmed his position as a creature and his place in the order of creation; in other words, *beyond the neurotic there stands only the saint*. This enables us more easily to understand the frequent occurrence of neurotic episodes, or of phases bearing an extraordinary resemblance to them, in the lives of so many saints. This should not lead us to the foolish and pseudo-scientific conclusion that saintliness is in itself a true or modified neurotic attitude to life. The neurotic phases are always only episodic, as can be proved from the study of such lives; they represent periods of transition, in which the battle against the "dark despotic self" is fought out to a victory, raising the man to a higher plane of life. The repetition of such episodes is thereby rendered more understandable, for they correspond to the various stages in the man's upward progress and lead to a more and more complete absorption into the Godhead. On the other hand, it must not be forgotten that in dealing with the spiritual life, psychology can only proceed very cautiously and tentatively in its attempts to explain things, for there factors and forces are involved that are outside the categories of this science, and even the most delicate psychological analysis and description prove inadequate. It seems, for example, to be altogether mistaken to interpret "the night of the soul" and similar phenomena in terms of neurosis or of purely natural categories.'—*Psychology of Character*, by Rudolf Allers, pp. 346-7 (Sheed & Ward).

3. (p. 39). In his last farewell address to the Visitation Sisters of Lyons, 1622, St. Francis of Sales says:

'. . . I say then that we must neither ask for anything nor refuse anything, but leave ourselves absolutely in the arms of divine Providence, without busying ourselves with any desires, except to will what God wills of us. St. Paul practised this self-abandonment most excellently at the very moment of his conversion, for when Our Lord had smitten him with blindness, he cried out instantly: "Lord, what wilt thou have me to do?" and from that time forth he continued in absolute dependence upon the will and commands of God. Our whole perfection lies in the practice of this; and the same St. Paul, writing to one of his disciples, forbids him, among other things, to allow his heart to be engrossed with any strong desire, so well did the great Apostle know the danger of this failing.

'You say: "You must not then desire virtues, although Our Lord says: Ask and it shall be given you." Oh, my daughters, when I say that you must ask for nothing and desire nothing, I am speaking of earthly things; as for virtues, we may, of course, ask for them, and in asking for the love of God, we comprise all, for it contains them all.'

4. (p. 48). 'The invasion plan decided upon, he [Field-Marshal Montgomery] abandoned the details to de Guingand and the Americans and devoted himself entirely to the soldiers. He had a special train, and Addison Road, Hammersmith, was his private station. From here he set out each week with the intention of seeing and talking to every soldier and officer who was destined to go on the invasion, something like a million men. . . . The Army Intelligence reports had made it clear that the average young officer was expecting to die in the assault, and among the ranks there was the same heavy weight of apprehension and dismal foreboding. Very well. He would conquer this despondency. He would preach a new gospel of faith and hope. Let him get among the soldiers and they would understand. They would turn this invasion into a new crusade.

'Up and down the country Montgomery went, talking sometimes to five or six meetings, addressing thirty thousand men in a single day. First he marched round the ranks peering into the soldiers' faces one by one. Then they came running in thousands towards him, to sit at his feet and listen to the thin religious voice : "Finish the thing off . . . you and I together . . . with God's help we will see the job through to the end." It was the same with each meeting, the same brand of faith and conviction, and he talked with the same assurance to Americans and Canadians, even to Norwegians and Poles. . . .

'Quite early in his morale campaign he had addressed a large gathering of the most eminent men in England at the Mansion House in London. It had been a great testing-point for Montgomery. Possibly there is no more urbane and long-headed assemblage in the world than that which gathers from time to time at the Mansion House ceremonies. With the Cabinet, the ambassadors, and the aldermen of England watching him in open curiosity, Montgomery rose and spoke as though he were addressing a platoon of soldiers on the heath. As always it was the way he spoke, his manner, his note of pronounced conviction— even his tense and ascetic appearance—which won the day and roused them to an exuberant and youthful cheering over the glasses of port. The words he used, in part, were these: "It must forever redound to our shame that we sent out soldiers into this most modern war with weapons and equipment that were hopelessly inadequate; we have only ourselves to blame for the disasters that early overtook us in the field. Surely we must never let this happen again. Nor will we.

' "*But it is the man that counts and not the machine* . . . and you must have mutual confidence between the commander and the troops; any steps you take to establish this confidence will pay a very good dividend.

' "A study of the military disasters that have overtaken us in our history will reveal that they have been due, basically, to faulty command, or bad staff-work, or neglect of the human factor, and sometimes possibly all three. . . .

' "Can you imagine this conversation in after years? 'What did you do in the World War?'

' " 'I pulled hard to start with; but after a time I began to lose interest and let go the rope. I thought I wanted a rest; and I wanted more pay.'

' " 'And did you win?'

' " 'No, we lost. I let go the rope and we lost the match. God forgive me; we lost the match.'

' "Is it possible that such a conversation could apply to us British? No. It is impossible. Thank God it is impossible.

' "Then let us stand-to and get on the rope." '—*Montgomery* by Alan Moorehead, pp. 187 seq. (Hamish Hamilton).

'One of the first responsibilities of a C.-in-C. in the field,' Montgomery writes in one of his pamphlets, 'is to create what I would call atmosphere, and in that atmosphere his staff, his subordinate commanders and his troops will live and work and fight.

'Above all, commanders must have a moral courage, that resolution and that determination which will enable them to stand when the issue hangs in the balance.

'The battle is, in effect, a contest between two wills, his own and that of the enemy commander.

'It is absolutely vital that a C.-in-C. should keep himself from becoming immersed in details. He must spend a great deal of time in quiet thought and reflection. He will refuse to sit up late at night conducting the affairs of his army; he will be well advised to withdraw to his tent or caravan after dinner at night.

'He must trust his subordinates. The only orders issued from a commander's Tactical Headquarters are those given verbally to army commanders by the C.-in-C. These are never confirmed in writing.

'Every single soldier must know, before he goes into battle, how the little battle he is fighting fits into the larger picture. . . .

'When the issue hangs in the balance radiate confidence in the plan and in the operations even if inwardly you do not feel too certain of the outcome.

'And finally: Never worry.'

5. (p. 57). 'This "sloth" (*acedia*) is not leisure, but the incapacity for leisure. Sloth is the real source of restlessness and the cause of work "for work's sake". "Work for work's sake" is an escape from one's own being. *Acedia* means that a man prefers to forgo his human rights, his own nature: that he does not want to be as God wants him to be. *Acedia* is despair from weakness. It is the not giving the consent of one's

will to one's own being. And its opposite is not feverish hard work but acquiescence in the world, in God, in love. *Acedia*, far from being simply refusal to face work, is in essence disobedience of the Third Commandment, which commands rest, cultivation of the peace of mind in God. And this *acedia*, the deep-seated lack of calm which makes leisure impossible, is a deadly sin from which others flow. We do not know how to be silent, how to let things happen. But silence is the soul's power to answer the reality of the world. It is not grabbing the reins, but leaving them loose, letting oneself go. There is a sleeplessness which comes from the lack of capacity for leisure. Sleep itself is symbolic; "God giveth songs in the night". All this is interestingly connected with the idea of Holy-days and Feast Days. Secular humanism, if we may define it as including the denial of any meaning beyond man's human effort, cannot properly understand leisure. For leisure is feeding; it is to feast, and to feast is a religious act identical in its fulness with divine worship. Historically there are no real feast days without gods; feast days and holidays are historically in essence times for receptiveness, for worship, for grace. The extreme of the secular humanist's denial of this is Baudelaire's: "One must work, if not from taste then at least from despair, for, to reduce everything to single truth: work is less boring than pleasure."'—Louis Arnaud Reid in *British Journal of Educational Studies*, Vol. I, No. 1. Cf. also *Leisure the Basis of Culture* by Josef Pieper, a German Catholic writer (Faber and Faber).

6. (p. 59). 'For what, after all, do we—do I—admire St. Simeon so enthusiastically for? It is for that terrific talent of his for doing nothing. There is no finer slap in the eye to the modern world than that. It is a phenomenon that the modern world finds not only incomprehensible, but reprehensible and even criminal, and there are strong reasons for thinking that the modern world needs a good slap in the eye. St. Simeon stands—or sits, or perches—as the pure contemplative, the eagle up aloft in his eyrie gazing at the sun, the look-out man in the crow's nest. I know that the textbooks will tell you—and the lives of most saints truly witness—that the life of contemplation does not mean a life that is physically inactive; that the great contemplatives have been great men of action. But it is the other kind of contemplative life, the other kind of sanctity, that I think the modern world needs.

> Teach us to care and not to care
> Teach us to sit still.

St. Simeon had certainly learned to sit still, and he if anyone amongst the saints of Christendom can teach us how to do the same.

'For why can't we sit still? Why must we be always doing? It is because the active life of the West does not feed the soul, because it so destroys our spiritual resources that even the briefest respite from it brings a sense of boredom. I am sure that most of the restlessness of the West arises from this fear of boredom, and boredom means being brought face to face with our own emptiness. Therefore that childish question: what did old Simeon do all day?—is highly relevant. If we could say no more about him than that he faced boredom, wrestled with it, did not succumb to it—did not descend from his pillar—but conquered it and remained up there, DOING NOTHING, then I think that would be sufficient to make him a worthwhile study and counterblast to the present day.'—*Saints For Now*—St. Simeon Stylites, by George Lamb, p. 58.

7. (p. 60). 'The true psychologist will, then, be very cautious in this matter. The well-known investigation of Heymans and Vierzma on the character of 2,757 boys and 701 girls simply concluded that there are certainly more females than males who are emotional. But even there, what part does education play? There is a strong convention that men must not give way to demonstrativeness which is unbecoming to their sex; also that women are more free in this respect—and many of them take full advantage of it. A greater show of emotion does not necessarily imply a greater power of emotion, as a certain theory called "peripheric" would have us believe; but the resolution to repress emotion and its nervous reaction has an effect on the formation of character. However this may be, girls are more demonstrative than boys (boys 14·5 per cent, compared with 20·3 per cent of girls), more excitable and sensitive (boys 9·8 against girls 10·7 per cent). The girls react more often by crying or sulking when rebuked (15·6 against 8·5 per cent). They enthuse more quickly (9·8 against 7 per cent). But it must be noticed that the differences in proportion are slight. To sum up, the enquiry finds 59·8 per cent of the females as emotional and only 45 per cent of the males; the figures for the non-emotional types are 39·3 per cent males, against 26·5 per cent females.

'As for activity and intelligence, the differences between the sexes are practically negligible if one goes by the data provided by the investigation; but what is more serious than all the characteristics current in feminine psychology and feminine literature, is that the following qualities come undeniably under the heading of emotivity: inconstancy of moods, anxiety, uneasiness, lack of courage, morbidity, sudden bursts of temper, need of change, frequent shifting of sympathy, propensity for laughter, a narrowing of conscience, suggestibility, concrete imagination, insight, but lack of reasoning power, little aptitude for mathematics, greater aptitude for languages, a dislike for abstractions, intuitive thought, impulsiveness, tendency to fanaticism, manual dexterity, vanity, domineering spirit.'—*Jean Plaquevent, Lumen*

Vitae (International Centre for Studies in Religious Education). Rudolf Allers is much more cautious, cf. *Psychology of Character*, Ch. 5.

8. (p. 62). 'The importance of marriage in the lives of the Israelites has found its expression in the two accounts of the creation of man. When the world came into existence, and the order of the world was created, all was crowned by the creation of man and woman. On their union was laid the blessing to which later generations owe their existence. In both accounts man and woman are indissolubly bound together, but the closeness of the connection is differently expressed. The Priestly Code expresses it in the manner that man and woman together make '*ādhām* (man). The passage reads: God created man (*hā-'ādhām*) in His own image, in the image of God created He him, male and female created He them (1. 27).

'Singular and plural are used indifferently about the same being. Man is a whole consisting of two parts, the man and the woman. Nothing is said of the relation between them, except that they are indispensable to each other, and not till they are united do they together form a whole human being.

'The Yahwist, on the other hand, relates how Yahweh first created man, i.e. the man. The man is in himself man, but he lacks something that he may be so wholly. It is not good that man should be alone. He must have someone to help him, and this help-meet he finds in woman. She is taken out of him, and thus she must be there, in order that he may be man wholly. She is part of him; that which makes her fit to make him whole is that she is of the same flesh as himself. When the parents have brought up the son so far that he is becoming a man, then he leaves the house of his father and founds a new house, thus uniting himself with the woman and becoming a man, man wholly.

'Thus, the shade of difference between the two accounts is that, according to the former, the man and the woman together make man, while according to the latter the man is man proper, though the woman is necessary in order that he may be man wholly. This shade of difference cannot be explained through a difference in time between the two narratives. The relation between man and woman was considered in rather the same manner throughout the whole of the history of Israel; and, like other Israelitic authors, the priestly writer in his genealogies exclusively reckons with men. No more can it be explained by the fact that the priestly account should be of foreign origin, whereas the Yahwist represents the Israelitic point of view. There are certain things which seem to point in the direction that both accounts are due to foreign influence; but they both describe something which the Israelite can recognize. The difference originates in the different points of view of the two narratives. The priestly writer wants to describe the creation of the various genera. Man—woman make a separate genus as contrasted with plants, birds, fishes, etc. The genus man is of dual sex, just as male and female specimens are required to represent the genera of the animals. The Yahwist wants to describe the order of the world in which man lives, the centre of gravity and distribution of power, and then the man must necessarily occupy a prominent position. The man is the ruler; it is he who provides the bread and makes the soil yield up its wealth. The woman is dependent upon him, but not like the animals; she is closely connected with him and part of him. Her task is to bear him children. She is his indispensable help-meet in the maintenance of the family.

'The man's position in the family is expressed by his being its *ba'al*, the meaning of which word is the possessor and the master. But these two meanings spring from another still deeper. *Ba'al* always presupposes a psychic community, a whole, and *ba'al* designates the ruling will within this. The word does not mean one-sided sovereignty; wherever that is meant, *'ādhōn* is used. The conqueror who sets his foot on the neck of the enemy will never be called the *ba'al* of the vanquished. In order that a man may become a *ba'al* there must be an intimate relation, and he exercises his power within its limits. Therefore the word is hardly ever used in an isolated sense; the relation in which the person in question is *ba'al* is always mentioned, unless it appears directly from the context.

'When the father of the household is called its *ba'al*, then it implies that he is the strong will within the narrow circle. He is the *ba'al* of his wife and she is *ba'al*-taken by him. He is the *ba'al* of his domestic animals, of his field and the whole of his property. It is probably due to chance that he is nowhere called the *ba'al* of his slave, even though the word *'ādhōn*, master, is also here appropriate.

'The word *ba'al* therefore not only characterizes the man as the master of the house, but also tells us something of the character of his rule. He is not an isolated despot, but the centre from which strength and will emanate through the whole of the sphere which belongs to him and to which he belongs.

'When a man is called father, it really implies the same thing, kinship and authority, also being expressed by the name of father. To the Israelite the name of father always spells authority. Naaman is called father by his servants (2 Kings 5. 13). The priest is called the father of the cultic community, of which he is the head (Judg. 18. 19), and Elijah is called father by his disciple (2 Kings 2. 12).

'Round the man the house groups itself, forming a psychic community, which is stamped by him. Wives, children, slaves, property are entirely merged in this unity. Nearest to the father are to a certain extent the children. They are his flesh and bear his name. The slaves are either born in the household or foreigners; in the former case they belong more intimately to the circle than if they are bought or captives. But they never leave their impress upon the house, the man being strong enough to counteract any foreign influence. The foreign characteristics of the slave only leave insignificant traces, and he falls quite into line with the house in its entirety. The position of the house-born slave in many ways closely resembles that of the children: he is "the son of the house" (Gen. 14. 14; 15. 2f.; 17. 12, 27; Jer. 2. 14); and if he has belonged to the house for a long time, he may as the "elder of the house" come to stand in very close relationship to the father of the house. He performs important tasks on behalf of the house-father (Gen. 24), and even the possibility that he may inherit is hinted (Gen. 15. 4). The slave is subject to circumcision (Gen. 17) and is admitted to the family worship. How closely he is received into the household appears from the fact that the slave of a priest may eat of the holy thing which is forbidden to the strange guest or the paid labourer, nay, even to the daughter who is married to a stranger (Lev. 22. 10–12).—*Israel—Its Life and Culture*, Vol. I–II, pp. 60 seq., by Johs. Pedersen, Professor of Semitic Philology in the University of Copenhagen (Geoffrey Cumberlege, O.U.P., London).

9. (p. 85). 'A. On its physiological side habit springs from a definite organic context which appears as a condition and antecedent before the performance of an act. The process is chiefly neurological, involving a series of working units in the nervous system with their respective synaptic connections. Close study of these last-named structures gives us the clue to the physiology of habit. Thus it is a special characteristic of the synapse that it always offers resistance to the original passage of an impulse. Once, however, a nerve current has managed to cross the barrier, it automatically lowers the resistance of the synapse to future crossings. If the connection between receptors and effectors has not been established by the inner growth of the nervous system, it is possible within limits to construct one by training. This is a necessary preliminary to all conditioning. Thus from the organic point of view, learning consists in the laying down of new pathways through the gradual elimination of obstacles presented at the synapses. If a pathway becomes disused, resistance is restored and the procedure must be gone through again. Two stages, therefore, are revealed in the physiological development of habit; first, the acquisition of preferred tracks of conduction; secondly, the strengthening of newly acquired synaptic connections so that the preferred tracks may become permanent.

'B. On its psychological side habit is explained as a phenomenon of revival. It is a fact of common observation that past mental states, and particularly those of the very recent past, have a tendency to recur. Even if it is only a partial content which reappears, the inclination of mind is to bring back the total experience to which this partial content belongs. The amount which actually recurs is dependent upon the extent to which our associative impulses harmonize with the present tendencies of consciousness. The general law is to revive the presentations of sense in the order and arrangement of their original occurrence. This naturally leads to facility of mental processes, especially when, through repetition, we accustom ourselves to the same modes of response. . . .

'For the student of mind there are three general systems to which all habits may be reduced. First there is the physiological series, including manual habits, such as those involved in dressing, writing, and forms of mechanical dexterity; laryngeal habits, like talking and singing; and motor habits, associated chiefly with walking, running, and so on. Next in order is the psycho-physical series, represented for the most part by habits of memory, perception, and emotional response. Finally there is the purely intellectual series, covering our habits of thought and volition.'—*General Psychology*, by Robert E. Brennan, O.P., pp. 392–3 (New York, Macmillan).

10. (p. 88). 'My father was poor, and had only a small farm, but he would not send me to the local school of Flavius, although rich boys, the sons of high and mighty Centurions, used to go there, with their slates and satchels hung over their arms, and their light pennies in their hands on pay-day. No, he boldly took his boy off to Rome to be taught what any man of equestrian rank or indeed any senator, would have his own children taught. If any one in so big a city noticed how I was dressed, and the slaves who took care of me, he would have thought that some great ancestral estate must have defrayed the expenses of it all. Further, he himself, the faithfulest of all guardians, went with me to all my teachers. Why should I say more; he kept me chaste, which is the first grace of manhood; he kept me not only from wrong-doing, but even away from the breath of it. He was not afraid that anyone should twist it to his discredit if some day I should follow a humble occupation like his own.

'Never while I retain my reason could I regret having such a father.'
—*Horace*, Alfred Noyes, p. 25.

11. (p. 94). 'A habit is a permanent disposition which furthers or hinders the movement of a being towards its natural end. In the words of Aristotle, "habitus dicitur dispositio difficile mobilis, secundum quam bene vel male disponitur dispositum aut secundum se aut in ordine ad aliud".

'Strictly speaking only a spiritual nature and its immaterial faculties of understanding and will are the subjects of habits. Adaptations of the material faculties go rather by the name of dispositions than that of habits. Indeed a habit, according to the idea of the Scholastics, means a permanent modification of the faculty itself, and of this material things do not allow. To be the subject of a habit, the powers of a thing must be capable of being directed in different ways "potentia determinabilis ad diversa". Now if we examine bodies we find that they do not admit of any subjective modification, for each is drawn blindly towards its special end. Chemically simple bodies thus have neither habits nor dispositions. As for complex bodies resulting from the combination of simple bodies we find them capable of acquiring "dispositions" for action: the sensitive faculties become more or less serviceable instruments of the higher faculties; animals can be habituated to certain actions, we can train them to behave in certain ways; organs adapt themselves to their functions; exotic plants become acclimatized; metals become pliant and easy to work in respect of some shape impressed upon them, an organism has its dispositions of health or sickness, of weakness or strength. Nevertheless all these dispositions do not merit the name of "habits", for they lack that characteristic stability which is essential to the notion. This is wanting to them precisely on account of the nature of the material subject which acquires them. Every material thing is the resultant of a happy combination of diverse elements with a view to some end; but so numerous are the elements and so great the complexity upon which this concurrence depends, that of necessity its stability is extremely slight. They must not, then, be denominated habits but rather dispositions; and so, too, must be termed health and sickness and the acquired adaptation of organs or of tissues. Habit, in virtue of its characteristic of permanence, implies a subject that is substantially unchangeable and incorruptible.'—*Manual of Modern Scholastic Philosophy*, by Cardinal Mercier, Vol. I, pp. 493–4 (Kegan Paul).

12. (p. 109). 'Because it thus makes real and incarnate the unity of the human race, married love is worthy of the respect and veneration due to all that is noblest in our nature which is summed up in this unity. God, "who has so wonderfully created and more wonderfully restored the dignity of human nature", by the same obligation which He imposes on us to respect that dignity, obliges us to respect love, in which our nature is thus summed up and its unity realized in the world of fact.

'We have reached here the corner-stone of all social morality. It cannot be shaken without endangering the whole structure. Respect for the life of our neighbour, for his property and for his good name, is an obligation which arises from this wider and deeper commandment which includes all those particular precepts: "Remember that thou respect human nature". To fail in this duty by insulting human nature where it finds its unity and its source, and to treat as a plaything the august function which alone guarantees its existence, is to sin grievously against the first principle of all human society, and against the law of essential subordination of individuals to the race. The result is that the individual who acts thus, cannot escape without psychological and moral injury to himself which may wound him mortally. Precisely because it is an act of the race, love affects the individual profoundly. It even perfects and exalts him so far as to make him in a manner identical, for the time being, with the human race itself, and to constitute him an active principle in the existence of a human being like himself.

'This is the reason why love plays the tremendous part which we see it play in human psychology. It is one of the most constant and active stimulants of human energy, one of the never-failing sources of interest and solicitude in life, and emphatically one of the most important factors in human morality. It is love which, by the interaction of one sex upon the other, and by the common interest of rearing a family, develops and perfects the mentality of both. It is love which leads man and woman by a movement imperceptible but inevitable, from the more or less selfish concerns of individual life, to the nobler life of devotion and self-forgetfulness.

'We can easily imagine what respect and care is demanded by such a central, essential and delicate element of human psychology and morality. So much begins here, that the slightest disorder here may involve a catastrophe later on. Therefore anything that would turn this delicate and powerful machinery against itself by distorting into an act of selfish pleasure the urge towards self-surrender, gives a violent wrench to one of the mainsprings of a true attitude towards life, thereby attacking oneself and wrecking one's soul. Nothing degrades as does this kind of disorder; when it has established itself in the human heart, respect for oneself and for others is driven out, and one grows by degrees into a state where the sacrifice of human dignity, and even human life in all its stages, no longer causes remorse or is even felt. Hence the worst punishment of those nations who pervert love—the worst, that is, after the eternal sanctions of the moral law—does not consist in falling birth-rates nor in deterioration of public health, but in degradation of the national character. The courage to live is lost; the very will to live is weakened, because it has been attacked by a disease more virulent than any physical infection.'—*Love, Marriage and Chastity*, by E. Mersch, S.J., pp. 9–12 (Sheed & Ward).

13. (p. 111). 'A precept has the nature of a duty . . . Now, a duty may bind in two ways: first, it may need to be fulfilled by an individual, and this duty cannot be neglected without sin. But there may be another duty, which has to be fulfilled by the multitude, for many things are necessary for the multitude or community, which one individual does not suffice to fulfil, but which can be fulfilled by the multitude, in that one individual does this and another does that. The precept of the law of nature concerning eating has to be carried out by each individual, for otherwise the individual could not be conserved. But the precept concerning generation applies to the whole multitude of mankind. Now, it is necessary to the multitude not only that it should be multiplied bodily, but also that it should progress spiritually. And hence the multitude will be provided for sufficiently if some give themselves to the work of carnal generation, and others, abstaining from this, give themselves to the contemplation of divine things, for the glory and well-being of the whole human race: just as in an army, some guard the camp, some carry the flag, and some fight with weapons; all these things being required by the multitude, but they cannot be fulfilled by one person.'—*Summa Theol.*, 2–2, 152, 2 ad 1.

14. (p. 128). It would be absurd to pretend there was no such thing as mental illness, which requires highly specialized treatment by competent psychotherapists. In spite of every precaution mental disorders find their way into religious institutions, and should be dealt with prudently. Two extremes have to be avoided in this matter. First, the attitude of superiors and at times even of priests and retreat fathers who take the view that psycho-analysts and others working in this field 'talk a lot of nonsense'. It is all too easy for the religious superior to adopt the rule of thumb that all sisters have to do in their distress is 'to pull themselves together'. The amount of avoidable suffering caused by this lack of insight on the part of superiors is truly appalling. Even more harm can be done by superiors and priests who presume to know all about mental illness. More than any other specialization psychotherapy suffers from well-intentioned amateurs of little or no clinical experience. Religious superiors and priests can be instructed to recognize the initial symptoms of mental disorder which calls for prompt and specialized attention but they should never presume to give such treatment either inside or outside the confessional. The risk is too grave. On the other hand the right people must be consulted when such maladies are suspected or diagnosed. It is true to say that the safest, soundest and most successful psychotherapy is undertaken by those who have the Faith and humility to know their own limitations, and who know when the spiritual care of the priest is needed. But unfortunately so many 'experts' outside the Church do not recognize

their limitations precisely because they have no appreciation of purely spiritual forces and values. Such people are a kind of new priesthood conjured up to cope with the difficulties of this new age.—Catholic parents and above all religious superiors should consult Catholic practitioners in these difficulties. Any good, sound Catholic doctor will be able to advise when such specialized treatment is necessary. The competent Catholic G.P. is a God-send to many of our convents.— But we should never lose sight of the fact that many of these cases of acute or chronic mental illness are brought on reactively by the religious environment itself. Where there is a whole life in Christ and a right-functioning religious authority few of these cases would ever burden the religious life. The inception of most of them can often be traced to a grave lack of prudence and common-sense in receiving unsuitable subjects into religion and to moral coercion of the kind described in the early chapters of this book.

15. (p. 139). It is tempting to interpret the vocation of the religious sister as a kind of participation in the motherhood of Our Lady. It would seem possible to envisage the life and apostolate of the religious sister as the extension of this divinely appointed prerogative of Mary. Sisters will sometimes say or imply that their relationship to Christ is essentially that of Mary His spouse and mother though of course immeasurably inferior in degree, and that therefore their dignity as a religious derives from a certain sharing in the Bridal Maternity of Our Lady. But this is true only by analogy. The motherhood whereby Mary brings forth the Mystical Body is more sublime than that of the Mystical Body or that of individual members partaking of its fruitfulness, because the essence of Mary's spiritual motherhood is that she brings forth the Mystical Body as an organism to be the Spouse of Christ; and it cannot function as an organism without Mary's continued activity as mother. The Church's begetting of individual souls, as Spouse of Christ, depends too on Mary's causal maternal activity by virtue of her privilege as mother of the Incarnate Word. But she carries on her maternal work in and through the Church.

16. (p. 139.) 'C'est une conclusion théólogique certaine, que Marie coopéra, de quelque manière, à l'acte principal du sacerdoce de Jésus-Christ, en donnant comme l'exigeait le plan divin, son consentement au sacrifice de la croix, tel qu'il a été accompli par Jésus-Christ. Selon l'enseignement de saint Thomas l'acte principal du sacerdoce de Jésus-Christ a été l'acte par lequel Jésus s'est offert en sacrifice pour la rédemption du monde. Dès le premier moment de son incarnation, il eut la volonté d'accomplir ce sacrifice; mais la parfaite consommation à laquelle, selon le plan divin, était attachée notre rédemption, eut lieu

seulement sur le Calvaire. Ce fut par ce sacrifice suprême que Jésus remplit veritablement sa fonction de prêtre ou de réconciliateur du monde avec Dieu, qu'il expia tous les péchés de l'humanité, et qu'il mérita pour elle *de condigno* tous les dons divins.—A cet acte principal du sacerdoce de Jésus-Christ, Marie coopéra par le consentement qu'elle donna, au moment de l'annonciation, à l'incarnation telle qu'elle devait être réalisée avec le sacrifice de la croix comme conséquence, et avec la communauté de souffrances qui devait exister entre la mère et le Fils pendant toute la vie de Jésus, jusqu'a la consommation du suprême sacrifice du Calvaire.' (*Dict. de Théol. Cath.—Marie*, col. 2396-7.)

'La dignité de la maternité divine l'emporte donc aussi sur celle du sacerdoce chrétien. Le prêtre, administrant les sacrements ou prononçant les paroles de la consécration, tout en agissant avec intelligence et liberté, agit seulement comme cause instrumentale par la vertu et sous la dépendance immédiate de Notre-Seigneur qui est la cause principale. Plus relevée est l'action de Marie dans l'accomplissement du mystère de l'incarnation. En donnant la nature humaine à son divin Fils, elle agit par sa vertu propre, bien qu' avec l'aide du Saint-Esprit, suivant la parole de l'ange lui annonçant qu'elle concevrait du Saint-Esprit. C'est ainsi qu'elle donne à Notre-Seigneur sa chair adorable et contracte avec lui cette parenté sublime qui la place dans l'ordre hypostatique, bien au-dessus de toutes les autres perfections créées.—Toutefois à ne considérer que certains effets immédiats de l'action du prêtre comme la consécration eucharistique ou la remission des péchés par le sacrement de pénitence, il est vrai que le prêtre peut accomplir des actes que Marie, ne possédant point le pouvoir sacerdotal, n'aurait jamais pu accomplir. Mais, en ceci, il ne s'agit plus de la comparaison des dignités, mais seulement d'effets particuliers, procédant d'un pouvoir que Marie ne possédait point, mais qui ne comportent pas une dignité supérieure.' (*Loc. cit.* col. 2366.)

17. (p. 152). Billuart writes: 'The Blessed see all things, or at least the chief things, that belong to their state; whether these things are free or necessary or natural or supernatural acts, or are in this life or in the life to come.

'Thus St. Peter, and more probably every Pope, sees what regards the whole Church; a King, his kingdom; a religious Founder, his Order; a Father, his family.

'Hence, too, the most Blessed Virgin knows much more than the rest of the saints, especially the prayers and thoughts of men. As their special advocate she must have a deep knowledge of their state that she may bring them timely aid. Nevertheless, it does not seem that she knows all the thoughts and free acts of men, since not all these are her concern. This knowledge is the privilege of Christ, Who, as appointed

Judge of all men, must know all whom He is to judge, together with all their actions and thoughts in all their circumstances'—Billuart, *Summa, De Deo*; Diss. 4, Art. 10, 2.

18. (p. 157). In ordinary speech we understand by merit something which entitles us to a reward. We speak, for instance, of a well-merited honour. As there must be some equality between the deed and the reward if we are to merit the reward we see how impossible it was for man in his fallen state to merit the Beatific Vision. Only by God Himself becoming man could the reward be merited for mankind in strict justice.

Supernatural merit is of four kinds: first, condign merit, in strict justice (*merito de condigno*), which is that of the Incarnate Word whose least human act was worthy of our restoration to grace in strict justice, and which presupposes no favour on the part of God rewarding. Secondly, condign merit in the less strict sense, when anyone in a state of grace performs a supernatural act; but such an act presupposes the grace of divine favour. Thus those in a state of grace merit in God's sight since their actions confer a right to their own reward, whilst the grace enabling them to perform such good actions is a divine favour. Every voluntary act of a justified member of the Church Militant is therefore condignly meritorious; none of his voluntary actions can be indifferent. If they do not merit they are evil. Such an act to be meritorious must be informed therefore by grace and charity; the former to make it supernaturally vital, the latter to direct it to God from the motive of our love of Him. The increase of grace and charity make all our voluntary acts more meritorious. The Council of Trent teaches that the faithful of Christ, having been thus justified and made the friends and domestics of God advancing from virtue to virtue, are renewed day by day . . . by the observance of the commandments of God and the Church. They grow in the justice they have received and they are further justified. For it is written: He who is justified, let him be justified still; and, in another place 'Do not fear to progress in justice, even until death. . . .' The Church begs this increase from God when she prays: 'Grant us, O Lord, an increase of faith, hope and charity.' In the same session an anathema is proclaimed against those who dare to maintain that 'justice is not preserved or increased by good works, but that these latter are only fruits and not causes of the increase', or that 'They are not truly meritorious . . . of an increase of grace and glory'. (Sess. VI, cap. 10; can. 32). The third kind of merit is termed congruous in the stricter sense (*de congruo proprie*), and arises from the rights or rather the becomingness of friendship; that is to say such an act is meritorious only because the one who performs it is a friend of God. This is, therefore, not a reward in strict justice because there is no equality between the work and the recompense. It is in this way that we can merit such gifts of divine grace for one another, and that Our Lady can merit such gifts for all of us by reason of her unparalleled love of God. But even Our Lady cannot merit grace for others in strict justice. The fourth kind of merit is termed congruous in the wide sense (*de congruo improprie*), which arises from the liberality of God who rewards works as though they were prayers. Thus those who live unselfishly under the impulse of actual grace even though they be in mortal sin, can be said to merit their own conversion.

Of these four kinds of merit the one which concerns us here when speaking of Our Lady is the third-congruous merit, strictly so called, that is merit founded on the love of God. In the words of Pope Pius X: 'Since Mary surpasses all creatures in holiness and union with Christ, and since she has been associated by Him with the work of salvation, she has merited for us *de congruo*, as it is termed, all that Christ merited for us *de condigno*, and is the principal minister in the distribution of graces.' (Encyclical, *Ad Diem Illum*, 2nd Feb., 1904.)

It will be seen then that the difference between Our Lady's power to merit graces for others *de congruo* and ours is twofold: first, her congruous merit is universal. She is the Mother of all. In the words of the Pope she 'has merited for us *de congruo* . . . *all* that Christ merited for us *de condigno*'. And secondly, as the power of congruous merit depends on the degree of love between the one meriting and the one rewarding, her love for God is immeasurably greater than ours.

19. (p. 157). Some Catholic writers hold that Our Lady is an efficient cause of grace. But as competent theologians, after years of careful thought on this subject, are themselves sharply divided, it seems reasonable to conclude that the rest of us should be careful not to base our devotion to Mary on a theological opinion however probable it might be.

Father McNabb writes: 'To solve the question whether our Blessed Lady is an efficient cause of all grace, we must lay down a fundamental principle in the words of St. Thomas: "A sacrament in causing grace works after the manner of an instrument. Now an instrument is twofold; the one, separate, as a stick, for instance; the other united, as a hand. Moreover, the separate instrument is moved by means of the united instrument, as a stick by the hand.

'"Now the principal efficient cause of grace is God Himself; in comparison with whom Christ's humanity is as a united instrument; whereas the sacrament is as a separate instrument". (III, Qu. 62, Art. 4.)

From this it is clear that our Blessed Lady is neither the principal efficient cause nor the united instrumental efficient cause of grace.

'Nor would it seem consonant with theology and revelation to assert that our Blessed Lady is a separated instrumental efficient cause of grace. This would seem to be either the ordinary lay person in Baptism and Matrimony, or the priest (bishop) in the other sacraments.

'Now it seems clear that our Blessed Lady's prerogative as Mother of God is not that of being a sacramental priest. Here the authority of St. Alphonsus Liguori, one of our Lady's most devoted clients, is of force. He says: "The power of the priest surpasses that of the Blessed Virgin Mary; for although this Divine Mother can pray for us and by her prayers obtain whatever she wishes, yet she cannot absolve a Christian from even the smallest sin. 'The Blessed Virgin Mary was eminently more perfect than the apostles', says Innocent III; 'it was however, not to her, but only to the apostles, that the Lord entrusted the keys of the Kingdom of Heaven.' St. Bernardine of Siena has written, 'Holy Virgin, excuse me, for I speak not against thee. The Lord has raised the priesthood above thee.' " (*St. Alphonsus Liguori* Selva, trans. by Eugene Grimm, C.S.S.R.—Benziger, 1889, pp. 31–2.)

'This is but a dramatic statement of the theological fact that the Divine Motherhood of our Lady is not the sacerdotal power of being an instrumental efficient cause of grace.' (*Blackfriars*, April, 1923.)

20. (p. 158). There is only one way by which a man may become one with God—through the union of grace with Christ's humanity. The creature seeking God can only find Him through Christ and in Christ; the more we live in Him, the nearer we grow to God. Therefore, in our endeavour to attain to the ultimate goal of all religion, the possession of God, it is essential that there should be an intimate, ever-growing union with Christ.

The road to salvation has one definite direction. God is united with the human nature in Christ, Who carries out the work of redemption; He also incorporates each individual in Himself in order that all may share in the grace of adoption and that through our union with Him we may hope for perfect union with the transfigured Christ in Heaven, in the blessed possession of God. This is the way to salvation manifested in divine revelation: God—God Incarnate (Christ)—mankind in Christ (through incorporation)—mankind through Christ (through the practice of asceticism)—God.

21. (p. 168). 'After the Blessed Virgin had given her assent the Holy Ghost came upon her, cleansing her and giving her abundant strength to conceive and bring forth the Godhead of the Word. Then, the truly abiding wisdom and power of the Most High, the Son of God who is co-substantial with the Father, overshadowed her in the form of divine seed, and formed for Himself from her spotless and most pure blood

a body adorned with a rational and intellectual soul, the first fruit of our besprinkling; this, however, not by a procreation of seed, but, in accordance with the will of the Creator, by the Holy Ghost, so that the figure of the body was not achieved gradually by accessions, but was completed in one and the same moment—the same Word of God being made the hypostasis and person of the flesh; whereas the Word is not united with flesh in a person who already exists . . . Wherefore it is flesh at the same time as it is the flesh of the Word of God, as it is the flesh adorned with a rational and intellectual soul.'—St. John Damascene, *De fide orthodoxa*, Bk. III, ch. 2, *P.G.*, XCIV, 985 ff.— quoted in *Mariology*, Scheeben, *Vol. I, ch. 5.*

22. (p. 168). Vicarious satisfaction is reparation made for an offence, not by the offender but by a mediator with the consent of the person offended.

'The purpose of satisfaction is to repair the offence offered to God and to make Him once more favourable to the sinner. The offence offered by mortal sin has about it a certain infinity, since offence is measured by the dignity of the person offended. Mortal sin, by turning the sinner away from God, his final end, denies in practice to God His infinite rights as the Supreme Good and destroys His reign in souls.

'It follows from this that only the Incarnate Word could offer to the Father perfect and adequate satisfaction for the offence of mortal sin. For satisfaction to be perfect, it must proceed from a love and oblation which are as pleasing to God as, or more pleasing than, all sins united are displeasing to Him. But every act of charity elicited by Jesus had these qualities; for His Divine Person gave them infinite satisfactory and meritorious value. A meritorious work becomes satisfactory (or one of reparation and expiation) when there is something painful about it. Hence, in offering His life in the midst of the greatest physical and moral sufferings, Jesus offered satisfaction of an infinite and super-abundant value to His Father. He alone could make satisfaction in strict justice since the value of satisfaction like that of merit comes from the person, and the Person of Jesus, being divine, was of infinite dignity.

'It was, however, possible to associate a satisfaction of becomingness (*de congruo*) to Jesus' satisfaction just as a merit of becomingness was associated to His merit. In explaining this point, we shall show all the more clearly the depth and extent of Mary's sufferings.

'When a meritorious work is in some way painful it has value as satisfaction as well. Thus theologians commonly teach, following upon what has been explained in the previous section, that Mary satisfied for all sins *de congruo* in everything in which Jesus satisfied *de condigno*. Mary offered God a satisfaction which it was becoming that He should accept: Jesus satisfied for us in strict justice.'—*The Mother of the Saviour*, Garrigou-Lagrange, O.P., pp. 214, 215 (Golden Eagle Books, Ltd.).

23. (p. 178). 'Christ's sacrifice on the Cross was not only an individual, personal one, but was offered in the person of the second Adam, Who represents mankind. Christ, the second Adam, the Head of the new race, died "for us" and made the atoning sacrifice for our sins. This is a clear truth of dogmatic theology, expressed innumerable times in holy Scripture.—It was Christ's wish to renew His unique sacrifice on the Cross in order that the members of His Mystical Body could offer themselves as sacrifice to the Father with Him, thus giving the highest glory to the Father and simultaneously bringing about their own transfiguration.—The re-establishment of "all things in Christ, that are in Heaven and on earth, in Him" (Eph. 1. 10), is the object of God's divine economy of salvation, but this is not fully consummated through Christ's sacrifice on the Cross. It is only completed for Christ Himself, who has entered into glory through His suffering and death. Man, who is still a wayfarer upon earth, is destined to attain to perfection and transfiguration in the same way; the sacrifice of the Cross must be repeated by each individual Christian. Since Christ offered Himself in person to God, He is also destined (as a part of His sacrifice) to dedicate His whole mystical Body as an oblation to the Father, this being a sacrifice of Christ, the Head, in unison with His incorporated members.'—*The Mystical Body of Christ*, Jurgensmeier, p. 210 (Coldwell); cf. also *Mystici Corporis Christi*, par. 81.

24. (p. 184). 'Still it is not Mary, but Christ Himself who is the real Mystical Head of mankind. As mother of this Head she obtains towards the rest of men such a position by virtue of which she is the mother also of the Mystical Body of Christ; or as mother of Christ, mother of Christians also; and as bodily mother of the Son of God, spiritual mother of men with regard to their state as children of God.

'This universal motherhood of Mary, which is usually called the mystical motherhood, may not at all be considered as a purely moral or so-called motherhood. In its nature it is as equally real, organic, living and substantial a relation as that of the bodily motherhood. It rests on the maternal relation of Mary to Christ and the organic relation in which Christians stand to Christ as their Head. Ultimately this mystical motherhood is derived from the fact that Mary, as real bride of God, is seat and instrument of the divine light of grace.

'The cohesion of this secondary with the primary motherhood is so close that we may say: Mary receives in the conception of Christ the real, divine Word as *semen divinum*, in such a way that in Christ and with Christ men also must be born from it as children, and that consequently all men are virtually brought forth in her bosom through the conception of Christ.

'In Christ, Mary also receives and brings forth her own spiritual Head. As His bodily mother she is subject to Him as to a spiritual Bridegroom and is given to Him as His partner because as man He is in His mother's womb "man", not "child", according to the spirit. Likewise, in view of spiritual motherhood, she is also with regard to men subordinate and co-ordinate to her Son as to their spiritual Father. Therefore, as spiritual mother of men, she takes a position between these latter and Christ, in a way analogous to that which other mothers have between the father and the children.'—*Mariology*, Scheeben, Vol. I, pp. 232–3 (B. Herder Book Co.).

25. (p. 185). Our Lady was, of course, willing to accept this self-oblation. She knew that as her Son was the Saviour, she His mother would have in some way to share His sufferings; and that transfixion of which Simeon reminded her was to begin with the severing of the bonds uniting her to Christ her Son. He belonged to His Father; and she was the Bride of the Word. This mutual relationship of Mother and Son in God was stressed repeatedly by Our Lord during His public ministry. As from babyhood she had brought Him up as Saviour and Victim, so during His public ministry did Our Lord in His relations with His mother prepare her for her share as Bridal Mother in the sacrifice of Calvary. In His mercy and loving kindness He took her step by step towards her final self-oblation. On Calvary He was to be forsaken mysteriously by His divine Father as the culminating agony of His sacrifice, and she was to be forsaken by her Son, the Incarnate Word, as His Victim-Spouse.

26. (p. 189). What makes tiny, fugitive distractions in prayer so alluring? St. Augustine gives us the answer in his *Confessions*. He tells us that as a boy he stole fruit from a neighbouring garden. He knew quite well that he had better fruit at home. What attracted him was not the fruit but the stealing.

Doctor Allers, commenting on this, remarks: 'There is indeed a peculiar fascination in doing things forbidden; an old adage asserts that we always strive for the things forbidden and long for those denied us. The fact is well-known; St. Augustine supplies the explanation. By trespassing, by ignoring a commandment, by consciously acting in contradiction to what we know to be the law, man gives to himself the illusion of being greater than the law-giving power; he gives himself for a moment a feeling of superiority and even, when the commandment ignored be of divine origin, the illusion of being more than God

Himself. It is as if the words of the serpent were still resounding in man's ears: "You will be like gods."' (*Self-improvement*, pp. 181, 182.)

An apple may seem a trifling thing with which to encompass the ruin of the human race; but it was a *symbol*. There can never be any danger of thinking that man disobeyed God from weakness, in other words, that he fell by reason of the irresistible appeal of an apple. Not what the apple was, but what it signified brought about the fall of man.

So too with distractions in prayer. Things we deem hardly worthy of a second's thought outside prayer become almost irresistible when we are on our knees. We can see now why this should be, and why so much depends on our struggle against distractions. They are symbols. What makes them attractive and beguiling is not what they are, but the spirit of pride. (Cf. *The Science of Prayer*, by Vincent McNabb, O.P., p. 93; *Memorabilia*, by Bertrand Wilberforce, O.P., p. 150; *Summa Theol.*, 2-2, 83, 12 and 2-2, 83, 13 ad 3; The Divine Office by Bacquez, pp. 570 seq. *On Distractions; Conference* 34, St. Jane Frances de Chantal.

INDEX

Date Due

NOV 1 8 '59	DE 2 '67	
DEC 9 '59	MR 24 '69	
JE 10 '60	JY 28 71	
JY 18 '60	OCT 4 '73	
AG 16 '60	JAN 3 1 1976	
SE 6 '60	MAY 0 5 1992	
JE 10 '61		
OC 30 '61		
MY 6 '66		
JY 2 '66		
JY 1 8 '66		
JY 3 0 '66		
SE 30 '66		
OC 1 4 '66		
MY 3 '67		
JE 24 '67		
JY 3 '67		
JY 20 '67		

PRINTED IN U. S. A.